W9-CZI-848

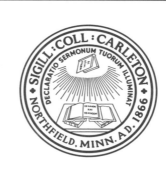

LIBRARY

Given for the
American Studies Program
by the
Fred C. Andersen
Foundation

ETHICAL THEORY & SOCIAL CHANGE

ETHICAL THEORY & SOCIAL CHANGE

The Evolution of John Dewey's Ethics, 1908-1932

Abraham Edel

Transaction Publishers
New Brunswick (U.S.A.) and London (U.K.)

Copyright © 2001 by Transaction Publishers, New Brunswick, New Jersey.

Library of Congress Catalog Number: 2001027889
ISBN: 0-7658-0055-1
Printed in the United States of America

Library of Congress Cataloging-in-Publication Data

Edel, Abraham, 1908-
   Ethical theory and social change : the evolution of John Dewey's Ethics, 1908-1932 / Edel Abraham.
       p. cm.
   Includes bibliographical references and index.
   ISBN 0-7658-0055-1 (alk. paper)
       1. Dewey, John, 1859-1952—Ethics.   I. Title.

B945.D44 E34   2001
171.2—dc21   2001027889

To Sima

"Philosophers are parts of history, caught in its movement; creators perhaps in some measure of the future, but also assuredly creatures of its past."
(in Dewey's *Reconstruction in Philosophy*)

Contents

Abbreviations and References to Dewey's Writings

Since the thirty-seven volumes of John Dewey's works published by Southern Illinois Press are divided into five volumes of the Early Works, fifteen of the Middle Works, and seventeen of the Later Works, reference will be to EW, MW, LW, in each case followed by the number of the volume, and a page number when necessary, all preceded by the year of the work in question. Thus, for example, the introduction to the 1932 *Ethics* would be referred to as 1932, LW 7: 7–35.

Where reference is necessary to the original volumes of the 1908 *Ethics* and the 1932 *Ethics*, both by Dewey and Tufts, they will be referred to as *08* and *32*, used almost as proper names.

Brief Bibliography

Bullert, Gary. *The Politics of John Dewey*. Buffalo, N.Y.: Prometheus Books, 1983.

Campbell, James. *Understanding John Dewey*. Chicago and La Salle, Ill.: Open Court Publishing Co., 1995.

Dykhuizen, George. *The Life and Mind of John Dewey*. Carbondale, Ill.: Southern Illinois University Press, 1973.

Hook, Sidney. *John Dewey, An Intellectual Portrait*. New York: The John Day Co., 1939.

Rockefeller, Steven C. *John Dewey, Religious Faith and Democratic Humanism*. New York: Columbia University Press, 1991.

Ryan, Alan. *John Dewey and the High Tide of American Liberalism*. New York and London: W.W. Norton and Co., 1995.

Welchman, Jennifer. *Dewey's Ethical Thought*. Ithaca and London: Cornell University Press, 1995.

Westbrook, Robert B. *John Dewey and American Society*. Ithaca and London: Cornell University Press, 1991.

Acknowledgments

This book has been long in the making, and went through a variety of complicated changes. For many years, in teaching philosophy at the City College of New York I had used Dewey's part of the 1932 Dewey and Tufts *Ethics* as a representation of modern ethical theory. I selected it rather than other modern works because he had a sense of time—he did not write as if ethical beliefs were eternal or unchanging—and he saw ethics as part of an ongoing culture, not intelligible if isolated.

In doing this, Dewey was in effect taking an anthropological approach to human culture. He was influenced by Franz Boas, who was at the time Professor of Anthropology at Columbia, where Dewey was then Professor of Philosophy. He attended a course given by Boas in the early part of the second decade of our century. As a result he dropped, in the 1932 edition of the Dewey and Tufts *Ethics*, all notions of ethics having evolved from a group ethics to an individualistic ethics, ideas that are found in the 1908 *Ethics*. He maintained that the ethics of a people is always a social matter, and that all an individual's moral decisions take place in a social matrix.

My early work in ethics was strongly influenced by the anthropological treatment of ethics. My first wife, May Mandelbaum Edel (deceased in 1964) was an anthropologist, a student of Boas, and the first modern anthropologist to do field work in East Africa.[1] In fact we collaborated on a book entitled *Anthropology and Ethics*, published in 1959.[2]

I am also greatly indebted to my second wife, Elizabeth Flower, (deceased 1995) who cooperated in the present work in two ways. One was by critical discussion of the text. The other was by bringing to our reflection the results of her own research which she had done for *A History of Philosophy in America*, by Elizabeth Flower and Murray Murphey [1977]. In this work she went back to Dewey's early history and traced the development of his philosophical interest and the writing of his works, his attempt to reconcile philosophy and the religious spirit, and his final break with all non-naturalism—in his article "The Reflex Arc Concept in Psychology" (*The Psychological Review*, July 1896). More generally, she developed in writing history of philosophy the idea that the philosophical writings of an author should not be treated in isolation, but should be dealt with together with his or her view of or presuppositions about science and its place in human life. Thus she studied William James's moral theory in the light of his psychology. Implicit in this approach is the view that a moral philosophy rests on a scientific background consciously used or else taken for granted.

In turn, both Elizabeth Flower and I were deeply indebted to Jo Anne Boydston, editor of the twenty-seven volumes of *The Works of John Dewey*. At her invitation we went to the Center for Dewey Studies in Carbondale, Illinois, worked on materials there, and prepared an Introduction to Volume 7 of the Later Works in which the 1932 *Ethics* appeared. Both in Carbondale and in later extensive correspondence we discussed many detailed points with her. Even more, as our discussions located gaps in our sources, she several times reexamined the original materials in Carbondale to locate what would provide answers to the questions that had arisen. And beyond all this, she gave us permission to quote, as extensively as we found necessary, from the thirty-seven volumes of John Dewey's Works, not only for our introduction to Volume 7 (1932) but for the present work.

I should also like to thank the following: my wife, Sima Szaluta, for countless hours spent working on the manuscript; my friend Professor Finbarr O'Connor, for so generously undertaking the onerous task of preparing the index; my publishers, Mary Curtis and Professor Irving L. Horowitz, for their encouragement and attention throughout.

Notes

1. Her work is reported most fully in May M. Edel, *The Chiga of Uganda*, second edition, Transaction Publishers, 1996. This book adds to her *The Chiga of Western Uganda*, International African Institute, 1957, her report on Chiga material culture, found among her papers.
2. It was published by Charles C. Thomas. A revised edition appeared in 1968—*Anthropology and Ethics: The Quest for Moral Understanding*, Cleveland: The Press of Case Western Reserve University. In 1996 Transaction Books published a full account of her African works, including her hitherto unpublished work on Chiga material culture, entitled *The Chiga of Uganda*.

Preface

Scope of the Book

This book is a case study in the thesis that ethical theory without sociohistorical background is blind, and sociohistorical theory without ethical understanding is empty. The case study consists in a comparison of Dewey and Tufts' *Ethics* (1908) with the second edition (1932) in the light of Dewey's life and activities in the intervening quarter of a century. During this period Dewey traveled widely—to Europe, Japan, China, Mexico, and elsewhere. In the academic sphere, he worked chiefly at the University of Chicago, then at Columbia University. In both cases he participated actively in community life: in Chicago largely in educational circles, in New York at Columbia in the intellectual life of the city as a whole. For example, he organized the founding of the New School for Social Research to provide philosophical and general education for adults; it also provided jobs for refugee scholars escaping from fascism and Nazism in Europe.

The quarter century between the two editions was a critical one in Europe and America. In 1908 only a few sensed the growing tensions that were to break out into World War I. After the war, one could not avoid the continuing battles (intellectual and physical) between socialism, communism, fascism, Nazism, and democracy. These tensions culminated in World War II.

Dewey lived and wrote during this whole period. His writing began early in his life (he was born in 1859 and died in 1953), but his development of pragmatism began only in the last decade of the nineteenth century, after he became acquainted with the work of C.S. Peirce and William James. From then on he gradually shed all religious and idealistic philosophies and gave a naturalistic shape to his pragmatism. His philosophical writing is distinctive on the American scene. Other philosophers expound their positions and show how they differ from one another's views. But Dewey goes further: he relates philosophical difference to the ongoing life of the society and the position that philosophers have in that life. In this, he is like Karl Marx—he gives the sociohistorical a constitutive place in philosophy.

Although this book is primarily a study of John Dewey, not of James H.

Tufts, the important role that Tufts played in their joint venture is not to be neglected. In both *08* and *32* Tufts did Part I, Dewey Part II; and in Part III Dewey did Chapters XX and XXI, Tufts XXII to XXVI. In general Tufts is more concerned with the historical development of ethics than Dewey is in this work. Dewey of course appreciates the necessity for the historical, but to see his historical views we have to consult the whole range of his writing. At some points in his chapter in *32* Dewey has doubts about Tufts' interpretation—for example, that the evolution of morality has been from the social to the individual. He is inclined to question the very distinction, since he sees morality as essentially a social matter, and the individual as coming to grips with the social throughout his or her life rather than fashioning an individual morality of one's own.

Dewey's Life and Times

John Dewey was born on October 20, 1859 and died June 1, 1952. His life was almost evenly divided between two centuries—forty-one years in the nineteenth century and fifty-two in the twentieth. When we consider the history of America—indeed of the world—in the two half centuries we find a marked difference in the physical and social background in which Dewey lived and worked during his "two lives". He was only two years old when the American Civil War broke out in 1861; eight years old when Marx published the first volume of *Capital* in 1867; ten years old when the first transcontinental railroad crossed the United States (1869); twelve years old when Darwin published *The Descent of Man* (1871); seventeen years old when the telephone was invented and the Suez Canal opened (1876). This was also the period in which Germany emerged as a dominant European power after winning the Franco-Prussian War. Dewey lived through the 1890s in which the Independent Labor Party was founded in England and in which the German Socialist Party came into being and split into a socialist and communist wing.

In general, the period from the late nineteenth century to 1914, when the war broke out, was a complex one. It was a time of national alignment in Europe—Germany and Austria on one side, France and Britain on the other. There was struggle over land, oil, and other resources, as well as emerging conflict over colonies. The nineteenth century wars between Germany and France left borders to become the setting for twentieth century wars. Imperial Russia was expanding and lined up against the central European powers. Africa—East, West, as well as South—was being divided among the imperial powers. And, of course, the British Empire extended over Egypt and India. British control of the seas was about to be challenged by Imperial Germany. The growth of industry—an age of industrialism was getting under way—made the struggle for iron and steel as important as that for agricultural land had been and continued to be. In sum, the causes for war were multiplied, and the spark might come at any time from the character of monarchs or governing chancellors. In fact it came from Germany's challenge of British sea-power.

These causes, of course, do not operate by themselves. The fighting in wars has to be done by people, either willingly or under coercion, or in a revolutionary upsurge, as in France of 1870–1871 or Russia of 1917. The early part of the twentieth century saw western invasions of the East, and by eastern powers of their neighbors—in Japan, China, India. The United States extended its controls in Latin America. It seemed more peaceful because, in some contexts, it used the power of money rather than of arms.

Dewey's part in these events was a tangential one. He was too young for participation in the Civil War in America, though he witnessed it—his father served with the cavalry in Virginia. When the United States entered the First World War in 1917, he was almost 58, too old to take an active part in the fighting. And of course by World War II in the 1940s, he was in his late eighties. His active life centered in the university milieu, and in the cities in which the universities were located. After graduate work at Johns Hopkins (1882–1884), his first university teaching job was at the University of Michigan, at Ann Arbor. Here he taught both psychology and philosophy. He stayed there ten years (1884–1894) with a slight interruption, a short period at the University of Minnesota. It was there that he married Alice Chipman in 1886, with whom he had three children. From Michigan he went to the University of Chicago, at the age of 35, where he stayed from 1894 to 1904, after which he moved to Columbia University in New York, at the age of 45. Here he taught till he retired at the age of 71. After that he lived in New York, and in his summer home in New Hampshire.

In the intellectual sphere Darwin's work had had the greatest influence on Dewey's thought. His mother had pressed a religious outlook so strongly on him that he developed a lifelong antagonism to religion. At first he substituted a religious attitude for religious belief, giving generalized sermons. Then he shifted to philosophical idealism, substituting an acceptance of the philosophy of Hegel, then of T.H. Green, for direct religious belief. But even this thinner religiosity did not last. Darwin conquered. Dewey's break with any form of religion or idealism is found in his article, "The Reflex Arc Concept in Psychology" which appeared in the *Psychological Review*, July 1896. This criticized the then-current analysis of behavior in terms of stimulus and response as separate events, and presented an integrated account of how problems are formulated in the unified process of dealing with them. An excellent detailed account of this work is to be found in Elizabeth Flower's chapter on John Dewey in *A History of Philosophy in America*, which she wrote with Murray E. Murphey (1977).

Dewey's Philosophical Writings 1908–1932

Dewey had begun philosophical writing as early as 1882. His earliest writing in ethics was in 1889. But in the period between that and 1908 he dealt more with psychology and education and the psychological basis of ethics. The 1908 *Ethics* presented Dewey's comprehensive thought on the subject. In the Collected Works the Dewey and Tufts *Ethics* comes in Volume 5 of the Middle Works. That means that before this there are five volumes of the Early Works and four of the Middle Works. Clearly Dewey, once he started writing in 1882, wrote continuously.

Dewey's writing between the 1908 and the 1932 publication of the *Ethics* was also continuous and varied. Clearly these works bear some responsibility for the differences that *32* exhibits from *08*—both the views that it abandons and the new ones it acquires

From 1910 to 1914 Dewey focussed on problems relevant to education, for example in *How We Think*[1] and *Interest and Effort in Education*[2]. But once World War I was on, he wrote *German Philosophy and Politics*[3] in which he tried to understand the German character in terms of its special history and its cultural features of dominance and institutions of coercion. From 1916 on, however, he turns to more positive themes of democracy and reconstruction in education and social life, and in philosophical thought itself. Among his best known works of this period is *Reconstruction in Philosophy* published in 1920 after his long tour of the East in which he visited Japan and China.[4] He had been repelled by Japanese militarism, but impressed by what the Chinese had done to maintain life under difficult conditions: for example, how they preserved their soil for centuries, whereas in the American midwest the soil was recklessly spoiled by over-cultivation. He is also critical of ancient western philosophy, particularly of the way in which it sought to behold absolute things-in-themselves rather than deliberate about directions in which people would have their lives go.

In 1922 *Human Nature and Conduct* appeared.[5] It had been presented as a set of lectures at Stanford University in 1918, but publication was delayed because of Dewey's prolonged absence in China and Japan. It proposes to deal with the place of impulse, habit, and intelligence in conduct. These appear in history as needs, custom, and reconstruction. This orderly scheme is upset when intelligence itself is interpreted as a set of habits, and impulse turns out to be shaped by social habits rather than be an independent dynamic source. Dewey's conclusion is that morality is unavoidably a social product, a product of socially conveyed habits.

Experience and Nature, one of Dewey's large and comprehensive works, was published in 1925.[6] In it he attacked the common assumption that experience goes on in human beings while nature is what is apart from human life. Instead he offers a kind of empirical naturalistic metaphysics. Experience is seen as a method of getting at nature: in natural science controlled experience furnishes the facts and laws of nature.

In 1927 Dewey published *The Public and its Problems*, consisting of lectures delivered at Kenyon College, Ohio. It does not take the state for granted, but sees it as arising and taking form under difficult conditions and problems of the public. It is not surprising that at that particular time the state should not be thought a necessary or indispensable part of the social structure. In America of the twenties, prior to the crash of 1929, the market was reaching new heights and speculation was rampant. Even the social sciences were affected by the political scene. For example, some sociologists drew a sharp distinction between the social and the political, and assigned to the state the task of keeping order in the society, so that business enterprise could operate successfully. The state should not, however, trespass in the economic realm: that is a "free enterprise" zone left to individuals in their pursuit of profit. The state prevents crime and regulates social structure, for example, to protect women and children from outsiders, while not itself interfering in the family. Interestingly, in Britain at the time, under the impact of broad labor strikes, particularly in mining, the ideas of Guild Socialism were developed: property should belong to the workers as public property and be managed collectively. Instead of the state, the country should be governed by workers' councils. Indeed by 1930, the British Labor movement was ready to take power, and engaged in a prolonged strike to bring down the government. But the length of the strike—no terminal date had been set—brought suffering to the public as industries shut down, supplies dwindled and prices rose. The public turned against the strikers. Labor did not have the resources to take over and run industry—for example, to pay for imported raw materials. It yielded finally and entered a coalition government run by the Conservative Party. By now there was no alternative to cutting the standard of living. The left wing of the Labor Party called for immediate socialization of industry, but it was overruled.

In America of the late twenties, Herbert Hoover, as president, kept government out of any economic activity, following the policy of his predecessor Calvin Coolidge. But whereas Coolidge, serving after the depression of the early twenties (which had followed the end of World War I) had the advantage of rising productivity, Hoover kept the government out of any economic activity even when the great depression of 1929 struck the country and brought industry to a standstill. In 1930 banks closed, beggars were found on every corner in New York City. Childs Restaurant put out a sign reading "All you can eat for 60 cents", but even the present writer (who came to New York in 1930 and had a Columbia fellowship in Philosophy for 1930–31) could not afford to have a meal at Childs.

Dewey was well aware of the situation in both Britain and America. His book, *The Quest for Certainty*, published October 11, 1929, was based on his Gifford Lectures, delivered April-May 1929 at the University of Edinburgh. Dewey rejects the absolute certainties humans have sought and the partitions between absolute knowledge and fallible belief. All knowledge is of one sort and all is fallible. Clearly such an approach would open the door to social experiment, particularly under trying situations.

It is not surprising then that *Individualism Old and New*, which included essays Dewey published in 1929–30 (to which some essays were later added) focuses directly on the social, moral, and scientific attitudes pertinent to a time of economic depression and controversy about the desirable directions of social change. It appeared at the height of the Great Depression. 1929 witnessed the great crash in the Stock Market, about which the British journal *Punch* published a cartoon showing stock brokers jumping out of skyscraper windows. And indeed there were numerous suicides on a particular day when many a man woke up rich in the morning and died a pauper at night. Hoover did nothing to help the situation; he apparently assumed that depressions were cyclical phenomena and the economy would recover in due course. It is not surprising under these conditions that he lost the presidential election. Indeed it was quite clear, after banks closed early in 1931, that the governor of New York State, Franklin Delano Roosevelt, would be elected in the coming elections.

What Dewey saw clearly was that the issues America was facing were not only political; they concerned the character of American culture, the problems of a profit-system, and the type of individualism that would be morally acceptable. Some of the titles of the essays in the volume themselves show this central concern: for example, "Toward a New Individualism", "Capitalistic or Public Socialism", "Individuality in Our Day", "From Absolutism to Experimentalism". And the text bears out the titles. For example, he says directly "Anthropologically speaking, we are living in a money culture" and refers to our "rugged or is it ragged?"—individualism. He finds that industry and business for profit are nothing new, but it is the invention of machinery that has given them a power they never had in the past. This is going on in Europe too. Interestingly, Dewey defends Americans against the charge they are grasping or mercenary by asking what Europe has done for the peasant and the proletarian.

1932, the year Roosevelt was elected president, was also, as we have seen, the year of the publication of the second edition of the *Ethics*. We may recall that it was two years after Dewey retired from teaching at Columbia, and he was now 79 years old.

Notes

1. 1910–11, MW 6.
2. 1911–1914, MW 7.
3. in 1915, MW 8.
4. 1920, MW 12.
5. 1922, MW 14.
6. 1925, LW 1.

1

Introduction

Dewey and Tufts' *Ethics* was first published in 1908; the revised edition appeared in 1932. Dewey's part in the latter was wholly re-written, and in effect constituted a new work. It might seem a mild academic exercise to compare the versions and see what had been changed. In the traditional isolation of academic thought it might even appear a quixotic project—why not attend rather to which was a more adequate moral philosophy, which had more correct answers to the theoretical problems of ethics, which brought us closer to the pulse of contemporary ideas? At best, ship the project over to those who are interested in intellectual history and don't bother the philosophers with it. They are too busy with philosophical truth to worry about philosophical history.

On the other hand, there is the gnawing possibility that the events, the social structure, the beliefs and attitudes of a period, its models of science and human history, all have some constitutive role in its philosophical theory. In that case the comparison of *1908* and *1932* offers an exciting vista. 1908 is in the period when industrialism is moving into higher gear and putting greater pressure on the social institutions that had not sufficiently accommodated its demands, when people still look on the future as an era of unfolding progress and extending democratic growth, when the next revolution in science is only getting under way and has not yet affected modes of thought, when philosophic thought about human life is still reflecting in abstract form the effort to reconcile Darwinism and traditional religion, when imperialism and the struggle for the division of the world among European powers has begun to change the temper of political relations and na-

1

tional outlooks but has not yet permeated general consciousness as a new era. By 1932 all this is changed. Industrialism is in high gear and urbanization has shifted the balance, but it is a period of world depression. The hope of peaceful progress has been shattered by the first World War, and the vista of slow democratic growth at least interrupted by the advent of Russian communism, Italian fascism, and the imminent threat of German nazism. A new physics has definitely replaced the Newtonian outlook and a new logic has shaken philosophic thought. The balance is shifting toward secular philosophy and philosophy itself is becoming a profession. The social sciences are staking claims for the study of human life and thrusting different perspectives of method and research into the arena. An ethics that had coasted on the comfortable assumption that people agreed about morality but only argued about how it was to be justified was startled into the perception that there were fundamental moral conflicts and the threat of relativism in the answers.

Dewey is an ideal case for comparing the changes in an ethical theory over a quarter of a century, just as that period itself encapsulates a packed budget of changes. Unlike many philosophers Dewey appreciates change, many of his basic ideas are geared to the problem of human control under change. Moreover, he is concerned with the relation of theory and practice, and much of his work in metaphysics and epistemology is devoted to discovering the role that doctrines in these fields play and how they reflect the movement of social life. He is constantly concerned with ethics, with the history of ethics, with the presuppositions of an ethical theory that are studied in the social sciences and applied in the normative disciplines of politics, education and law. While no person can be fully conscious of all the sources of change in his thoughts at least Dewey's theory of ethics would offer no barriers to the attempt to see what growth in the various domains of knowledge and what happenings on the historical scene prompted theoretical revision. We can even assume that he would be likely to be very conscious of what entered into changing views of ethics since he had himself gone through one earlier profound change of thought. In the 1890s he moved from his *Outlines of a Critical Theory of Ethics* (1891) to *The Study of Ethics: A Syllabus* (1894) under the impact of William James's *Principles of Psychology*.[1] If an ethical theory could change under a revised psychological theory, why not continually—as ideas grew and were transformed in anthropology, social psychology, sociology, law, education, politics, as well as in the response of philosophers to new ideas in physics and logic, in biology and in linguistics? The project of comparison in ethics thus may reveal how an ethical theory is crystallized in the processes of the growth of knowledge in all fields and the human vicissitudes in history. And in doing this it may plausibly show the place of presuppositions from all these areas in the structure of an ethical theory itself.

Our story begins with a lecture given by Dewey to the French Philosophical Society in 1930. It was translated from the French by Jo Ann Boydston and published in *Educational Theory* in July 1966, and entitled "Three Independent Factors in Morals".[2] Its theme was, to put it almost starkly, that there is a basic indeterminateness in morality, reflected in the theoretical struggles of good, right, and virtue. This is because morality has three independent roots in human life and these in moral decision are a source of systematic conflict.

Boydston writes in her introductory comment "In 1930, Dewey and Tufts must surely have been working on the revised edition of the *Ethics* which was published two years after the present 'communication' was read to the French Philosophical Society . . . The present statement may well have been, as remarked in the Society's discussion, a premiere presentation of those ideas. In any case, it took those members of his audience who had followed Dewey's previous writings completely by surprise. In the discussion, the anthropologist Mauss says: 'I believe Professor Dewey has given us quite a new perspective on new points, because in the works which he has published, he has not before expressed so definitely the opinions he presented today.' And E. Leroux, who is introduced by the chairman as one who knows Dewey's philosophy well and called upon for comment says that his authority refers to past work and not to the presentation of that evening. The past works 'are not at all the same ideas he has just presented here. I had forgotten that Mr. Dewey is a man who renews himself incessantly and that he does not like to rely on his writings.' Dewey replying (with an obviously keener eye for his own principle of continuity) describes the change as a broadening."

Actually, it may not have been the first presentation. In a letter to Professor Horace S. Fries, who had apparently written him to inquire about the differences between the 1908 and 1932 editions, Dewey mentions a paper he had written about 1926 or 1927 for a small club to which he belonged. (This was probably the New York Philosophy

Club at Columbia.) A portion of a paper unearthed by Boydston seemed at first to belong to this presentation. It had two distinct parts, the second of which overlapped the 1930 paper, and so suggested it was a precursor of the latter. However, Boydston concluded on the basis of a calligraphic study that it was a later paper that used part of that study. Now it seems to us doubtful that Dewey would have presented this later paper after the full development of the ideas in the revised edition of the *Ethics* in 1932. Hence we may think of the manuscript, which it is useful to compare with the 1930 paper, as giving us ideas that flank the latter from the 1926 date mentioned in the Fries letter to the 1932 publication of the *Ethics*.

Our cast of textual characters for our inquiry is beginning to take shape, and it is well to spare our labor by giving them names for reference. Let us title them the *three roots paper*, the *Fries letter*, the *club paper*. And of course the main characters are the two editions of the *Ethics* for which almost as proper names we will hereafter employ *08* and *32*. Now the first three of these, to be discussed in the next chapter, all concern a shift in conceptual structure from *08* to *32*. All the sources here are addressed to philosophers and so it is almost natural that structural questions should be in the forefront. But what would have been Dewey's reply if instead of the philosopher Fries a social scientist had written him a letter of inquiry about the changes between *08* and *32*? We get some inkling of a direction of inquiry in the discussion of the *three roots paper* on the occasion of its presentation. The historian of ancient philosophy, Robin, questions whether there is really a sharp distinction in Greek thought between the idea of the good and the idea of law, that is, between the ideal of the good and the search for a jural order. Bouglé is reminded of the pluralist strands in the sociological thought of Lévy-Bruhl and Durkheim. Leroux finds a kind of unity in Dewey's psychology as expounded in Dewey's own *Human Nature and Conduct* and wonders whether that militates against a pluralism in moral decision. Jean Wahl makes a comparison to ideas of political pluralism, even in Dewey himself, and calls attention to another philosopher who had believed in an irreducible plurality of moral principles. On the whole, French thought of this period finds no difficulty in passing readily between philosophy and what is later set off sometimes sharply in the Anglo-American tradition as the social sciences.

A direct answer can be found in the then prevalent view of the social-historical unity of human development that stands out clearly in *08*. The basic underlying picture, we shall see, is the emergence in the progress of civilization of a reflective individualism making continually greater inroads on an unreflective customary morality. This is certified by the anthropology of the day and is aligned with a psychology of individual development. All the studies of institutional change are brought into this circle of thought. Tufts bears the brunt of the historical exposition, while Dewey's attention is almost wholly absorbed in the theoretical changes wrought by the growth of reflection. By sharp contrast, in *32* this picture of a linear development in morality has disappeared. Yet this is not an isolated rejection of an anthropological thesis of the beginning of our century. It topples a reigning concept of individualism and leads to a reconsideration of the very idea of custom itself. It revises the theory of history and of social influence. And these in turn have an effect on the idea of reason in ethics, the scope of human learning and control, and the evaluation of genetic method in ethical theory. These developments took a long time in Dewey's thought. Indeed, in spite of many traces, we cannot be sure that the foundational shift is complete before his paper on "Anthropology and Ethics" which was a chapter in Ogburn and Goldenweiser's *The Social Sciences and Their Interrelations* in 1927. Here the linear view of moral evolution is definitely rejected, and its various forms tracked down and criticized.

Our three sources—the *Fries letter*, the *club paper,* and *three roots*—give us a clear idea of the shift in conceptual structure from *08* to *32*. We will not yet, at this point, have to look into the detail of *08*. Let us start with the relevant portions of the Fries letter. Dewey writes:

> I supposed my position in the early edition was that of a socialized utilitarian . . .
>
> As far as I can tell a large part of the change in the two editions was made for pedagogical reasons. The material of Part II [Dewey's theoretical part] I felt was too much couched in terms of ethical theories. I re-organized the material with a view to making the approach direct and criticism of theories secondary. The theoretical change is in the direction of a sharper distinction between different strands in morals. I wrote a paper about 26 or 27 for a small philosophical club to which I belong on the independent variables in morals, the good, right and virtue, end, standard, approbation [in Dewey's original statement he has 'end' written above 'good', 'standard' above 'right', 'approbation' above 'virtue'] and the ideas I expressed in that were the ones that expressed the theoretical change. I was a little surprised to find in going back over the early edition that the idea was at times implicit there; it must have been somewhere below express consciousness . . . .

[Dewey goes on to say that the change was connected with] a perception that there are three independent factors which have influences [influenced] the development of morals & that many of our moral problems come from the necessity of uniting them when we act. I fncy [fancy] that in the early tradition [edition?] I followed the tradition in making ends, the good, the basic idea, and in that sense the end was made primary. I became convinced that in the actual development of morals the concept of right had in fact played an independent role. I do not now reverse the roles but hold that it is a moral problem—one of conduct—to adapt the concepts of right and virtue to that of the good end. Theoretically they are distinct and independent.

[A postscript adds] As far as I can recal [recall] any specific influence in changing my views it was reading more carefully the English moralists. I saw that they determined the good in terms of approbations or identified it with the virtuous; of course I knew already that Kant determined it in terms of obligation. The consequence was that I was led to the idea of three independent concepts.

The *club paper* is a 13 page paper entitled "Conflict and Independent Variables in Morals" and begins to coincide on its page 6 with the latter part of *three roots*. While both start with conflict and uncertainty as basic in the moral situation, the *club paper* headlines conflict in its title; three roots limits its title to the independence of the factors. The failure to recognize conflict is traced to postulating a single principle to explain the moral life. With moral action having only one source, the moral choice becomes viewed as between the moral and the immoral. The *club paper* illustrated this with choices between the more immediate and the more important good; a particular good and a general; the personal and the social. Such conflicts are not denied for some cases but declared not to advance the theoretical problem.

The *three roots* are related to three major traditions in the history of morals. Their theoretical forms are as follows. The morality of ends, with the central idea of the good, is based on impulses, appetites and desires. Without foresight only differing strength determines action, but with foresight of consequences they become measurable in terms of their results. Comparison, judgment and correction enter. In time two moral concepts were formed in such processes: *reason*, introducing order and system, and *ends* culminating in a hierarchy of goods up to a final good. The second theoretical form is the morality of laws. This comes from the basic phenomena of group life, each trying to secure the acceptance of his purposes and plans by others, and generates an established system of order or right, that is, requirements clothed with authority. Dewey says: "The point that I want to emphasize is this: there is a difference in nature, both in origin and in mode of operation, between an object which seems capable of satisfying desire and which is thereby a good, and an object which sets up a demand on our conduct which we must acknowledge. One cannot be reduced to the other."3

A third independent variable in morals is based on the phenomena of praise and blame, spontaneous approval and disapproval. These are natural responses to the acts of others, and out of them come our ideas of virtue and vice.

Dewey traces finally the conflict of the three factors. What is desired may be prohibited, and what is prohibited may happen to be approved; to recognize the reality of conflict would be a gain in theory and morality.

In the *club paper* the formulation is sometimes blunter, and to that extent clearer. For example, after asserting the genuine independence of the three variables, he says: "The three things I regard as variables are first the facts that give rise to the concept of the good and bad; secondly, those that give rise to the concept of right and wrong; thirdly, those that give rise to the conception of the virtuous and vicious." Obviously it is not the concepts that are the variables but the facts or range of phenomena that give rise to the concepts. His mode of analysis thus seems to presuppose that in the phenomena of life tasks are generated and concepts develop in carrying out the tasks. Presumably this was what he meant in the *Fries letter* by a direct approach, with criticisms of theories secondary. This basic reference to facts and forces is what leads us to use the term "three roots" for these independent factors.

The theories in the history of moral philosophy are not, however, neglected. Indeed, different schools in their historical origin are seen to express one of the variables and to some extent to be bringing the others within the scope of that variable. Thus we have the Greek and utilitarian development of the good, the Roman-Stoic and Kantian development of the right, and the British eighteenth century sentiment theory development of sympathy and approval into virtue and vice. A further feature of Dewey's thought here is significant, even though so briefly developed. Just as he has looked to universal psychological and social phenomena as a base for the concepts and theories, so he offers suggestions about the socio-historical conditions that incline thinkers to go along one or another of the variables. For example, the Greeks developed moral theory in teleological terms in a unified way because "it was a natural consequence of the peculiar nature of the Greek city for Greek philosophers to consider social obligations and claims among the ends subject to reason. Because there was an intimate and vital relation between the problems of state and the interests of the citizens in Athens, which has served as a model for philosophers, legislation was discussed and considered to the point that (theoretically at least) it was the manifestation of reflective intelligence. Greek cities were small enough so that it was possible to consider formal political decisions as an expression of the reasoned thought of the group, that is to say, directed toward purposeful goals, whereas laws based on the *fiat* of the will were considered arbitrary and tyrannical and those born of passion, confused and perverse."[4]

While the Greek political and social atmosphere made it possible to identify law and obligation with a rational adaptation of means to ends, Rome provided far different conditions and developed different ethical ideas. In its large and conglomerate empire with the needs of central control and order, "Reason became a type of cosmic force constituting the structure of things, forcing them to adapt to each other and to exert themselves in the same direction: law was simply the manifestation of that great ordering force. Functions, duties, relations— not of means to ends but of mutual adaptation—of correspondence and reciprocal harmony, became the center of moral theory."[5] And ordinary experience with its demands for mutual control and influence in numerous standardized situations (as in the parental) falls into similar patterns of authority.

Both ethical concepts and the selective play of ethical theory at different points in the history of morals thus express the tasks and forms of actual life and its central problems. That Dewey is giving this primacy to actual life is underlined by the way in which, in the *club paper*, he speaks of *forces* : "The three concepts in question represent forces that have different roots, not a common and single one. Because these forces pull different ways there is a genuine conflict—and a problematic quality pervades the whole situation."[6]

The general facts of conflict and problem and reconstruction had of course been fully recognized in *08*. Indeed generic conflict and generic reconstruction are the essential features of consciousness which shape the operation of intelligence. What we have in these new papers is the discovery of *systematic* conflict between the basic idea-systems and so between the forces in human life and experiences that underlie the idea-systems, for example between the pursuit of ends and the satisfaction of desires and the group needs for control and order. Such conflicts are much more serious than that of two desires which necessitates an ordering of ends. For the latter, individuals may develop preference orders, but for the former they have to develop whole character structures. What we shall see in examining the three idea-systems in *32* is that each has its own ideas of rationality, its own sanctions, and to some extent its own key or leading conceptions—the final end, authority, benevolence.[7]

It is one thing to discover systematic conflict, it is another to tell us how to relate the conflicting parties, in effect, how to deal with the underlying conflicts. The new papers do not really tackle this question. *Three roots* pleads for the recognition of the basic problematic character of morals, so that the creative and active character of moral judgment will be recognized. Presumably this is what Dewey meant in the *Fries letter* when he said that "it is a moral problem – one of conduct – to adapt the concepts of right and virtue to that of the good end." But what form will the solution take? "A moral philosophy which frankly recognizes the impossibility of reducing all the elements of moral situations to one single principle, one which would admit that every human being can only do his best to shift for himself among the disparate forces, would throw light on our real difficulties and would help us make a more accurate estimate of competing factors."[8] The *club paper* ends on a more upbeat note. At least he draws the lesson of "the assimilation of judgment and choice to the experimental point of view in knowledge."[9] And more heroic than the individual shifting for himself is that "we choose and act morally as well as prudentially at our peril." Now between the time of these papers and the revised Part II in *32* Dewey must have grappled with this question, for there is a proposed solution. Let us first, however, look at the broad contours of *08* and ask how they were changed by the point of view of the new papers. And let us do this without trespassing too far on the specific discussion of each of the three ethical idea-systems.

In the Fries letter Dewey says that he supposed his position in *08* to be that of "a socialized utilitarianism." That means that he operated within the framework of a primacy of the good and interpreted the concepts of the other systems within the framework of the good. Even a casual reading of *08* cannot miss this, particularly of course of Part II. Conduct as moral is defined as activity directed by ideas of value where the values are so mutually incompatible as to require reflection and selection before action is begun.[10] The distinctive intellectual tradition from which the Kantian view emerged is recognized but it tends to be subsumed under a different perspective—the problem of the relation of the inner and the outer. Moreover the chapter on Typical Divisions of Theories (chapter 12) multiplies perspectives—not only the teleological contrasted with the jural, but the individual and the institutional, the empirical and the intuitional. The division of voluntary activity into the inner and outer in examining theories makes it easy to see Kant and Bentham as one-sided and to look for an intellectual synthesis. In general, the emphasis is on the one-sidedness of theories as compared to the continuities found within conduct. Eventually, after the critique of utilitarian and Kantian conceptions, the final statement about duty in *08* is that "Duty is what is owed by a partial isolated self embodied in established, facile, and urgent tendencies, to that ideal self which is presented in aspirations which, since they are not yet formed into habits, have no organized hold upon the self and which can get organized into habitual tendencies and interests only by a more or less painful and difficult reconstruction of the habitual self."[11] In short, duty is reinterpreted as an aspiration phenomenon in a growing self. Similarly, the definition of virtues is steered toward the good: "The habits of character whose effect is to sustain and spread the rational or common good are virtues; the traits of character which have the opposite effect are vices."[12]

Dewey says about the idea of the three roots in the Fries letter: "I was a little surprised to find in going back over the early edition that the idea was at times implicit there; it must have been somewhere below express consciousness." In looking at the three idea-systems in subsequent chapters we shall try to find these traces; it is not implausible, since the notion of the centrality of conflict was there, and there were occasional genetic references to the actual sources of ideas. But the multiplicity of points of analysis tended if not to obscure, at least to detract from a sharp recognition. As for ideational influence toward the recognition of the three roots, Dewey attributes it in the letter to his restudy of the British moralists and the recognition of virtue alongside of good and obligation. "I saw that they determined the good in terms of approbations or identified it with the virtuous." Presumably this showed that each system could play at the game of reduction. What Kant alone had not been able to reveal, Kant and the moral sentiment theorists side by side suggested.

That the structure of Part II in *32* is reorganized to conform with the new ideas is very clear from the classification of problems in the last section of chapter 10, after it has discussed reflective morality and ethical theory and the continuities in moral conduct conveying the old warnings against the separation of conduct and character, motive and consequences, etc. The classification [13] of theories that center around Good as ultimate, Duty and Right as ultimate, and Virtue and Vice as central, are briefly introduced by presenting their basic phenomena— purposes and the realization of ends, control of desire and appetite, approbation and condemnation. These are to be examined not so much from the point of view of truth and falsity as "to see what factors of permanent value each group contributes to the clarification and direction of reflective morality."[14] We shall see later how in each case the independent character of the roots is maintained and the problems of conflict studied. The general conclusion is that the roots are permanent in human life. The summary at the end of Part II recapitulates the pervasiveness of human desires, wants and needs demanding satisfaction; the unavoidability of associated living with its companionship and competition, its relations of cooperation and subordination; and the mass of phenomena of approval and disapproval, sympathy and resentment. And it concludes:

> "We cannot imagine them disappearing as long as human nature remains human nature, and lives in association with others. The fundamental conceptions of morals are, therefore, neither arbitrary nor artificial. They are not imposed upon human nature from without but develop out of its own operations and needs. Particular aspects of morals are transient; they are often, in their actual manifestation, defective and perverted. But the framework of moral conceptions is as permanent as human life itself."[15]

What now is the proposed solution in *32* for the relation of the three roots and their idea-systems? It is to maintain the distinctness of the categories and their underlying phenomena, but to make the content in each responsible to the idea of the good. This is how the right and the good are related:

> "In short, while Right as an idea is an independent moral conception or 'category', this fact does not solve the question of *what* is right in particular. Law and lawfulness are not all one with *a* law. Law is necessary because men are born and live in social relationships; *a* law is always questionable, for it is but a special means of realizing the function of law in general, namely, the institution of those relations among men which conduce to the welfare and freedom of all."[16]

Whether such a solution is satisfactory or whether it is a disguised form of reduction remains to be seen after we have examined the three roots in detail, as well as what elements were continued in the interpretation of the good from *08*.

Notes

1. For a sketch of this transition, see Elizabeth Flower's chapter on Dewey in Elizabeth Flower and Murray G. Murphey, *A History of Philosophy in America*, vol. II, chap. 14, esp. pp. 827–46.
2. LW 5: 279–88.
3. *three roots*, 203.
4. Ibid., 201.
5. Ibid., 202.
6. *club paper*, 41.
7. An important fragment in Dewey's notes on Ethics (102/64/9, Ethics, notes, 1925 January. AMs and TMs, 4pp.) strikes a keynote to the new ideas. One item on the relation of right to good, dated January 5, 1925, provides evidence that will be examined in Chapter 6 below. A second, dated January 7, 1925, shows Dewey thinking hard about the nature of conflict and its significance: "No possibility of making a complete theoretical synthesis—too many disparate and incompatible factors in conduct—the integration or synthesis is (1) found only in action and (2) is recurrent, because individualized. The meaning of morals is missed unless it is recognized that such unity as is attainable rests upon deliberation and choice-acts, and is not found in the nature of things apart from such interventions.

   Hence the experimental and unique character of moral conduct, and its peculiar connection with judgment, and of judgment with choice."

   He goes on to suggest some points of the conflict: "First, conflict of values, of good . . . Second, conflict of claims, requirements, heterogeneity of social groups . . . Third, conflict of claims and values. Social and individual; morality and self-sacrifice." The third is obviously on the verge of recognizing the conflict of roots, not just within each root.

   In the surviving notes and lectures, the early days of 1925 would seem to be the beginning of the ferment that led to the *three roots* and the *club paper*.
8. *three roots*: 204.
9. *club paper*: 13.
10. John Dewey and James H. Tufts, *Ethics* (New York: Henry Holt and Co, 1908), 194. This edition of the *Ethics* is hereafter referred to as *08*.
11. *08* : 326.
12. Ibid., 359.
13. Dewey and Tufts, *Ethics*, revised edition (Holt, 1932), 193–96 (hereafter referred to as *32*).
14. *32*: 196.
15. *32*: 309.
16. *32*: 227.

Part I

Fashioning the Conceptual Structure of *O8*

2

The Difference Between Customary and Reflective Morality

In this chapter we examine the difference between customary and reflective morality and the part played by this distinction in *08* and *32*. A major concern is the thesis presupposed in *08* but dropped as erroneous by *32* that the evolution of morality in the progress of civilization is from a customary, unreflective group morality to an individual reflective morality. It is only the historical-evolutionary thesis that is abandoned, not the distinction between the customary and the reflective. But we shall see that the thesis is what held together the several components in the idea of the customary and that this unitary character of the customary imparted a special character to its opposite, the individual reflective morality. With the weakening of the thesis the components flew apart and conceptual reconstruction was forced on the ethical theory. There lies the importance of the historical thesis and why we have to examine it carefully.

The general contrast of customary and reflective morality is basic to both *Ethics*. The very first sentence of *08* finds the significance of the work to lie in the effort "to awaken a vital conviction of the genuine reality of moral problems and the value of reflective thought in dealing with them."[1] Two theoretical keynotes are here sounded. The first, the genuine reality of moral problems, involves vindicating the character of the moral situation as one in which decision in made in face of a problem, not simply rules followed in the face of temptation. On this there will be a consistent path throughout. So too on the second keynote, the importance of reflective thought. But the character of reflective thought itself, though its general contours may be clear enough, is

15

assigned specific components that depend on the contrast with customary morality. Thus reflective thought is in some sense an *individual* matter; but is that to be interpreted by contrast with *social* or with *group*? And in what is the contrast to lie?

In *08* the contrast involves the convergence of three different contexts: the genetic context of the historical evolution of mankind, the comparative context of sociological differences in the state of society, the developmental context of individual growth. The first page of the Preface of *08* speaks of following the moral life "through typical epochs of its development."[2] This, we are told, "enables students to realize what is involved in their own habitual standpoints." There is an epoch of customary morality which precedes the emergence into an epoch of reflective morality. This is set off clearly in chapter 19 when in a discussion of the virtues Dewey contrasts virtue with mere conformity to custom. In a footnote he says: "This is, of course the point made in ch. 4 on 'Customs or Mores', save that there the emphasis was upon the epoch of customary as distinct from the reflective morals while here it is upon the customary factor in the present."[3]

The customary in the present points us to the comparative, as distinct from the genetic, study of societies, for it can be carried out independent of any succession of epochs. Thus in chapter 20, on "Social Organization and the Individual"—perhaps the clearest analysis of the idea of the social in *08*—Dewey speaks of *customary society*[4] and contrasts a *stationary society* with a *progressive society*. The central difference is between relying on custom and relying on exercise of the intellect. These bring along a contrast between the group and the individual, since customs are ways of a group and intellectual reflection is an individual or personal matter. It is necessary to add how customs are conceived: customs are habits in the group of which the group approves. In general then, both in genetic-historical and comparative-sociological study we begin to see the emergence of contrasting constellations: group, custom and habit, as against individual reflective. (The habitual and the customary are often roughly equated when the individual's habits are thought of as an outcome of the customs under which he or she has grown up.)

The third context, that of individual moral development as seen in *08*, raises serious problems, but at the same time enables us to make some clarifying distinctions. Three stages are found in conduct: "(a) Instinctive activity, (b) Attention; the stage of conscious direction or control of action by imagery; of deliberation, desire, and choice, (c) Habit; the stage of unconscious activity along lines set by previous action."[5] Consciousness is placed between hereditary reflex and automatic activities on the one hand and acquired habitual activities on the other. (The view that consciousness appears where the system has no ready-made responses is of course already long familiar in Dewey's writings.) When the new responses have become automatic, habitual, consciousness goes off elsewhere. In morals it is the habits formed at an earlier stage that prove inadequate to the complexity and conflict of a new situation. That is when struggle, effort, and deliberation take place. If successful, new habits are formed on a higher level. "For the new habits, the new character, embody more intelligence."[6] The first stage is not moral. The second shows morality in the making, including the process of transition from impulse through desire to will. "It will be illustrated in our treatment of race development, by the change from early group life and customs to the more conscious moral life of higher civilization. The third, well-organized character, is the goal of the process. A good man has built up a set of habits; a good society has established certain laws and moral codes." But it is not a changeless world. New choices and new valuations are needed. Therefore the focus will be on the second stage—of active moral consciousness.

Such a focus is certainly to be expected, for the whole work is set upon the role of reflection in morals. But what are we to infer from the fact that habits, the genus of custom, appear at the end as well as the beginning—let us call them pre-reflective habits and post-reflective habits respectively—and that while the first set are already outworn and so inferior to the reflective process, the second set might have been regarded as the triumphant end-product? It looks as if the latter are prospectively inferior since their day will soon be over; change can be counted on and there will be the continued need for reflection. Now the habitual at both ends can be seen as the customary, for the initial habits were approved in the pre-reflective stage and the outcome habits win approval. It would look then as if the general contrast of the customary as a whole and the reflective is putting all the habitual together under the rubric of what requires (has required or will require) change. On the other hand, we have been told that the new habits, the new character, *embody more intelligence*. (We do not yet raise the question that will come much later when we consider Dewey's *Human Nature and Conduct* : how the general contrast of custom and intelligence will hold up when intelligence itself is seen as a set of habits.) How, faced with an account of two different habits, shall we tell which embodies more intelligence? A minimal answer might be that one came into being out of deliberation while the other did not, either by continuing a habit acquired in the socialization process or taken over in some imitative way. A more substantive answer might look to the subject-matter of the situation—whether one habit fits the situation or answers to its problem more than the other does. But such a greater embodiment of intelligence might be found where there has been no previous deliberation. Obviously the contrast of the customary and the reflective, approached through the third context (that of moral growth or development) raises difficulties which have to be solved—for the other two contexts as well—by *specific differentiating criteria* rather than in a wholesale manner.

Most of such analysis comes through consideration of the historical development of morality. In the Introduction, even the terminological remarks about "ethics" and "morals" set us off in that direction. "Ethics" is derived from the Greek *ethos* which originally meant customs, just as "moral" is from the Latin *mores* which means the same, and likewise the German "sittlich" from *Sitten.* The moral or ethical began to appear in customs which were not merely habitual ways of acting but ways approved by the group or society. Today's use of ethical and moral stems from a far more complex and advanced type of life—"just as economics deals with a more complex problem than 'the management of a household'."[7] The implication is that there has been a change in the phenomena—an increase in the complexity of life—and that the moral shift was from approval of the ways of society to individual reflection about approving or disapproving the ways of society. But beyond this general vista by far the greatest specificity about the differentiation between customary, and reflective morality comes in Part I which, cast in historical form, is entitled "The Beginnings and Growth of Morality." This part is wholly the work of Tufts. There is little point in asking whether Dewey agreed with every distinction that Tufts here makes. We shall see in a later chapter that he did hold at that time to a generally similar thesis. What we can see here is what Dewey used or ignored or developed in Part II when he was on his own.

At the outset of Part I chapter 2 we are sent back to understanding primitive society in order to understand the origin and growth of moral life. The central fact there is the dominant influence of group life. One mark of this is clearly phenomenological, the sense of identification: the feeling that one is first and foremost a member of a group rather than an individual is furthered by kinship relations.[8] The degree of control exercised by the group over the individual is another mark. It is membership in the group that gives the individual whatever rights he has. This is seen by Tufts as still largely true of legal rights. At the beginning of chapter 5 "customary morality" is defined: "The organization of early society is that of group life, and so far as the individual is merged in the group the type of conduct may be called 'group morality'. Inasmuch as the agencies by which the group controls its members are largely those of custom, the morality may be called also 'customary morality'."[9] We are told later on that the individual takes the standard as a matter of course. "He cannot begin to be as selfish as a modern individualist; he simply hasn't the imagery to conceive such an exclusive good, nor the tools with which to carry it out."[10] Again, as to character, "In the organization of stable character the morality of custom is strong on one side. The group trains its members to act in the ways it approves and afterwards holds them by all the agencies in its power. It forms habits and enforces them. Its weakness is that the element of habit is so large, that of freedom so small. It holds up the average man; it holds back the man who might forge ahead. It is an anchor, and a drag."[11]

In general, the view expressed in these quotations may be labeled, in Bagehot's familiar phrase, "the cake of custom" conception of early man. It was, of course, very prevalent in the writings of the late nineteenth and early twentieth century that were intent on finding a line of evolution in morality, as they sought also in the family, the economy, law, art, etc. (We shall examine this intellectual atmosphere in chapter 8 below.)

The very title of chapter 5 reveals the thesis: "From Custom to Conscience; From Group Morality to Personal Morality." The criteria of moral advance offered help clarify the distinction of types: "Advance then must (1) substitute some rational method of setting up standards and forming values, in place of habitual passive acceptance; (2) secure voluntary and personal choice and interest, instead of unconscious identification with the group welfare or instinctive and habitual response to group needs; (3) encourage at the same time individual development and the demand that all share in this development—the worth and happiness of the person and of *every* person."[12] It is added that these advances bring on collisions that were only implicit before: that of authority and group interests with the independence and private interests of the individual; and that of order with progress, between habit and reconstruction.

Since chapter 9 is entitled "A General Comparison of Customary and Reflective Morality" we should expect a sharp setting off of the two ideas. But there is much that begins a retreat from their distinctness as epochs. Perhaps when both are looked at together the elements of the common begin to compete with the elements of distinctness. In any case, the first focus is on agreement and continuity.

Two continuities are offered. One is the partial persistence of the previous customary morality. The second, which we will consider later in the conceptual structure of ethics, is the fact that morality in the later stages does not find new concepts but takes them from the group life or its various spheres.[13] In spite of the proliferation of social groups and institutions and professions in the later stages, each has its own habits and customs. There is a certain ambiguity in this formulation, for what seems to persist is simply the habit of having habits. Nevertheless, the formulation is in accord with the theory of deliberation examined above, since the outcome is to be the reconstruction of habits into the new habits of character. Still, something more is intended: "In other words, group morality does not vanish in order that conscious and personal morality may take its place. Group and customary morality is still the morality of many of us most of the time, and of all of us for a good deal of the time."[14] This refers not only to childhood, but to the vast area of life in which we do not think out our standards, plus the pervasiveness of social influences, traditions accepted without challenge. Indeed it is fortunate that this is so, for to build all morality anew is as melancholy as to build all science anew.

Turning to contrasts among the stages, a first and obvious one is the separate emergence of the moral, now distinguished from the conventional, the political, the legal, etc. In the earlier stage the quality that the moral conveys attended all of custom, and clear distinctions were not made between the violation of manners and that of morals.

A second difference is found in epistemological source. Custom is tied to *observation* as against reflection. (To observe has its double sense: to see or to conform to.) The morality of custom—at that stage the approved character—stands out for perception, and the element of intelligence is reduced to a minimum. In the reflective stage the moral is no longer equated with the customary but has to be recognized *in* custom. This requires intelligence, and by the separation makes possible a critical component. This epistemological formulation is bolstered by an argument which might have been offered as a causal account of the conditions under which reflection is stimulated, but instead is apparently an ontological suggestion about the differences in subject-matter between the two stages. The example and its conclusion require quoting in full:

> A child may be shown in a pretty direct and physical fashion the difference between *meum* and *tuum* in its bearing upon his conduct: a fence may be pointed at which divides his yard from that of a neighbor and which draws as well the moral line between what is permissible and what is forbidden; a whipping may intensify the observation. But modern business knows also of intangible property—good will, reputation, credit. These, indeed, can be bought and sold but the detection of their existence and nature demands an intelligence which is more than perception. The greater number of duties and rights of which present morality consists are of just this type. They are relations, not just outward habits. Their acknowledgment requires accordingly something more than just to follow and reproduce existing customs. It involves power to see *why* certain habits are to be followed, what *makes* a thing good or bad. *Conscience* is thus substituted for *custom*; *principles* take the place of external rules.[15]

This argument seems to shift from what is required for encompassing the material to a critical assessment of what is grasped. There may well be more intelligence embedded in the understanding of credit and paying by check than in gold and barter. But the same might be said of an earlier complex kinship system on which moral obligations depend as against the obvious biological relations of the nuclear family today. Moreover, moderns accept customary property systems of a complex sort with no more thought than an earlier person accepted complex kinship systems and their obligations. It is surprising therefore that Tufts goes on to make this argument so central in his exposition: "This is what we mean by calling present morality reflective rather than customary."[16] Social customs have not, of course, disappeared but on the contrary, increased in both number and importance. "But the individual has to grasp the *meaning* of these customs over and above the bare fact of their existence, and has to guide himself by their *meaning* and not by the mere fact noted."[17] The remaining differences raise less difficult problems of interpretation. Customary morality is static. Reflection may find a meaning in custom which leads one to alter its present form. The idea that a custom may be wrong comes to the fore, and there is a readiness for transformation. A deepening of meaning in the moral concepts employed also takes place. Conflicts arise between the individual and the existing standards. Insofar as change of custom is more likely, a reflective morality marks a progressive society, whereas customary morality marks a stationary one. The general effect is multiple—individualism with both its enhancing and its egoistic consequences, emphasis on the personal and the subjective, tendencies to reconstruction, and so forth.

As Part I comes to a close, customary morality stands out not wholly clearly, but at least as a complex of several features. Among them are:

> Group cohesion and domination
> The weight of the habitual
> Automatic or unquestioning acceptance
> The lack of differentiation of the moral from other aspects of social life
> Can be directly grasped and does not require intellectual scrutiny
> Deals with simpler situations
> Static rather than dynamic
> Historically a prior period, but custom continues into the present as an important part of life and morality.

We may well ask, in going on to Part II and Dewey's theoretical inquiry into ethics, which of these will in fact be *used*.

For a long time, once Part II ("Theory of the Moral Life") is under way, the custom side of the custom-reflection contrast makes no entry on the stage of the inquiry. It is not surprising, for the topic is itself reflective inquiry and its place in morals, and it deals with concepts and theories. Nor would we expect it in discussions of Kant, for whom all existent tendencies as such are non-moral, nor in the Utilitarians whose attention is largely on the form of reconstruction. Of course character involves habits. But it is defined initially in a more general way: "we mean by character whatever lies behind an act in the way of deliberation and desire, whether these processes be near-by or remote."[18] When habit does enter into character in the concept of virtue, the reference is to the habits that are the cumulative outcome of reflection, the *post-reflective* as distinguished from the *pre-reflective* habits. Any customs that might have been invoked here would have been the ones established as a result of the reconstruction. Thus "The genuinely moral person is one, then, in whom the habit of regarding all capacities and habits of self from the social standpoint is formed and active."[19] This definition, we may note, should not be turned into a paradox of the truly moral person as one who goes back to custom, for this embodiment of the social approach is itself post-reflective, not the original group absorption.

Custom and pre-reflective habit enter on the scene again in chapter 16 which is concerned with moral knowledge. In criticizing moral intuitionism, Dewey concedes that "a large part of the acts, motives, and plans of the adult who has had favorable moral surroundings seem to possess directly, and in their own intrinsic make-up, rightness or wrongness or moral indifference."[20] But variation in such *perception* is evident enough, and direct perception of this sort does not guarantee moral validity. Such perception involves the funding or capitalizing of results of past experience, and takes place only under usual circumstances. (In short, it is the habitual at work.) New occasions coming on, however, compel the reflective process.

The more serious return to custom comes in considering the place of general rules in moral knowledge. We need not enter here into the careful analysis Dewey gives of different kinds of rules (the empirical, arising from actual cases of conduct and those which are simply given), problems in recognizing likeness classes, effects of rigidity and fixity on the moral life, and so forth. These will be considered in our later methodological discussions. The return to a consideration of custom comes in connection with the critique of empirical rules. Mill had met the objection that people do not have time to do a utilitarian calculation in a moral decision with the retort that this was equivalent to asking the sailors to recalculate the nautical tables on shipboard. Instead, Mill concluded, "Being rational creatures, they go to sea with it already calculated; and all rational creatures go out upon the sea of life with their minds made up on the common questions of right and wrong, as well as on many of the far more difficult questions of wise and foolish."[21] Dewey, while agreeing that the intuitionist's ultimate deliverances are generalizations in Mill's sense, complains that "the truth brought out by Mill does not cover the ground which needs to be covered. Such rules at best cover customary elements; they are based upon past habits of life, past natural and economic and political environments." Such customs, he adds, can include trivial elements and worship of idols; and in our own time "tolerate and sanction many practices, such as war, cruel business competition, economic exploitation of the weak, and absence of cooperative intelligent foresight, which the more sensitive consciences of the day will not approve." Again, "To take the rules of the past with any literalness as criteria of judgment in the present, would be to return to the unprogressive morality of the regime of custom—to surrender the advance marked by reflective morality."[22] The Nautical Almanac has been scientifically calculated. But custom's rules are "a confused mixture of class interest, irrational sentiment, authoritative pronunciamento and genuine consideration of welfare."

The spotlight now having focused on custom, Dewey says: "Custom still forms the background of all moral life, nor can we imagine a state of affairs in which it should not. Customs are not external to individuals' courses of action; they are embodied in the habits and purposes of individuals . . . " Quoting Grote he says "they reign under the appearance of habitual *self-suggested* tendencies."[23] Without customs the individual would be helpless; they provide a way of approaching each state of affairs that requires action. But customs are in conflict as opposite habits set up incompatible ends. Hence principles, not rules, are needed in judging. They are intellectual, not imperative: "Rules are practical; they are habitual ways of doing things. But principles are intellectual; they are useful methods of judging things."[24]

In Dewey's reckoning, then, intuitionism and rules become the methodological surrogates of custom, while intelligence and principle operate in reflection. Looking back to the list of features elicited from Tufts' account in Part I, intuitionism lines up with the directly grasped or the observed, and rules with the weight of the habitual and the static.

In the next chapter (17) which deals with the place of duty and the subjection to authority, the habitual rather than the customary plays its part. Dewey is considering the common (and Kantian) setting of the problem of authority—the conflict of duty and inclination—as one of duty versus appetite and unreflective impulses. This is too narrow; he points out that even reflectively formed habits, as in the case of professionals, may encroach upon other concerns and lead the individual to slight other responsibilities. Hence a more generic explanation is needed, to cover such habits as well as appetites. His formulation of the problem is accordingly that habit—like an instinct, habit is second nature—represents something formed and set, and it is this against which the reconstructive demand of duty is directed.[25]

There is only one more context in Part II in which custom is directly discussed. This is in considering changes in virtues.[26] Dewey points out that the actual meaning of virtues (e.g., chastity and patriotism) is widely different in different periods. But because minor changes are going on all the while, there is a lag between the community's formulated code of esteem and "its practical level of achievement and possibility. It is more or less traditional, describing what used to be, rather than what are, virtues. The 'respectable' comes to mean tolerable, passable, conventional. Accordingly the prevailing scheme of assigning merit and blame, while on the whole a mainstay of moral guidance and instruction, is also a menace to moral growth. Hence men must look behind the current valuation to the real value. Otherwise, mere conformity to custom is conceived to be virtue; and the individual who deviates from custom in the interest of a wider and deeper good is censured."[24] The footnote is the note we have already quoted earlier, but it is important to repeat here: "1.This is, of course, the point made in ch. 4 on 'Customs or Mores,' save that there the emphasis was upon the epoch of the customary as distinct from the reflective morals, while here it is upon the customary factor in the present." It is not unfair to say that in the whole of Part II Dewey has limited himself to the customary *in* the present. However, as noted earlier, this limitation may come from the topics of concern in Part II and its theoretical character. We have then to supplement the account with the treatment of the customary in the two chapters he wrote in Part III ("The World of Action") on Social Organization and the Individual and on Civil Society and the Political State. Only the first of these has relevant material for our present topic.

In some respects the relevant parts of this chapter seem to be accepting the historical thesis, just as the footnote mentioned above did. But in other respects it seems to be correcting that very account. He calls attention to a twofold movement in the history of morals. One is the "constantly increasing stress on *individual* intelligence and affection."[27] The change from customary to reflective morality is from an injunction to do what kin, class, or city do to being a person with certain habits of desire and deliberation. But at the same time "The moral history of the race also reveals constantly growing emphasis upon the *social* nature of the objects and ends to which personal preferences are to be devoted."[28] While moral quality resides in the habitual dispositions of an agent, it consists of the tendency to secure socially shareable values.

Granting that there has been increasing liberation of individual powers from rigid social control, Dewey at the same time recognizes that "emancipation from one sort of social organization means initiation into some other social order; the individual is liberated from a small and fixed (customary) social group, to become a member of a larger and progressive society."[29] What we have is really the formation of more complex and extensive social organizations, in short a rich and varied society. It is the multitude of groupings that brings out the multitude of individual powers.

Dewey can still say: "In customary society, it does not occur to any one that there is a difference between what he ought to do, i.e., the moral, and what those about him customarily do, i.e., the social. The socially established *is* the moral."[30] But in the same paragraph he says that the distinctively personal morality which reacts against custom "is simply the means of *social* reconstruction. It is treated as if it were an end in itself, and as if it were something higher than any morality which is or can be socially embodied." In this he seems to be cutting down any view that had a distinctive individual morality as the antithesis of customary morality. There is apparently no individual morality, all morality is social; there is individual reflective participation in reconstructing the social morality. And the causes of the individual growth are themselves social. Dewey enumerates various ways in which social institutions determine individual morality[31] and says emphatically (that is, in italics): *The very habits of individual moral initiative, of personal criticism of the existent order, and of private projection of a better order, to which moral individualists point as proofs of the purely 'inner' nature of morality are themselves effects of a variable and complex social order.* " Surprisingly for a work in which there have been repeated distinctions between an earlier customary epoch and a later reflective epoch, Dewey goes on to say: "If then we take modern social life in its broadest extent, as including not only what has become institutionalized and more or less fossilized but also what is still growing (forming and re-forming), we may justly say that it is as true of progressive as of stationary society, that the moral and social are one. The virtues of the individual in a progressive society are more reflective, more critical, involve more exercise of comparison and selection, than in customary society. But they are just as socially conditioned in their origin and as socially directed in their manifestation."[32]

The situation we are left with in *08* is briefly this: the distinction between the customary and the reflective as types of ethics, developed as an historical one as well as a sociological one with few hesitations in Tufts' chapters, is touched in Dewey's part only on a couple of methodological sides and begins to be undermined in his treatment of the pervasive character of the social in Part III. We have now to look at *32* to see what emendations and reconsiderations take place and on what grounds.

A number of retreats from the historical-evolutionary hypothesis are evident in the Introduction. For one thing, the method of investigation is now described as "comparative and genetic methods"[33] and the emphasis shifts to the comparative: "We cannot assume that our own morality is the only type that needs to be considered. Customs of primitive folk are doubtless not an adequate guide for present-day conduct, nor are our problems identical with those of ancient Hebrews, Greeks and Romans. Yet despite civilization we are still fundamentally human." In short, the first lesson is less the location of our sources than the recognition that in a comparative view ours is not the only type of morality to be considered. And the first lesson of primitive study is not origins but finding the common human. The more general lesson—that a historical approach enables us to see morality in a more dynamic way than a merely present study—is maintained.

As for the context of moral development in the individual, *32* continues to assume some similarity of the historical and psychological growth—almost but not quite ontogeny recapitulating phylogeny. In both editions the individual process is seen as one of successive rationalizing, socializing, and finally a moral stage of reflection, valuation, and criticism. But *32* has an element of reservation about the historical which it does not have for the psychological: "we look at the process of growth as it now goes on in a child, and as to some extent it has gone on in the history of those peoples which had had most to do with the present moral life of Europe and America . . . "[34]

Again, it is interesting to note that *32* drops the account of successive stages of instinct, attention and habit, as a basis for contrasting the reflective and the habitual and so the customary. Instead, we are given three levels of behavior and conduct in a macroscopic or observational manner, yet differentiated by motives. The first is motivated by non-moral (biologic, economic) impulses such as family or work, but which have important results for morals. In the second, the individual accepts "with relatively little critical reflection the standards and ways of his group as these are embodied in customs or *mores*..."[35] In the third, "the individual thinks and judges for himself, considers whether a purpose is good or right, decides and chooses, and does not accept the standards of his group without reflection." In short, the criteria of the reflective are the act of reflection and the employment of moral concepts. We are warned also that no individual of maturity is wholly at any single level. And the growth in which these stages are then discussed is that of the child primarily. The distinction between rationalizing, socializing, and operating at a moral level considered in this context (and found in both editions) is briefly as follows: Rationalizing is identified with the more efficient or intelligent satisfaction of the level one needs (but ends of course change in the process). Socialization provides an increased capacity to enter into relations with others (it also broadens the span of activities and calls out new powers and ends), a social self is built up. On top of the first two levels, the moral aspect involves the more rational and social conduct being itself "valued as good, and so be chosen and sought; or in terms of controls that the law which society or reason prescribes should be consciously thought of as right, used as a standard, and respected as binding."[36] And of course it is consolidated as habit and character.

In spite of the shifts in the Introduction with respect to the general picture of origins and the toning down of the historical thesis, when we get to Part I by Tufts, the greater part is maintained. Let us briefly note the changes.

The chapters retained are: 2 ("Early Group Life"), 4 ("Group Morality—Customs or Mores"), and 5 ("From Custom to Conscience; From Group Morality to Personal Morality"). These have been largely unchanged. The introductory paragraph of 2 does reflect a hesitancy. *08* said:

> To understand the origin and growth of moral life, it is essential to understand primitive society. And while there is much that is uncertain, there is one fact of capital importance which stands out clearly. This is the *dominant influence of group life*. It is not asserted that all people have had precisely the same type of groups, or the same degree of group solidarity. It is beyond question that the ancestors of modern civilized races lived under the general types of group life

which will be outlined, and that these types or their survivals are found among the great mass of peoples today. (*08*, p.23)

In *32* the first two sentences have been changed to:

To understand the growth of moral life, whether in the history of civilization or in a child, it is helpful as a first step to look into the life of certain more primitive societies. For these show clearly the great influence of groups on their members.[37]

The remainder is unchanged.

Beyond the retention of these three chapters in *32*, there is the significant fact that chapter 9 of *08*, "A General Comparison of Customary and Reflective Morality," has been eliminated in *32* in its entirety. Instead there is an expansion of materials that appeared in the earlier account of the modern period. It will accordingly be worth keeping an eye later on what has disappeared from the analysis, as well as the changes in the other chapters of Part I. (The addition of a chapter on "The Roman contribution to the Modern Moral Consciousness" is important for the structural shift, but not directly for the historical-evolutionary hypothesis.)

What looks like the final and decisive theoretical reckoning with the historical-evolutionary issue comes in *32* in the first few pages of Part II, Dewey's theoretical part.[38] Here the issue is no longer ignored. Indeed, the distinction between the customary, and the reflective is declared to be relative rather than absolute.[39] What is more, there emerges from the discussion a clear statement of the continuity of reflective morality and ethical theory. This had not been dealt with in *08*, and its significance can best be appreciated retrospectively even for *32*. For within a few years after 1932 there came on the scene the extremely sharp and absolute distinction between normative or substantive ethics and metaethics. The latter was declared to be a quite separate treatment of moral discourse, without normative elements (other than logical clarity and precision) and capable of being studied in isolation from the problems of normative ethics.

In these pages Dewey does not disown the distinction between customary and reflective morality. "The former places the standard and rules of conduct in ancestral habit; the latter appeals to conscience, reason, or to some principle which includes thought."[40] It thus shifts the center of gravity in morality. But it is nonetheless relative. For reflective thought could not be wholly absent in the one type, and certainly in the latter "there is an immense amount of conduct that is merely accommodated to social usage." It will therefore be regarded as a difference in principle rather than trying "to describe different historic and social epochs." A critical shift, as in Hebrew and Greek thought, is the necessity of criticizing existing customs and institutions from a new point of view.

Such necessity, on Dewey's view, should obviously come from conflicts in the society, and the changes of habits required. That is what prompts both systematic moral theory and reflective morality. For it is the questioning of the old that generates both of these. Children start in that direction by seeing parental injunctions as arbitrary, and adults start when in perplexity. As long as there is a positive belief as to right and wrong neither has occasion to arise; "what is called moral theory is but a more conscious and systematic raising of the question which occupies the mind of any one who in the face of moral conflict and doubt seeks a way out through reflection. In short, moral theory is but an extension of what is involved in all reflective morality."[41] New issues precipitating such a situation may come to a whole community in a given period. "The difference between customary and reflective morality is precisely that definite precepts, rules, definitive injunctions and prohibitions issue from the former while they cannot from the latter."[42] Confusion arises when appeal to rational principles is regarded as a substitute for custom. It is merely changing the source of moral commands and of authority, not making a genuine shift in the way of solving moral problems. The whole task of Part II is to work out the way that embodies reflection, not to replace one authority by another.

Without the historical thesis, the difference between the reflective and the non-reflective might very well have been raised in other terms. For Dewey's purposes, the crucial point was the criticism of existent ways. Whether the existent ways represented custom and were justified by appeal to custom, where justification was needed, would have been an empirical question to be compared to religious justification, justification by beliefs about social stability, and a host of other possibilities. The all-encompassing conception of custom obviously is something that has to be understood in terms of intellectual history of the time. We shall investigate this hypothesis later.

And yet the apparent ease with which Dewey left aside the aspects of custom which did not touch his methodological thesis raises the question whether it can be treated as an isolated matter, whether indeed it has any significance for the ethical theory that was being constructed. It could still be just a collateral historical belief that could not hold up in analysis and was gradually shed. The issue is whether it had any other consequences in the theory than the ones we have so far examined. The leading idea we are suggesting is that it did reach into the interpretation of habit, into the picture of individualism and the accompanying contrast of the individual and the social, and into the place of history in ethical theory. All these threads will be worth examining in subsequent chapters.

Notes

1. *08* : 3.
2. Ibid.
3. Ibid., 361.
4. Ibid., 387.
5. Ibid., 13.
6. Ibid., 14.
7. Ibid., 7.
8. Ibid., 27.
9. Ibid., 54.
10. Ibid., 72.
11. Ibid.
12. Ibid., 74.
13. Ibid., 161.
14. Ibid., 162.
15. Ibid., 167.
16. Ibid.
17. Ibid.
18. Ibid., 188.
19. Ibid., 271.
20. Ibid., 289.
21. Ibid., 299.
22. Ibid., 300.
23. Ibid.
24. Ibid., 301.
25. Ibid., 309–11.
26. Ibid., 360–61.
27. Ibid., 383.
28. Ibid.
29. Ibid., 384.
30. Ibid., 387.
31. Ibid., 389–90.
32. Ibid., 389.
33. *32*: 10.
34. Ibid., 13.
35. Ibid., 12.

36. Ibid., 24; cf. *08*:16.
37. Ibid., 22.
38. Ibid., 162–66.
39. Ibid., 162.
40. Ibid.
41. Ibid., 164.
42. Ibid., 165.

3

The Structural Shift, Before *08*

In this and the following two chapters we turn to look at the structural shift in some detail, in the attempt to trace what brought it to pass. The focus is of course on the three areas of the good, obligation, and virtue, and how the initial supremacy of the good as the unitary root gave way to the three roots. One of the important questions we shall have to ask, indeed to unravel, is what part the evolutionary assumption of the development from customary to reflective morality played in the structural shift itself. We cannot, however, simply begin with *08* alone. It was itself a culmination of a shift that had been going on since Dewey wrote *The Study of Ethics:A Syllabus*[1] (hereafter referred to as the *Syllabus*). In some respects *08* completes that shift, while at the same time making some revisions. In this chapter we shall accordingly examine the salient points of this process up to *08*; in the next chapter, the picture as given in *08*; and in the third of this group, the development after *08* through *32*.

The handles by which we lay hold of the tasks of this chapter are several. The first is obvious: In the *Syllabus* Dewey offers a view of conduct and its nature that remains constant throughout his work. It is what integrates his whole approach to ethics, and it is taken for granted as well as expounded in various ways in his subsequent works. Now it is clearly a *psychological* analysis; indeed the greater part of the *Syllabus* (Part II) is entitled "Psychological Ethics" and specific discussions of Obligation or of Freedom and Responsibility begin with "The Psychology of Obligation" and "The Psychology of Freedom." It is important however to add that Dewey does not conceive of Psychological Ethics as one type or branch of ethics; it is the whole of ethics

33

analyzed psychologically, that is, ethics studied from the standpoint of individual agency. The hardened distinction so often found between Individual Ethics and Social Ethics is not Dewey's; his is between Psychological Ethics and Social Ethics as two ways of studying ethics as a whole.[2] Now the topic to which these remarks lead us is simply that his central analysis of conduct has to be seen in the light of the revolution that had taken place in his conception of psychology.

A second handle is found in Dewey's constant concern with the relation of the individual to his natural and social environment. It is, of course, part of the problems raised in his psychological theory, but it reaches back of his changed psychological outlook, for it is already found in the earlier *Outlines of A Critical Theory of Ethics*[3] whose revision changed into the *Syllabus*. Its root is the growth of his philosophical naturalism, the endeavor to see man in nature as against the traditional dualism of mind and matter or body and spirit.

A third handle is suggested by Dewey's remark in the *Fries letter* that the change from *08* to *32* was, on its pedagogic side, from couching the material too much in terms of theories in *08* to making the approach direct and criticisms of theory secondary in *32*. At first this is puzzling if it is supposed to play a part in the theoretical change of *32* : since theories are about phenomena and their organization, what does looking at the former do that looking at the latter does not? One possibility is that looking through theories narrows one's vision to the phenomena they regard as central. This suggests that we look at the theories Dewey selects for criticism in the earlier works; it may be that though they are in conflict with one another they nevertheless contained a common perspective of analysis, and this is what was later challenged in *32*. We shall accordingly have to see how Dewey dealt with Utilitarianism and Kantianism and with self-realization theory, and what he got out of this. Allied with this inquiry is Dewey's remark that the study of British sentiment theorists helped him see the independence of the third root. We have therefore to keep an eye on what Dewey or Tufts had done in that area before *08*; as a matter of fact, Tufts had done a great deal and it explains some features of *08*.

Dewey's Psychological Revolution and Its Theory of Conduct

The impact of James's *Principles of Psychology* on Dewey and the revision of his psychological thinking appears in a series of articles of which "The Reflex Arc Concept in Psychology"[4] provided the basic model. It criticizes the use of this concept in the current psychology. Although directed against associationism and body-mind dualism, it does not achieve its aim because it treats sensory stimulus, central connections and motor discharge as separate. They should be viewed "not as separate and complete entities in themselves, but as divisions of labor, functioning factors, within the single concrete whole, now designated as the reflex arc."[5] The paper both amplifies this interpretation and illustrates it in phenomena of consciousness and activity.

This paper marks a clear divide in Dewey's thought. It was a final break with any religious attitude to life, a matter that had a serious role in the greater part of his life. He early cast off any specific religious beliefs, replacing them with a favorable attitude to T.H. Green's philosophical idealism. But this too he dropped quite early. He continued to be sympathetic to a religious attitude to life, as treating life seriously. With the Reflex Arc paper, Dewey finally rejected any form of religious or philosophical non-naturalism.

The _Syllabus_ provides an integrated concept of conduct as a basis for ethics, and it is worth summarizing its often ponderous formulations on our topic. All conduct is at first impulse. But impulses have evolved in relation to the inclusive activity of maintaining life and so are interconnected. The ends for men are different and more complex. "The definite coordination of acts is thus, with man, not a _datum_ but a _problem_."[6] Each impulse that is expressed brings other experiences into consciousness and these react on the original impulse and modify it. "_This reaction of the induced experiences into the inducing impulse is the psychological basis of moral conduct._"[7] Dewey calls this back-reference of an experience the _mediation_ of impulse. Such mediation then constitutes the meaning of the impulse; thereby it is _idealized_. "The impulse mediated, that is given conscious value through the reference into it of the other experiences which will result from its expression, constitutes volition proper."[8]

Now this process is misrepresented if we separate impulse and induced experience, treating impulse as an independent act and induced experiences as external consequences. Dewey says that the consequences in the back-reference _are_ the act as a moral or conscious act. Note the close connection in this phenomenon of _learning_ and of significance or _value_. "Differences of moral value (as we shall see later) depend simply upon the range and thoroughness of this mediation—the completeness with which the 'consequences' of an act are returned into the structure of the natural impulse."[9]

Dewey derives the fundamental ethical categories from the psychological mediation of impulse. The mediation idealizes the impulse and gives it its value in the whole system of action; and it controls or directs it. The former constitute the goodness or badness of the impulse, its satisfaction or dissatisfaction. The control which operates through reaction of anticipated experience is the basis for obligation. "Thus we have, on one side, the moral categories of Satisfaction, Good (Summum Bonum), Value, and, on the other, those of Duty, Law, Control, Standard, etc."[10] He goes on: "Every concrete act unites, of course, the two phases; in its complete character, as affording satisfaction and, at the same time, fulfilling its organic interactions, it is right and the agent which it expresses is *free*. Thus we have three main sets of ethical ideas: those centering, respectively, about (a) the *Value*, (b) the *Control*, (c) the *Freedom* of conduct."

Three degrees of completeness of mediation are distinguished. In the most complete the original impulse is completely transformed— Dewey cites the way the impulse for locomotion is made over when we learn to walk or babbling when we learn to talk. This complete reaction is *habit*. In an intermediate completeness there are general lines or plans of action that become a framework for our conduct. In the least complete we have particular variable acts and numerous complex experiences in which there is no direct or organic reaction of consequences and so we do the best we can with the meaning of the act.

"Character" and "conduct" refer to the same situation. Character focuses on the mediated impulses as the source of acts. "It designates the *way* in which impulses (varying, of course, in every person) are directed and controlled—that is, mediated."[11] Conduct is the executed way. Motive is simply character in a particular instance—"impulse in the light of the consequences which may reasonably be supposed to result from acting upon it."[12]

We may note that conduct or character are taken by Dewey to be the *subject of the moral judgment*.[13] The *predicate of the moral judgment* is introduced by asking "When shall we call the character, or conduct, good or bad?"[14] The answer focuses on the mediation as a process of self-development in which one becomes aware of the meaning of one's impulses in terms of one's experiences. It is important to note that Dewey decries "the fiction of a distinct, deciding self, a self separate from the material estimated, the impulses competing."[15] The self is thus in effect the whole system of impulses.

Now the predicate, or moral value of an act, is identified by Dewey as *"the completest possible interaction of an impulse with all other experiences, or the completest possible relation of an impulse to the whole self."*[16] Thus in "this act is right" the subject is an act mediated by reference to the other experiences it occasions—its effect on the self. The wrong and right are distinguished by whether the self is narrowed and friction introduced into it or whether it is expanded and organized. Again, a good man is a whole self in his acts; a bad man has no unifying principle.

Other notions in the understanding of conduct are explicated in the course of analyzing moral approbation. For example, "Attention is an idea or set of ideas so completely bound up with an impulse that they demand realization."[17] They are organically connected with the impulse. Interest is related to attention. Intention, as what an agent means to do,"constitutes *reflection*, or the control of the impulse by *reason*."[18] Effort is in terms of emotion what reflection is in terms of rational content,[19] and occurs when impulses are striving for coordination and temporarily oppose each other.

Other psychological phenomena are also put in order within the same broad framework. There is of course a reckoning with pleasure during the critique of hedonism, and a complex analysis of desire in terms of partial activity, object, and feeling.

It is not difficult to see how Dewey's analysis of conduct shapes the interpretation of the moral categories. The process by which a choice is made and valued is a continuation of the process by which an end is purposed through mediation of propelling impulse. From the beginning Dewey regards every act that is consciously performed as already a judgment of value. The converse is also asserted: "every judgment about conduct is itself an act; it marks a practical and not simply a theoretical attitude. That is, it does not lie outside of the matter judged (conduct), but constitutes a part of its development; conduct is different after, and because of, the judgment."[20] The basic ethical category of value is thus inherent in all conduct. The moral judgment, as already seen, is in the first place about the goodness of character or conduct. It thus has already a reference to a systematization that reflects the phenomenon of mediation. Dewey has an interesting analogy in differentiating the natural good—the satisfaction which any impulse affords in its expression—from the moral good. He compares the former to the "value in use" of the economists, a value which is directly enjoyed without measurement. The moral good is like "exchange value" which involves measurement, "the measurement here also being through interaction or relation (namely, exchange) creating a tension of various impulses against each other, which makes it necessary to estimate the relative importance of each."[21]

The theory of obligation produces no utterly disparate phenomenon, in spite of the Kantian attempt to set off the ought against desire. Instead, "the consciousness of duty carries with it the sense of a fundamental underlying identity. The sense of obligation is not the sense of a stronger alien force bearing down; it is rather the sense that the obligatory act is something more truly and definitely one's self than the present self upon which the obligation is imposed. 'I ought to do this act,' implies that 'this act' is really 'I'; in so far as the idea of the act is felt as merely alien to self, it is felt as irritating, as something to be got rid of, not as authoritatively binding."[22]

Dewey expounds the sense of duty in terms of the by now familiar distinction of self as immediate and mediate. The initial impulse is, however, replaced by "a certain body of positive impulse and habit urging forward for complete expression."[23] It is thus the same principle of explanation, but with an extended initial state description. Progress in the situation does not call for destroying the old habits and desires but using them in new directions, which means a making over of the old habit. The sense of duty, in demanding the new, is thus a phenomenon of moral progress. (We can see in *08* how this type of argument is developed as a powerful perspective in the critique of Kant.) The point is made in more general terms in the summary:

"The consciousness of obligation arises wherever there is felt the necessity of employing an existent habit or impulse to realize an end with which it is connected on the basis of present need, though not of past history. Its peculiar double relationship arises from the fact that it is the nature of habit and impulse *in themselves*, or abstractly, to demand immediate discharge on the basis of their own past; thus they tend to resist readjustment, and go their own way. But habits and impulses are, after all, developed with reference to the needs of the organism; the habit is not isolated, but connected, and the consciousness of this functional connection comes out in the recognition that the required thing is somehow bound up with our own being, and not imposed from without."[24] The consciousness of duty is thus associated with critical periods of readjustment.

Now what of virtue? It is significant that in the listing of basic ethical ideas the third idea starts off not with Virtue but with Freedom. Dewey says: "The ethical conception of freedom is the recognition of the meaning for conduct of the identity of self and act, of will and deed. There is no factor in the act foreign or alien to the agent's self; it is himself through and through. No action is moral (that is, falling in the moral sphere) save as voluntary, and every voluntary act, as the entire foregoing analysis indicates, is the self operating, and hence is free. Impulse is self, the developing ideal is self; the reaction of the ideal as measuring and controlling impulse is self. The entire voluntary process is one of self-expression, of coming to consciousness of the self. This intimate and thorough-going *selfness* of the deed constitutes freedom."[25]

We should note also that he finds the basis of responsibility as well in the identity of self and deed. "We are responsible for our deeds because they are ourselves. Responsibility is a name for the fact that we are, and are something definite and concrete—specific individuals. I am myself, I am conscious of myself in my deeds (self-conscious), I am responsible, name not three facts, but one fact."[26]

Virtue is expounded in this framework: "Virtue may be considered either as a case of substantial freedom, of solid, thoroughly unified action, or as a case of substantial responsibility, of flexible, properly adjusted, interaction—the adequate intellectual recognition of, and adequate emotional interest in, the demands of the situation."[27]

It is this virtue in general that is first considered, "the wholeness of self, the full and definite manifestation of agent in act (the adequate mediation of impulse)."[28] The various specific virtues are then assigned to different phases of this total act. This kind of treatment of specific virtues—as phases of some process—remains throughout in Dewey's ethics, although (as we shall see) what they are phases of undergoes some transformation.

In this survey of the three ethical concepts in the *Syllabus*, it is clear that the good has primacy, that the other concepts enter in terms of the way in which the self works out the expression of mediated impulse under complex conditions. The primacy of the good was of course no new idea here. The relation of ethical concepts is no different from what it was in the earlier *Outlines*. But there it had been cast in terms of the play of ethical theories with their assigned meanings for the ideas. In the *Syllabus* the concepts have acquired a functional reference to aspects of the psychology of conduct.

The Quest for a Transactional View

In his much later correspondence with A. F. Bentley, beginning in the 1930s, and in his collaboration with Bentley, Dewey looks for a more fully integrated view of the relations of man and nature, man and man, than is conveyed even by the idea of *interpersonal* relations. He fears that the latter term may isolate the individuals and make their relations external to themselves. The notion of the *transactional* seems to convey more adequately the way of looking at unified goings-on. In the *Syllabus*, although there is an awareness of the total field as including conditions, natural and social, in the moral process, the spotlight remains fixed on the agency of the individual. Whether this is an unavoidable for ethics, or constitutes a special theory of ethics, is a fundamental question we shall meet on a number of occasions hereafter.

Quite possibly, in the *Syllabus* it is simply the consequence of dealing with Psychological Ethics. In chapter 2 (The Factors of Moral Conduct: The Agent and his Sphere of Action) Dewey says: "In analyzing conduct, it is just as important to consider the situation as the agent. While conduct proceeds from an agent, the agent himself acts with reference to the conditions as they present themselves."[29] For the role of conditions (environment), Dewey refers to the agent being molded through education into habits of thinking and feeling; and to the demands made upon one—custom, institutional expectations, as well as the stimuli of surrounding objects and opportunities. Again, ideas, plans and wishes require the power of the environment to issue in action; even more, the situation "reacts into consciousness, and strengthens or modifies the plan."[30]

Dewey also recognizes that the exclusive reference of conduct to the individual was a late development, due partly to the influence of Christianity and partly to the disintegration of local custom and interests under the Roman empire. (In short, it was a *historic* phenomenon.)

Nevertheless, the conclusion Dewey draws is not that an individual-in-environment focus should be operative in ethics. To secure right conduct we should pay equal attention to the agent and the conditions with reference to which he acts.[31] But external pressure or influence cannot secure right conduct, *"except in so far as it ceases to be external*; except, that is, as it is taken up into the purpose and interests of the agent himself."* Yet again, a person's plans have to reflect the requirements of the agent's situation. But the meaning of the situation depends on the agent's own capacities, resources and skill; he is himself a part of the conditions to be taken into account.[32] It is not quite a total transactional schema, so much as a recognition of two aspects each of which carries you to the other. As he puts it,"From the standpoint of the individual agent, *conduct is the coordinating, or bringing to a unity the different elements of a complex situation."* In the other direction,"From the standpoint of the scene of action, *conduct is coordinating, in an organized way, the concrete powers, the impulses and habits of an individual agent."*[33] Clearly both, in spite of difference of standpoint, point to the agent.

There is some movement toward a more integrated schema when he compares conduct to a biological function, the former being conscious. It is like respiration with the co-ordination of lungs as organ and air as environment. The immediate importance of the organ is explained by its being the point of initiation and of greater permanence than any particular part of the environment. But the nature of the function determines both; they are not each fixed in itself. Spencer is criticized for defining life, mind, and conduct as adjustment of inner relations to outer; the separation of inner and outer neglects the fact that we have not a parallelism, but the function includes and determines both organ and environment.

It is difficult to decide to decide whether Dewey has here fully moved into a transactional schema or whether at the last moment he turns it all toward the agent. Certainly in treating of the ethical concepts of the *Syllabus* the latter seems to be the case. If the organ is focused on in the biological function because of greater permanence and its initiating role, certainly these hold also for the individual in moral conduct, and in addition there is the unifying spotlight of consciousness. But at the same time we must remember that in the human situation the environment includes other people. In the *Syllabus* this part of the environment is still reflected through what goes on in the self of the agent. We can therefore appropriately ask why the agent focus is not overcome. Different considerations may be offered.

(i)   It is possible that the ethical theories Dewey is criticizing in bringing out various lessons for ethics are overwhelmingly individualist in their orientation, and though Dewey is constantly attacking their views for assorted dualisms and consequent isolation of ethics from bio-social relations, he may still be continuing their initial formulation of questions in spite of giving different answers. In the *Syllabus*, while focusing on the moral judgment of the individual, he has assigned to it both a subject and predicate that lead directly into conduct, and the content of the judgment is what is going on in the agent.

(ii)   The individual moral judgment is indeed a significant starting-point for the analysis that ethics carries out. If there were no such moral judgments there would be no subject-matter for ethics to go at. Or would there be no *distinct* subject-matter? This is a point the *Syllabus* has not clarified. Dewey's interest is always in reflective morality and reflection is a phenomenon of human individuals. Again, individual moral judgment is also the point at which conscious efforts at reconstruction emerge. It is not yet clear whether unreflective morality is simply unduly stationary morality, a wrong view of morality, or not morality at all.

(iii) Not only the syntactic properties of the moral judgment (subject and predicate) carry us to actual conduct, but every semantic reference (the content of the moral judgment) points the same way. But conduct is an individual's conduct. Dewey has gone far enough to set the individual in interactive relation to environment, and beyond that to see how given interaction takes place and how a constant feedback shapes both at a given time. The advance is to see all of this in consciousness. But it is a stretching of consciousness rather than a whole field function.

(iv)   The intellectual instrument in the advances have been biology and psychology. An evolutionary perspective almost unnoticed cast the initial enterprise of impulse not as just a phenomenon but as occurring in a complex of impulses directed to survival. Dewey did not start with ends (constituting the good) to be systematized on their own and to carry both themselves and their value concepts away from their grounding. Secondly, as we have seen, the whole view of conduct is the product of the new Deweyan psychology under the influence of James's psychology. Its weight then too, is toward the individual focus, for it is not yet a social psychology.

(v)   There is always the possibility that some influence in the individual focus stems from Dewey's own kinship with (not adherence to) the prominent self-realizationist view of the time. In April 1889[34] and

November 1892[35] he published articles on T.H. Green, and in November 1893 one on self-realization.[36] The last two date after the *Outlines* of 1891. Can we find there any clue as to why the moral concepts of the *Syllabus* still remain *self*-enclosed? The third paper sheds some light when it discusses Dewey's basic difference from Green, the relations of aspects in individual-environmental relations, and what Dewey regards as the central controversies in ethics of the time.

Dewey sees Green as having divided the self into an infinite ideal and a process of realization unrelated to it. "The notion which I would suggest as substitute is that of the self as always a concrete specific activity; and therefore, (to anticipate) of the identity of self and realization."[37] He wants to regard the self not as something *to be* realized, but as a reality in place and time, as "concrete as a growing tree or a moving planet."[38] In short, he wants a working conception of the self as against a fixed or presupposed self. The contrast that the self-realization theory finds turns out on analysis to be between "*a smaller and larger view* of the actuality."[39] This seems to provide for consciousness the task of enlarging the view.

To understand realization we are led into a metaphysical analysis of *capacity*. Capacity is itself activity, not the mere possibility of activity. Like Aristotle arguing for the reality of the potential, Dewey is treating the potential as a movement of an actuality. But instead of a movement toward a form, which has its definite essence, Dewey takes James's view of the essence as instrument—the essence as what is so important for one's interests that one may by comparison omit other properties. Hence capacity is a way of viewing actuality. For example we focus on the eye as an organ and make the attendant necessary factors in the situation of seeing into circumstances. The reality is the seeing; the eye is an abstraction, but by focusing on it we turn everything else into conditions of exercise. The eye then becomes the capacity of seeing. "Instead of the one organic activity, we now have an organ on one side, and environment on the other."[40]

In a footnote[41] Dewey refers us to his treatment in the *Outlines*.[42] There capacity and environment were analyzed as two sides of individuality. There, we may note, he referred to the *inner* side—the capacity as against the environmental side[43]—and showed how a function included the two sides, the *external* and the *internal*. The stage of philosophy in which internal meant mental and external meant physical is long behind him, but the retention of the language of internal and external is open to the same kind of criticism as Dewey in his *Reflex Arc* paper gave of the separation of stimulus and response as a dualistic survival. In the present article there is no misunderstanding: "We call any activity capacity, in other words, whenever we first take it abstractly, or at less than its full meaning, and then add to it further relations which we afterwards find involved in it. We first transform our partial conception into a rigid fact, and then, discovering that there is more than the bare fact which we have so far taken into account, we call this broken-off fact capacity for something more."[44] The future acts and conditions are thus seen as "*simply* the present act in its mediated content." This is a far cry from even the interaction of individual and environment, but Dewey is not intent here on fashioning new concepts. He is expounding self-realization, and he wants to substitute "a working conception of the self for a metaphysical definition of it."[45] He is content with rejecting action *for* the self in favor of action *as* the self.[46]

If Dewey is here content with bringing the self into present reality instead of leaving it an empty expression, we have to ask why he sets his sights so low. He gives at least one pragmatic reason: "The more one is convinced that the pressing need of the day, in order to make headway against hedonistic ethics on one side and theological ethics on the other, is an ethics rooted and grounded in the self, the greater is the demand that the self be conceived as a working, practical self, carrying within the rhythm of its own process both 'realized' and 'ideal' self . . . "[47]

On the whole, then, the spotlight in Dewey's ethical theory at this period still remains fixed on the individual agent rather than the transactional field, although he is perfectly clear about what such a field requires. Perhaps in spite of the weight of the reasons we have indicated, the simplest explanation suggested earlier is the most plausible—that the *Syllabus* is doing Psychological Ethics, which covers the whole field from the standpoint of individual agency. If so, we have to look as we move on toward *08* where and when he begins to look at the whole field from the standpoint of Social Ethics.

The Range of Theories to Contend With

The last of the topics outlined for this chapter is a glance at the theories Dewey grapples with in this period, and in fact into *08*. The list is a familiar one—largely the Kantian and Utilitarian, the self-realizationist (particularly T.H. Green, discussed above), and beyond that the evolutionary aspect of Spencer and an occasional reference to Stephen. Dewey and Tufts' attitude to criticism is stated in the preface to *08* : "Theories are treated not as incompatible rival systems which must be accepted or rejected *en bloc*, but as more or less adequate methods of surveying the problems of conduct. This mode of approach facilitates the scientific estimation and determination of the part played by various factors in the complexity of moral life."[48] The theories that are marshaled for criticism thus usually enter the scene because of their one-sided treatment of some aspect of the elements of conduct. They are lined up in their opposition and a synthesis is worked out not by adding the one lesson to the other but by undercutting their particular dualism, whether it be intention and consequences, or self and environment, or inner and outer, or feeling and action, or feeling and thought.

During this period, and into *08*, criticism of Kant plays a fixed role. It is to forestall any bid of right and obligation to conceptual independence from the good. As for Utilitarianism, we may recall that in the *Fries letter* Dewey said that in the earlier edition his position was that of "a socialized utilitarian." Criticism was accordingly directed to removing the fragmentized hedonism, the egoistic psychology, and (particularly of Mill) any tendency to equate empiricism with the fixity of custom. Of Green, as we have noted, criticism is directed to make a working rather than a dubiously transcendental or empty self; but the effect is still to keep the self as the boundary of the moral act. About Spencer's bringing the whole causal picture of evolution to bear upon ethics, Dewey raises the question whether it reconstructs the ethical arena or instead is running a parallel study of social and cultural change to explain the individual's consciousness. In his general essay "The Philosophical Work of Herbert Spencer"[49] he ends by denying Spencer's conception of evolution itself, for "A thorough-going evolution must by the nature of the case abolish all fixed limits, beginnings, origins, forces, laws, goals. If there be evolution, then all these also evolve, and are what they are as points of origin and of destination relative to some special portion of evolution." Spencer instead is projecting on the cosmic scene the ideals of later eighteenth century liberalism.

Now what of eighteenth century British ethics that played a pivotal part in leading Dewey to the independence of the third root? On the whole, even in *08* Dewey makes little use of it except for the general lesson that the affective there makes its bid for a place in ethical theory alongside of (and hoping to replace) the rational-intellectual; and the more specific point that it fashioned the individualistic misreading of human nature as the battle of egoism and altruism. The strange thing is, however, that Tufts had before *08* made a careful study of the British moralists of the seventeenth and eighteenth century in relation to the conditions of life of the period. [50] Why did not Tufts reach the conclusion about the independence of the third root?

The guiding idea of Tufts' survey can perhaps be conveyed by his own summary at the end of the 1904 work:

> The ethical theory of the eighteenth century has presented a view of the individual which reflects the economic and intellectual life of the age. Starting with thoroughly individualistic conceptions, measuring value in terms of feeling, conceiving reason largely as a mere means for obtaining the goods of feeling, and regarding desire and will as determined by feelings already experienced rather than by ideals of action, it never completely transcends these limitations. Nevertheless the conception expands to include new and more generous impulses. The abstractness of the older intellectualism is brought clearly into view; the dangers of the analytic method are in a measure recognized; the rational factor is introduced as an integral principle of control; the social forces are given an increasing recognition as the agencies which create and foster the moral life. The way is open for a system which will be enabled to assume the social good as the criterion and end of action, and rely on the social and immanent forces to make the social weal the motive to action.

The theme throughout has been the relation of individual and society. Tufts has examined them in motivations, in causal accounts, in religious and scientific ideas. For example, he compares Shaftesbury and Mandeville and finds that while the individual is more generally recognized as an individual by both, Shaftesbury gives the individual a far more social content, while Mandeville makes all social tendencies of man the consequence of social forces. It is clear that Tufts is finding a direction in the dialectic of ethical ideas and social conditions. While on the one hand the individual is winning fuller recognition, on the other the content of individual moral motivation is led more fully to the social good. This outcome is precisely the structure of the conceptual relations that we shall see unfolded, particularly in Tufts' part in *08* and taken for granted by Dewey in his theoretical sections.

The reason why Tufts' early study of the eighteenth century British ethics did not have the same result as Dewey's later restudy—that is, it did not lead to a third independent root for ethics—is thus fairly clear. Tufts was too intent on seeing it as a chapter in the evolution of morals from the customary to the individualistic-reflective. The underlying historical thesis of linear moral evolution is thus the mediating belief that imposed limits on the analysis of moral structure. The historically tantalizing thing is, as we shall see in the next chapter, that Tufts did at one point in *08* suggest the independence of the third root, but he passed by this idea. When Dewey by the middle-late 1920s restudied the same materials he could, being freed of the linear evolutionary theory, draw a fresh conclusion.[51] But much else by then had poured into the stream of thought.

We are brought to the portals of *08*. In proceeding now to the examination of its structure we have to approach it not simply as the first really large book on ethics as a whole that Dewey did, but a source in which we can ask what he added to the Psychological Ethics of the *Syllabus* and how this may have changed his conception of ethics as a whole.

Notes

1. 1894, EW4: 219–362.
2. Dewey states this point in different ways with some frequency. For example, in the lecture notes of a course on *Sociology of Ethics*, in the autumn of 1902 (02A3, Part I, pp. 1–206) he says (Oct. 2) that every moral question is a question for some individual, that social or sociological ethics is a misnomer. But when we ask what the individual is called on to do "the source of the ethical quality, the explanation of it, cannot be found in the individual." In a subsequent lecture (L3, p.18) he approaches the individual's role apparently through the relation of organism and environment: "its action is always interaction. There is no action which is simply the action of an organism." The organism is primary teleologically, but it is not an ontological primacy: "the organism stands for the beginning and end side and the environment stands for the means: and the life process is the complete reality." (p. 19).
3. 1891, EW 3: 237–388; (hereafter referred to as *Outlines*).
4. 1896, EW 5: 96–109. For a clear exposition of this paper and its ramification in Dewey's philosophy, see Elizabeth Flower's chapter "Dewey: Betting Against Dualisms" in Elizabeth Flower and Murray G. Murphey, *A History of Philosophy in America* (New York: G. Putnam's Sons, 1977), Vol. II, ch. 14, pp. 829 ff.
5. Ibid., 97.
6. EW 4: 236.
7. Ibid., 236–37.
8. Ibid., 237.
9. Ibid., 238.

10. Ibid., 239.
11. Ibid., 241.
12. Ibid., 242–43.
13. Ibid., 240–43.
14. Ibid., 243.
15. Ibid., 346.
16. Ibid., 244.
17. Ibid., 250.
18. Ibid., 251.
19. Ibid., 253.
20. Ibid., 224.
21. Ibid., 248.
22. Ibid., 311–12.
23. Ibid., 312.
24. Ibid., 315–16.
25. Ibid., 341–42.
26. Ibid., 342.
27. Ibid., 351.
28. Ibid., 353.
29. Ibid., 229.
30. Ibid., 230.
31. Ibid., 231.
32. Ibid., 232.
33. Ibid.
34. EW 3: 14–35.
35. Ibid., 155–73.
36. EW 4: 42–53.
37. EW 2: 43.
38. Ibid., 44.
39. Ibid., 45.
40. Ibid., 48.
41. Ibid., 48, n.4.
42. EW 3: 301–04.
43. Ibid., 302.
44. EW 4: 49.
45. Ibid., 50.
46. Ibid., 51.
47. Ibid., 53.
48. *08* : 4.
49. MW 3: 192–209.
50. The seventeenth century (including Hobbes, Cumberland and Locke) was treated in a work by Tufts and Helen Thompson entitled *The Individual and His Relation to Society as Reflected in British Ethics*, Part I: The Individual in Relation to Law and Institutions. It was published by the University of Chicago Press in 1896 (reprinted 1898): a note says that Thompson did the section on Cumberland, Tufts the rest. The eighteenth century was treated in a subsequent work by Tufts alone, with the same major title except that: "Of the Eighteenth Century" is added. It is regarded as Part II and goes through the full range of eighteenth century figures ending with Hume and Adam Smith. It was published by Macmillan in 1904.
51. We say "restudied" since of course there is ample evidence of Dewey having made use of the British moralists at many points before. For example, his early

article on "Moral Philosophy" in *Johnson's Universal Cyclopaedia* (1894, MW 4: 132–151) has a section on The English Development, and his article on Ethics in the *Encyclopedia Americana* (1904, MW 3: 40–58) has ample eighteenth century bibliographical listing for the British moral philosophers. The point is the use he makes of the eighteenth century materials in the particular contexts.

4

The Conceptual Structure of *08*

Two striking features of *08*, beyond the fact that it is a full text attempting to view the whole field, are: the place it gives to the history of the moral and attention to the problems of practice. The latter is a natural extension of the major task of morality. The former has been examined earlier for its impact on the relation of customary and reflective morality. Was the introduction of history an impact at all comparable to that of psychology in reconstructing the framework of ethical concepts?

On the whole we find that it has not so drastic a consequence. The treatment of ethical concepts in *08* is continuous with that of the *Syllabus* although there are changes. The drastic changes are to come in *32*. Those in *08* seem an almost natural extension of the previous account once attention is paid to the wider area of society and history. This suggests the thesis that since the *Syllabus* was almost entirely Psychological Ethics and since Dewey had declared the psychological and the social each to cover the whole field, *08* complements the *Syllabus* by presenting Social Ethics. It is Social Ethics in both the familiar sense of dealing with ethical problems of society and in the technical sense of looking at the entire field from the aspect of the natural and social conditions of action.[1] But the latter is done centrally by focusing on the historical development of morality with its twin features of the emergence of a reflective individual and the maturity of a social conception of the good operating as an individual motivation. In this chapter we test this thesis on the materials of *08*.

For the most part, morality is seen conceptually in terms of the two fundamental notions of good and right alone. The preface, referring to

Kant and Mill, Sidgwick and Green, Martineau and Spencer (not significantly to Hume and Adam Smith), finds a place in morals for reason and happiness, and so for duty and evaluation.[2] The opening definition for ethics in the Introduction is "the science that deals with conduct, in so far as this is considered right or wrong, good or bad."[3] These two concepts approach conduct from different points of view. In the case of right we think of conduct as before a judge, of a law that is authoritative; in the case of good we think of what is desirable, and a standard of what is to be sought or chosen. "I am to 'choose' it and identify myself with it, rather than to control myself by it."[4] More formally, when the work turns to theoretical analysis at the beginning of Part II, the tasks are to discover what in conduct it is that we judge good and evil, right and wrong, what these terms mean, and on what basis we apply them to their objects in conduct.[5] When the typical divisions of theories are listed, we find the teleological-jural contrast [6] but nothing indicative of a basic third force in virtue and vice.

There is one exception we have referred to in the last chapter, and this appears in a historical context of the comparison of customary and reflective morality (chapter 9). Tufts is expounding the view[7] that moral terms in customary morality came directly from group relations. The passage, full of speculative etymology, has almost a Nietzschean ring (reminiscent of *The Genealogy of Morals*). The 'kind' man is such because he acts as one of the kin. 'Noble' and 'gentle' first refer to birth in a superior-inferior setting; 'duty' is what was due to a superior. 'Honor' and 'honesty' were what the group admired; 'virtue' a manly excellence winning the praise of a warlike era. The economic ways add their contribution: "The conception of valuing and thus of forming some permanent standard of a better or a worse, is also aided, if not created, by economic exchange."[8] Jural ways add their concepts of moral law, authority, obligation, responsibility, justice, all with associations of group control and then organized government. Religion adds conceptions of purity and chastity. "'Wicked' is from witch."[9]

Etymologies (correct or spurious) apart, Tufts' thesis is that when morality becomes separated off as a distinct region, no fresh notions are required, but the terms taken from the different segments of life are refined and their meaning deepened. Thus the whole jural process is internalized and so becomes moral instead of jural: the same person becomes lawgiver, judge, and jury, as well as claimant and defendant.[10] (This picture is tightly reminiscent of Kant's depiction of conscience as an internal court of law; but Kant will not allow a person to judge himself and so postulates a God.) As for value concepts, Tufts amplifies the economic origin: "In the economic world things are good or have value if people want them. It is in the experience of satisfying wants that man has learned the language of 'good and evil,' and to compare one good with another; it is doubtless by the progress of science and the arts that objective standards of more permanent, rational, and social 'goods' are provided."[11] This process adds two fresh factors: the individual begins to consider his goods and values in relation to one another and to his life as a whole; and he goes beyond his natural appetites, and recognizes his own interests and the value that he can actively confer on things.

Now it is at this point that Tufts finds a third base in morals. "The term good where used in our judgments upon others (as in a 'good' man), may have a different history. As has been noted, it may come from class feeling, or from the praise we give to acts as they immediately please. It may be akin to noble or fine or admirable."[12] Again the refinement has two aspects: as moral such terms imply that we consider not merely outward acts but inner purposes and character; and our judgment is no longer in class or emotional terms, but social and rational and from a universal standpoint.

That Tufts got this wider perspective from his study of eighteenth century British ethics seems not unlikely. (There is a reference to the book of Tufts and Thompson in the Literature list at the end of chapter 8.) In any case, it is rooted in an historical outlook and in the derivation of ethical concepts from situations and problems and structures in human social experience. We noted above that in the *Syllabus* Dewey had only a brief look at the history of ethical ideas, and it gave him a valuable insight that the exaltation of the individual and the exclusive reference of conduct to him was a late development. But he looked upon this individualism as a side-tracking of sound theory into the Stoic and Christian inwardness with the dualism of spirit and the physical world. The many explorations of individualism in *08* show it rather to be a complex idea with different directions that it may take.

Let us now explore briefly the relation of duty to good in *08* and then pinpoint the position of virtue as compared to the *Syllabus*.

In some contexts good and right appear to be different indispensable aspects of conduct. But a definite primacy in some sense emerges for good. For one thing, all conduct is concerned with ends. Not all pursuit of ends generates a moral situation. This happens when we have an incompatibility of ends appealing to different kinds of interests and choice. Now the question is which is really valuable, or more desirable.[13] Competitions of values "for the position of control of action are inevitable accompaniments of individual conduct."[14] The reference to control opens the way to duty, but the definition of the moral does not include it: "Conduct as moral may thus be defined as *activity called forth and directed by ideas of value or worth, where the values concerned are so mutually incompatible as to require consideration and selection before an overt action is entered upon*."[15] Therein lies the primacy of good.

The idea of control that has here been in the offing is not, however, the only path in which the inquiry can go. When the individual has to decide, the appeal, says Dewey, is to himself, but the supreme appeal is to the sort of person he is to be, that is, to character. And this is the direction in which, when a standard for choice is developed, we shall see that the idea of virtue gets its entry. So the primacy of good, once choice between incompatibles is necessary, points to the development of a standard, but also has alongside the way a need for control.

Neither of these is initially separated from the situation of choice. Both are kept on short leash. Character is not an outside concept: "we mean by character whatever lies behind an act in the way of deliberation and desire, whether these processes be near-by or remote." And reason too, in which control formulates its principles, is basically and preponderantly taken to be concerned with the deliberative situation and the resolution of its conflicts. (But of this, later.) Historically, too, the problem of the knowledge of the good comes first, as in the Socratic quest.[16] Indeed, the problem of control comes to mean in the individual how to handle the natural appetites and desires that turn one to false goods, and in the society how those who know the good can structure law and training to develop appropriate habits in those who have to be trained.[17]

The analysis of duty (chapter 17) is no different from that in the *Syllabus* and has the same objective, namely to undercut the separation (particularly in the Kantian theory) of duty from the desires and interests that are central to the analysis of conduct and the Deweyan (as against the Kantian) conception of the good. It is, in brief, to restore the position of right and duty as an aspect of the deliberative situation emerging from within rather than as an external force. The strategy of the demonstration is an expansion of the similar point made in the *Syllabus*: duty is not directed against desire or impulse but against something more general.[18] Take the carefully formed and cultivated habits of a professional. They may become a preoccupation that encroaches on other goods, e.g., domestic and civic responsibilities. If we think of the opposite of duty as inclination, then inclination is not to be identified with appetite and desire. Dewey's candidate for what duty attacks is thus habit, whether it concerns appetite or anything else, *"the inertia or momentum of any organized, established tendency."*[19] So too the control of appetite or desire is a matter of practical readjustment *"within the structure of character, due to conflict of tendencies so irreconcilable in their existing forms as to demand radical redirection."*[20] Thus the phenomenon of obligation is brought back within the ambit of reflection and deliberation in their normal reconstructive function.

In dealing with the content of duty, the social aspect is stressed. Duties come from relations to others, socially established connections and roles. "Every relationship in life is, as it were, *a tacit or expressed contract with others*, committing one, by the simple fact that he occupies that relationship, to a corresponding mode of action."[21] But Dewey connects these relationships with selfhood as entering into the makeup of the individual and leaving him not morally free to pick and choose. In the end, the intra-self perspective dominates: "Duty is what is owed by a partial and isolated self embodied in established, facile, and urgent tendencies to that ideal self which is presented in aspirations which, since they are not yet formed into habits, have no organized hold upon the self and which can get organized into habitual tendencies and interests only by a more or less painful and difficult reconstruction of the habitual self."[22] The conflict of duty and desire is thus found to accompany a growing self. "The phenomena of duty in all their forms are thus phenomena attendant upon the expansion of ends and the reconstruction of character."[23] Since Dewey here refers to all forms, it is worth noting that rights and obligations, not merely right and duty, are later[24] analyzed as social phenomena and so brought into the same framework, as protecting goods and advancing goods.

Whatever the similarities of the analysis of duty in *08* and *32* it is clear that in *08* it lacks independence as a basic separate factor in the moral life.

The road to virtue in *08* is markedly different from that followed in the *Syllabus*. In the latter it ran through freedom or responsibility; virtue lay in the completeness of the self in conduct. In *08* the road winds through the social as the standard for character. It is interesting to follow the emergence of this view in the occasional references to virtue prior to the chapter on the topic (chapter 19), and in the more extensive search for the standard for character.

There is no inkling of the eventual outcome in an earlier examination of what virtue is under different theories; here virtue is considered under the various forms of attitude-theory, and Dewey is most intent on criticizing the separation of inner and outer. That distinction, we are later told, is involved in the growth of character and conduct. If these were fixed, a separation would be possible. But there is no fixity and so there is no separation, "only a contrast of different levels of desire and forethought of earlier and later activities. The great need of the moral agent is thus a character which will make him as open, as accessible as possible, to the recognition of the consequences of his behavior."[25]

Concern with the consequences is only the beginning. As the search for a standard gets under way through a critique of happiness theory, further features are added. "If happiness is to be the same as the moral good, it must be after the right kind of happiness has been distinguished; namely, that which commends itself after adequate reflection."[26] For not all forms of happiness commend themselves to us; we want to regulate the formation of desire so that the present and permanent good will coincide, good in desire and good in reflection, present and permanent satisfaction. The standard becomes happiness as rightly conceived.[27] At the end of this discussion (chapter 14 on happiness and conduct), the stage reached is still formal: "What is the good which while good in direct enjoyment also brings with it fuller and more continuous life?"[28] The moment, however, that the inquiry turns to substance (at the beginning of chapter 15, on happiness and social ends) we are told: "In substance the only end which fulfills these conditions is the social good."[29] The good moral character, it turns out, is that of a person "in whom the habit of regarding all capacities and habits of self from the social standpoint is formed and active."[30] He forms plans, regulates desires, and performs acts with reference to effects on social groups of which he is a part. His dominant interests and attitudes are tied with associated activities. The outcome is a concept of moral democracy[31] which embraces the active capacities of voluntary agents and the congruous exercise of the voluntary activities of all concerned. Much later, when Dewey is discussing the growth of democracy, he says that morally, "it is the effective embodiment of the moral ideal of a good which consists in the development of all the social capacities of every individual member of society."[32]

It is to be expected that the importance assigned to the social in the standard for character will permeate the analysis of the place of the self in the moral life (chapter 18). The actual self is contrasted with the abstract self by including social relations and offices, both actual and potential.[33] The attack on a ready-made self is an old theme, but to regard as the essential factor in morality not just "the constant discovery, formation, and reformation of the self" but to add "in the ends which an individual is called upon to sustain and develop in virtue of his membership in the social whole"[34] is to give a specific substance to a formal picture. It is in effect a transition from the wholeness of self to participation in a whole community.

The consequence is that when at the beginning of the chapter on virtues (chapter 19) virtue is defined, it is no longer brought under prior notions of freedom or responsibility. Instead it is related directly to the social: "The habits of character whose effect is to sustain and spread the rational or common good are the virtues; the traits of character which have the opposite effects are vices."[35]

In the detailed treatment of virtue and the virtues, two striking features call for explanation. Dewey treats approbation and disapprobation as secondary phenomena of affective recognition and response to the common good. And he treats virtue in general as the central concept and specific virtues as explicable with relation to its dimensions or aspects.

Approbation and disapprobation, Dewey says, are never purely intellectual, but also emotional and practical. "We are stirred to hostility at whatever disturbs the order of society; we are moved to admiring sympathy of whatever makes for its welfare."[36] The emotions express themselves in appropriate conduct—to reprove, blame, punish, etc. Now the judgments of approval and disapproval express the character of those who utter them, and support or encourage the recipients or dissuade and affect them as part of forming their character. Dewey adds that this is not a conscious design: it issues from "natural, instinctive response to acknowledge whatever makes for its [society's] good."[37]

The structure of Dewey's account here is reminiscent, although he does not use that term, of the treatment of *sanctions* in Bentham and Mill. First comes the determination of traits that advance the general welfare; then the application of phenomena that are found among people which support or discourage such traits—Bentham's physical, political, moral (i.e. social), religious sanctions and Mill's internal and external sanctions. There is also the recognition in both the Utilitarians and in Dewey that the use of specific sanctions need not be automatically accepted as good, that the use of specific sanctions itself requires moral evaluation. Mill carefully distinguishes the natural desire for retaliation or revenge from anything in its use that may be moral; he compares it to sexual desire on which the family is built but the moral element follows a different (utilitarian) formula. Dewey says that "to approve or to condemn is itself a moral act for which we are as much responsible as we are for any other deed."[38] And he warns that in general the sanctions are directed to supporting "what used to be, rather than what are, virtues."[39] For changes are going on, minor as well as larger ones, and the apparatus of public approval tends to be directed toward the conventional rather than the emerging or growing. Hence mere conformity to custom is conceived as virtue. Neither the Utilitarians nor Dewey (in *08*) treat approbation and disapprobation phenomena as primary moral sources or phenomena out of which morality grows. This kind of view is found more in the tradition of Hume and Adam Smith, as well as in the general emphasis on the sentiments as the root of morality in eighteenth century British moral philosophy. It is not surprising that Dewey in the *Fries letter* says his restudy of British moral philosophy played a part in the shift from the picture of virtue in *08* to that in *32*.

The approach to specific virtues through a general concept of virtue rather than regarding the general as an abstraction or generalization from the specific appears to be held over from the treatment in the *Syllabus*. The aim is first to discover what makes any conduct *virtuous* and the answer is that it expresses the self with wholeness or completeness. Of course, as we have seen, completeness has veered to expressing the well-being of the whole community. But the primacy of this emphasis on virtue-in-general remains. It is strengthened by the tremendous variety to be found in specific traits that people regard as virtues. "Every natural capacity, every talent or ability, whether of inquiring mind, of gentle affection or of executive skill, becomes a virtue when it is turned to account in supporting or extending the fabric of social values; and it turns, if not to vice at least to delinquency, when not thus utilized."[40] The conclusion that virtues are numberless seems to turn Dewey away from approaching the subject through such pluralism, though he does suggest how we might try to classify virtues. Instead, he looks to the main aspects of virtue in general which capture the features of the moral life. For example, interest must be whole-hearted: "The whole self, without division or reservation, must go out into the proposed object and find therein its own satisfaction. Virtue is integrity, vice duplicity."[41] Similarly, interest must be persistent, sincere, etc. Dewey thus reinterprets traditional virtues from courage to conscientiousness in terms of the attitudinal requirements of human interests.

It is worth adding that in this broad shift in the treatment of virtue from the *Syllabus*, freedom and responsibility are dislodged from their earlier centrality. They find a new place in relation to the social good, to which virtue has been attached by definition.[42] Here their discussion is a more concrete one, rather than simply a categorial one.

In all three ethical concepts that we have examined, the growing role of the social in *08* stands out clearly. It is, however, an uneven growth and does not affect equally all parts of the ethics. The theory of the good is still cast formally in terms of the satisfaction of the self in conduct. It barely goes beyond the demand for permanently satisfying as against presently satisfying ends. But it has the hypothesis that permanently satisfying ends will prove to be social ends. As the moral involves character in the choice of goods and a standard is sought for character, the social moves more boldly into the standard. In the consideration of virtue the social already enters in a definitory way. In the case of duty, there is a move to the social in looking at content, although even there the interpretation of relations with others as contractual maintains the individualistic orientation. In any case, the treatment of the nature of duty as a relation of ideal and present self brings it back to the same focus as in the good.

This emergence of the social is, of course, seen by the authors as constitutive of the moral in a mature reflective individual. There is thus an intimate relation in *08* between the emergence of the social and the historical development of morality. In subsequent chapters 8 and 9 we shall examine separately the idea of the social and the individual and the fate of their historical framework in the years that followed *08*. In the next chapter we turn to the changes that were brought about between 1908 and 1932 in their thought and the modifications they forced, bit by bit, in the conceptual structure of *32*.

Notes

1. Dewey's article on Ethics in *Encyclopedia Americana* (1904, MW 3: 40–58) distinguishes social or sociological ethics from individual or psychological ethics in a detailed way (41) and it is doubtless the conception that governed *08*. Social ethics "deals with the habits, practices, ideas, beliefs, expectations, institutions, etc., actually found in history or in contemporary life, in different races, periods, grades of culture, etc., which are outgrowths of judgments of the moral worth of actions or which operate as causes in developing such judgments. Up to the present, social ethics has been developed mainly in connection, (1) with discussion of the evolution of morality either by itself or in connection with institutions of law and judicial procedure, or of religious cult and rite; or (2) with problems of contemporary social life, particularly with questions of philanthropy, penology, legislation, regarding divorce, the family and industrial reform—such as child labor, etc."

   Psychological ethics is concerned with "tracing in the individual the origin and growth of the moral consciousness, that is, of judgments of right and wrong, feelings of obligation, emotions of remorse, shame, of desire for approbation; of the various habits of action which are in accord with the judgment of right, or the virtues; with the possibility and nature, from the standpoint of the psychical structure of the individual, of free or voluntary action. It gathers and organizes psychological data bearing upon the nature of intention, and motive; desire, effort and choice; judgments of approbation and disapprobation; emotions of sympathy, pity in relation to the impulse of self-preservation and the formation and reformation of habit in its effect upon character, etc."

   Dewey also distinguishes ethics as an art which discovers and formulates rules of acting "in accordance with which men may attain their end." The rules may be considered as prescriptions or as technical formulae giving the best way to a desired result.
2. *08* : 4.
3. Ibid., 7.
4. Ibid., 13.
5. Ibid., 187.
6. Ibid., 207.
7. Ibid., 163–65.
8. Ibid., 164.
9. Ibid., 165.
10. Ibid., 170.
11. Ibid., 171.
12. Ibid.
13. Ibid., 192.
14. Ibid., 193.
15. Ibid., 194.
16. Ibid., 200.
17. Ibid., 201–03.
18. Ibid., 308–11.
19. Ibid., 310.

20. Ibid.
21. Ibid., 312.
22. Ibid., 326.
23. Ibid., 327.
24. Ibid., 394–95.
25. Ibid., 240.
26. Ibid., 245.
27. Ibid., 251.
28. Ibid., 259.
29. Ibid., 261.
30. Ibid., 271.
31. Ibid., 276–77.
32. Ibid., 424.
33. Ibid., 342.
34. Ibid., 356.
35. Ibid., 359.
36. Ibid.
37. Ibid., 360.
38. Ibid., 362.
39. Ibid., 361.
40. Ibid., 360.
41. Ibid., 363.
42. Ibid., 390 ff.

Part II

On the Road to 32

5

The Conceptual Transformation: From *08* to *32*

The general shift in conceptual structure from *08* to *32* was described largely on the basis of Dewey's account in the *three roots*, *club paper*, and *Fries letter*. Now that we have examined more detailedly the structure in *08*, we have to do the same for *32*. We shall follow the same order in dealing with good, right, and virtue. There is, however, the additional effort to see what light is thrown with respect to each by significant statements of Dewey's in the intervening period. Before all this, some remarks are also necessary on the development of Dewey's general focus and on his view of the role of ethical categories.

General Focus and Ethical Categories

We have had enough occasion to note that Dewey's outlook on man and the world is a naturalistic one. This means rejecting the sharp dualism of mind and nature, spirit and body; offering some positive view of the processes of thought as events in nature—in effect, not that mind thinks but man thinks; tracing the character of the interaction among the parts of the natural world—in particular with respect to the organism, its environment, the appearance of thought, the changes wrought at each point in all the others. In Dewey's time it was very hard to express all this, for the dominant approach even of those who shared his naturalism was largely in terms of gross causal determinisms. Nowadays, after the growth of such concepts as cybernetics and feedback, of teleological mechanisms, of microscopic interactions productive of macroscopic interactive regulation, there is a much readier vocabulary for depicting transactions in nature. We have seen that his outlook on organism-environment interaction was already matured in the *Outlines* and the *Syllabus*. But at least in the ethical context the focus was on the self, and interaction was in some sense filtered through it. This was fundamental to the interpretation of the good and since good held the primary place in terms of which the other ethical concepts were understood, the self focus held the whole structure, as it were, in harness.

After *08* there seems to us to be a gradual loosening. We read it from the very clear statement of Dewey's in his entry on "environment and organism" in the *Cyclopedia of Education* (1911).[1] These terms, he says, are strictly correlative, instancing brother and sister, buyer and seller, stimulus and response. But he does not leave it there; he goes on to show the functional character of the connection. (In his entry on function he gives the illustration of digestion, just as in his earlier works he several times referred to breathing.) Dewey says:

> Wherever there are correlative terms, there is a third medium to which both refer. In the case of organism and environment, this more comprehensive matter is life as a self-conserving, expanding activity. (See Function.) Life is a process which includes environment as well as organism within itself; if we are apt to connect life with the organism and not the environment, this only means that its connection with the former is direct, and with the latter indirect, or by means of the organism. But this indirect connection, when examined, is readily interpreted to mean that the organism itself is only a device for making the environment an included part of a life activity.[2]

He explains this, pointing out that environment is not simply the physical surroundings, since parts of them may have no relevance to the responses of the organism. But as the organism develops the environment changes. As special structures develop, free locomotion and a nervous system, the environment then expands: "There is then a genuine sense in which the evolution of life, the increase in diversity and interdependence of life functions, means an evolution of new environments just as truly as of new organs." The greatest change comes "when living beings become conscious of the fact that their reactions to preexistent stimuli modify the old forms in such a way as to create new or different stimuli."[3] Now deliberate ends emerge and lead to modifying the environment. Dewey illustrates by the history of tools that become "extra-organic organs", and brings these reflections to bear on education as control of direction of communal growth."From the biological standpoint, accordingly, the school with all its subject-matter, apparatus, and guiding personalities (teachers, etc.) constitutes a set of specially selected and arranged stimuli for the sake of evoking and forming certain standard types of response on the part of the life functions."[4]

This is a far cry from filtering everything through a self; instead, any filtering by the self is itself just a part of the process of determining what is the effective environment. The focus has moved from the individual and his agency to a view of all life in which group demands as readily play an active role.

Doubtless the growing attention to the social in addition to the psychological has played its part in this relaxation in focus. In chapter 8 below we will trace that side of the development and the evidence for Dewey's early attention to the growth of social psychology. After *08* provided the foundations of social ethics, the focus on the whole field of human life, approachable in different ways in different contexts, seems a natural replacement for the focus of the single individual expanding the self.

Dewey's view of the role of ethical categories is developed early, before *08*. It did not require the expansion of ethics from the psychological view to the social view; it was enough that the ethical judgment was seen as an active expression of consciousness modifying the situation that called for judgment. In the section on "The Categories of a Science of Ethics" in *Logical Conditions of a Scientific Treatment of Morality*[5], Dewey complains of the current way of treating ethical concepts. Instead of seeing the terms as tools for the active task of judgment, they "are generally taken as somehow given ready-made and hence as independent and isolated things."[6] Debates go on about their validity and specific significance, which without reference to functions can only be arbitrary; there is no check upon the meaning nor recognized standard for judging validity. This can come only by attending to the operations in which the terms are involved. It is important to note that, in the study of conditions for controlling ethical judgments that follows, Dewey considers both a psychological analysis and a sociological one. In this respect we have a program that *08* was soon to attempt to carry out.

Good

In *32* we do not expect a basic alteration in the theory of the good, but it is trimmed in a number of respects. We cannot in some of these be sure whether they are changes in doctrine or simply greater brevity, while in others they appear to involve a greater pluralism consonant with the broader focus.

The root of the good is that men have desires and wants.[7] This time there is no attempt to derive them from an evolutionary survival effort, but perhaps that can be taken for granted. It is enough that men are led to reflection when customs fail to guide, old institutions break down, and invention and innovations alter the conditions of life.[8] The stimuli to reflection are more socially or macroscopically presented. "And reflection upon what one shall do is identical with the formation of ends."[9] Reflection on conduct is also equated with developing inclusive and enduring aims. The ends that issue from impulse and provide meaning to guide action are ends-in-view. Again, Dewey makes the point for the relation of desire and reason similar to that established in *08* for the relation of desire and duty: they are not fundamentally or essentially opposites, but reason and duty adhere to the longer-range desire that has brought remoter consequences into view. The conflict is then between two ends, not an end and something else.

The cultivation of interests is seen as the human end. This is pluralistic and not forced into a single framework. As compared to *08*, the focusing of the good upon the moral good, the reference to character and through a standard for character upon the realizing of a whole self, has been removed from the account of the good. The several problems raised by such topics are discussed in other contexts. Character is of course important, but it is seen more as an instrument than a supreme end. "Selfhood or character is thus not a *mere* means, an external instrument of attaining certain ends. It *is* an agency of accomplishing consequences, as is shown in the pains which the athlete, the lawyer, the merchant, takes to build up certain habits in himself because he knows they are the causal conditions for reaching the ends in which he is interested."[10] But of course the consequences attained react on the self. The shaping of the self is a pervasive component in evaluation. "But to make self-realization a conscious aim might and probably would prevent full attention to those very relationships which bring about the wider development of the self."[11] In any case, the diverse problems of the self are discussed in a separate chapter (15) almost as a miscellaneous set. They are not the integral extension of the good, just as the right is no longer an emergent from the conflict of goods which leads to control, ordering and reason. The good remains strictly moored to the first of the *three roots*—desires and wants and the like—from which ends emerge, and its task is to usher in reflection and its process of end-formation. Self-realization as such has been reduced to a specific (and dubious) procedure.[12]

The resulting pluralism is itself not new in Dewey's thought. It had already long permeated his analysis of men's situations and found ready expression in practical issues. A fascinating example, even before *08,* is his controversy with Hugo Münsterberg over the proposed plan for the St. Louis 1903 Congress of the Arts and Sciences.[13] Münsterberg outlines a ground plan that would give each discipline its assigned place in a system. Dewey objects to such a philosophical postulation antecedently providing a unity of human knowledge. This could only curb the vital activities in the cooperative pursuit of truth. What is more explicit in ethics after *08* is that the pluralism has extended itself on the theoretical level, not only on that of the content of the good. There is no more systematic routing of the concept of the good to any one constricting interpretation. The cultivation of interests as the good, as noted above, keeps the theoretical field wide open.[14]

Another theoretical broadening that begins early in the second decade is Dewey's prolonged concern with the concept of *value*. It finds expression in a set of papers and controversies that extends well over two decades before culminating (after *32*) in his *Theory of Valuation* (1939) and continues intermittently even after that. At the same time, Dewey's books, particularly in the 1920s, contain discussions of the *good* as an ethical concept. We have thus to scan his treatment during this period of these two related concepts.

Attempts to formulate a general theory of value constitute a lively chapter in the history of ethics in the twentieth century, especially in its first third. Three sources may be indicated. The first is the hedonism of Bentham which had broadened the idea of the good into the whole range of pleasure and the avoidance of pain. This furnished the theme of measurement in the comparison of values or goods; it was intensified by the use of hedonistic theory in nineteenth century economics, in the utility theories, in which exchange value rather than use value carried the theoretical burden. The second and third sources stem from Darwinian evolution but in contrary directions. One is the attempt of philosophical idealism to find a generic mark of the spiritual to combat the reduction of human striving and aspiration to biological impulses. This is seen, for example, in T.H. Green's argument for a spiritual principle that is evident in both knowledge and practical life; it focuses on the self and its value character. The other accepts the Darwinian story fully and begins with the selective character of impulse in all life, human as well as animal. It goes on to trace the evolution within morality itself: reflective preference, and eventually obligation, grow out of primary selection. Its net effect is then to naturalize the moral life, not to set it off against the natural world. A general shift engendered by all three movements is to set questions of ethics in a more abstract framework. The concept of value is highly general, while morality becomes one of its provinces—usually that of values of character in terms of which the sense of duty and obligation are considered—alongside of aesthetic, economic, religious, social, and other value fields. In effect, then, the concept of the good is replaced by that of value, while virtue and obligation are left to dominate morality. One consequence was that when methodological interests became central, in the 1930s, they too were expressed in a highly abstract way. Thus it would be asked whether judgments of value were verifiable, as if a single answer could be given for all value as such.

The year 1909 marked a significant point in the advance of value theory in the United States. In that year Urban's work on *Valuation*[15] appeared, calling for a systematic treatment of all types of human values. He noted the march of science, taking over the whole "choir of heaven" as well as the "furniture of earth" and in effect called on the fields of value to unite rather than divide the human spirit. (In Britain, the position of philosophical idealism was well represented for value theory in Bernard Bosanquet's *The Principle of Individuality and Value* that appeared in 1912.) On the other hand, 1909 also saw Ralph Barton Perry's *The Moral Economy* which used an economic model to depict the proliferation of human interests and their modes of organization; Perry still stayed with the concept of the good, but extended it over all needs and demands. It was not till 1926 that his major work on value theory was published.[16]

With such contrasting approaches, yet both attempting to broaden the treatment of ethics, and with the impact of value theory in Germany on many American philosophers, it is not surprising that the Executive Committee of the American Philosophical Association in 1913 formulated the Problem of Values for discussion at its next meeting, and invited additional formulations of the question. Dewey's brief reply[17] submits a list of eight questions for consideration. They raise issues of the status of values, the role of reflective inquiry, the relation of value to organic behavior. One of his aims is clearly to set off the metaphysical underpinnings as separate issues. For example, his first question asks "Can the question of the status of values in philosophic discussion be approached apart from the question of the status of qualities?" Apparently then, issues of subjectivity would not be charged against values as such. And with respect to the relation of values to organic behavior or the equation of desires and aversions with consciousness, he suggests the use of a neutral term such as *selections* and *rejections*, or the connection of value with the *behavior* of organic beings, without specifying in advance how "behavior" is to be taken.

Perhaps the most important questions that Dewey raises, in the light of the direction that his own papers on value took thereafter, are the third and fourth: "Do values antecede, or do they depend upon valuation—understanding by valuation a process of reflective estimation or judgment?" and "If they antecede, does valuation merely bring them to light without change, or does it modify antecedent values? Does it produce new values? If the latter occur are the modification and production merely incidental or are they essential?"[18] These questions touch the basic conceptual question how the notion of value is itself to be construed. For Dewey's own answer at that time we can look to his entry on "Values, Educational" in the *Cyclopedia of Education* (1912–13)[19]:

> Value is in reality an abstract noun denoting not just one undefinable thing but the entire complex of valuable things. The conception of valuable things throws us back upon the attitude of individuals in choosing and pursuing. Things are valuable when they are valued; that is, when they are esteemed and chosen; they are not chosen because of some external trait of value contained in them. Want, effort, and choice are more fundamental concepts than value. Hence the significance of the term "invaluable." Strictly speaking, it denotes the negation of value, not in the sense of lacking value but in the sense of representing that which, in the given situation, is outside the sphere of valuation. It is not compared at all with other ends, but is that which effectively controls the comparing and weighing of consciously considered ends. In other words, we value, or evaluate objects only when in doubt and in the process of choosing. Value is a category of reflective comparison, or choice, not one of things in themselves. All values are instrumental, for the ultimate of any situation is invaluable.

Clearly Dewey's interpretation of value is in term of active reflective choice that refashions or creates outcomes in human demands, desires, satisfactions, enjoyments, etc. That the central phenomenon is the valuation process remains unchanged in Dewey's thought. What he wavers on is how to employ the term "value". As a verb, "to value" is readily seen by him as an equivalent to "valuating" or the process of valuation. On the other hand, there is the temptation to see the noun "value" as the product of the process, in a more immediate sense of the object enjoyed or approved. On the whole this seems to him a useless duplication for the more concrete attitudinal terms. But at times he is led to make distinctions between what is *prized* as value and what is *appraised* as undergoing a valuation process. At other times, *prized* itself becomes a process term, sometimes on the underlying assumption that prizing is an answer to the situation that generates desire.

It is worth noting that the waverings about "values" characterize not only twentieth century philosophical thought but also the use of the term in social science. Those who employ "values" for the description of the presence of some pro-attitude have to find some other term for the standards in the critical process of valuation. Philosophers invoked concepts of the organization of values, or standards of evaluating values. (The term "evaluating" seems to have come from a back-reference out of "evaluation" as the outcome of the process of valuation; it came to be used for the higher-level process of criticizing or reconsidering the outcomes.) Sociologists and social psychologists who used "values" in the sense of existing pro-attitudes tended to use "norms" for the more critical standards; some, however, in the same way as Dewey's early usage, employed "values" directly for the standards of criticism or judgment about attitudes and choices.

Dewey's experience with his major paper "The Logic of Judgments of Practice"(1915)[20] showed the confusions that could readily arise from these complexities in the then current philosophical milieu. His central point should have been straightforward enough in the light of his general position up to that time. He wants to examine "a kind of judgment, having a specific type of subject-matter"[21]—and he calls it practical judgment, since it is about what is to be done in situations demanding action. This subject-matter if we do not follow Dewey's account and simply ask what is going on in such a situation, is a passage of time in which a situation that Dewey describes as incomplete or indeterminate becomes completed or determined by a person's decision in which novel or creative elements are brought to bear upon it through reflective thought. Of course it is assumed that the initial situation, incomplete as it is, is already limited or demarcated by purposes and conditions; it is not a blank slice of existence. And the distinctive part of Dewey's approach is the active and creative role of the decisional process; it is this that prompts him to identify the process of choice as *valuation*. Now construed in this general way, Dewey's analysis is a scrutiny of the process of choice and its conditions and the role of reflective judgment in it, plus an implicit proposal that "valuation" be defined in terms of this process. Had Dewey simply given such an account of the material or subject-matter we suspect there would have been no confusion. Other philosophers might have disagreed, but they would not have misunderstood. They might, for example, have wanted "value" to designate the products of the process, the rules or attitudes or habitual interests that resulted; and Dewey could have objected that such identification would give too stable a role to post-reflective habits. His argument might have been that a more fruitful theory of meaning is geared to historical or genetic process rather than its temporary outcomes at a given point. In short, he would be advocating what we shall later examine as his genetic method.

Dewey, however, did nothing of this sort, although it is made clear enough here and there in his argument. Instead, he formulated practical judgment as *propositions*, an additional and neglected kind:

> To assume in advance that the subject-matter of practical judgments *must* be reducible to the form SP or mRn [the subject-predicate type of classical logic or the newer relational logic] is assuredly as gratuitous as the contrary assumption. It begs one of the most important questions about the world which can be asked: the nature of time. Moreover, current discussion exhibits, if not a complete void, at least a decided lacuna as to propositions of this type. Mr. Russell has recently said that of the two parts of logic the first enumerates or inventories the different kinds or forms of propositions. It is noticeable that he does not even mention this kind as a possible kind. Yet it is conceivable that this omission seriously compromises the discussion of other kinds.[22]

Dewey was thus challenging the whole approach to propositions that had emerged in the early twentieth century among the logicians and that was at the time producing its greatest triumph of Russell and Whitehead's *Principia Mathematica*. This rested on an atemporal view of the proposition in which any temporal reference would be part of the content; for example, "Socrates is sitting" would be expanded to

"Socrates is sitting at time t_1" rather than locating the proposition in time or resorting to a collateral statement of the time of utterance. Later on there were to be attempts to grapple with *agenda* propositions of Dewey's type by developing within a modal logic different kinds of logic of imperatives or of prescriptives. These were still of the same atemporal kind as the basic logic of propositions. The nearest to Dewey's active propositions came, when ordinary language analysis also attacked formal logic, in J.L. Austin's conception of performative utterances. But these were the active powers of the use of words, not wearing the robe of propositions.

What is more, the atemporality of the new logic was tied in with a wider movement to separate logic from psychology, the forms of validity from the processes of thought. Doubtless the new Frege-Russell approach to logic took on a realistic (often Platonic) metaphysics and was thought to be exploring the logical structure of the world. But retrospectively we can see it now as a great experiment that was studying the objects of thought (knowledge) without regard to the human vehicle of thinking. To put psychology aside was very much like what is now being done in the study of artificial intelligence which puts aside the vehicle of intelligence in the human (the processes of physiology, for example) and attends only to structural properties. Thus it is able to examine the thinking process of machines. On a Deweyan view, such a large experiment in abstraction could only be judged by its successes or failures, by the extent to which it developed fruitful tools for organizing and refining knowledge, a judgment that is to be considered in the light of questions of application of theoretical models. Dewey's attack in 1913 was apparently bewildering; to ask propositions to take part in action and fashioning the outcome was doubtless like asking abstractions to dance.

Let us return to Dewey's exposition. He says of the kind of propositions he is exploring: "Their subject-matter implies that the proposition is itself a factor in the completion of the situation, carrying it forward to its conclusion."[23] Now judgments of value are subsumed under practical judgments. There is, however, the familiar ambiguity about "value". In the first place, "*finding* a thing good apart from reflective judgment means simply treating the thing in a certain way, hanging on to it, dwelling upon it, welcoming it and acting to perpetuate its presence, taking delight in it. It is a way of behaving toward it, a mode of organic reaction."[24] But this is only one of the meanings.

For "'to value' means two radically different things: to prize and appraise; to esteem and to estimate; to find good in the sense described above, and to judge it to be good, to *know* it as good."[25] To prize is a practical, non-intellectual attitude, while to appraise is a judgment. To call things values in the former sense adds nothing; the latter involves reasons. Or again, he speaks of the contrast between "a good or an immediate experience and an evaluated or judged good."[26] Now on the assumption that action is required when the situation is incomplete or indeterminate, Dewey begins to speak of the former as "definite values" that would need no estimation.[27] On the other hand, the latter institute "a determinate value where none is given."[28] The factor of the new is stressed: "The express object of a valuation-judgment is to release factors which, being new, cannot be measured on the basis of the past alone."[29] That is why the value-judgment should not be construed as the application of an antecedently determined standard.

We are not suggesting that Dewey was unaware that he was opposing a major trend of logic in his time by his analysis of practical judgment. He had a different theory in mind: "I wish, of course, to suggest that logical traits are just features of original existences as they have been worked over for use in inference, as the traits of manufactured articles are qualities of crude materials modified for specific purposes."[30] This is an instrumentalist interpretation as against an ontological interpretation of logic. And what Dewey was especially worried about was an ontological reification that led back into a metaphysical dualism. But we may speculate whether, if the conflict had not been so overtly ontological, the degree of independent development required for logic might not have been formulated as an internal question in instrumentalism itself—perhaps as the length of the loop required before one got back to the objects for which the instruments are being prepared, or, as comparable to the contemporary issue in scientific work of the degree of independence required by basic research so that it will not be swamped by demands for immediate application.

In a brief paper on "The Objects of Valuation"[31] Dewey tried to meet the objections to his interpretation of value raised by Ralph Barton Perry and Wendell T. Bush.[32] Perry found Dewey's failure to be precise about what constitutes the identity of a judgment of value making his discussion too elusive and fluid to criticize; he denies that a value is constituted by a judgment of it. Bush is more intent on finding a place for judgments of intrinsic value. Dewey seems ready to concede that there is prizing or esteeming which is not reflective. But even with such he goes back to the mistrust that we have seen he showed all along toward post-reflective habits as well. "Sometimes every immediate or intrinsic good goes back on us. We do not confront any indubitable good. We are in the dark as to what we *should* regard with passionate esteem; we are beginning to suspect that something which we prized unquestioningly and directly in the past is no longer worth our while, because of some growth on our part or some change in conditions."[33] And that is when deliberation and judgment are called forth.

The battle was not over. Dewey, in spite of apparent concessions about two contrasting meanings of value, is not ready to concede parity to value in the sense of immediacy or intrinsicality. It was not till 1922 that he resumed the attack directly as a continuation of his 1915 analysis of judgments of practice. But in the intervening period he restates and develops a foundation in the two significant books, *Reconstruction in Philosophy* and *Human Nature and Conduct*. Here, however, the discussion is carried on less with respect to the general concept of *value* than with the ethical concept of *good*. Let us examine briefly the shape that his argument takes.

In a syllabus outlining what was to come in *Reconstruction in Philosophy* prepared for lectures in Tokyo,[34] Dewey presents clearly what is to be the keynote of his treatment of ethics. He is to emphasize that "Each situation requiring action has its own good depending upon its peculiar needs and conditions"[35]; that principles and standards are tools of analysis for the particular, not direct rules of conduct; that intelligence thus has increased responsibility; that goods lie within each situation; that ends are not fixed; that happiness is to be found in the process of striving. In the book itself, the chapter on "Reconstruction in Moral Conceptions" draws lessons from the character of scientific thinking for moral ideas. It exhibits the same pluralism and particularism. "Rules are softened into principles, and principles are modified into methods of understanding."[36] Goods and ends are plural, changing and individualized. The "unique and morally ultimate character of the concrete situation" is of primary significance and this is what throws the burden of morality on intelligence.[37] Just as rules do not settle what is good, neither do lists of general goods, for such ends are sure to conflict with one another. Once again we are told that moral goods are to be found only when something has to be done because deficiency characterizes the existing situation.[38] There is a reconstruction also in the idea of *intrinsic* good. It is no longer identified with something separately and isolatedly good that can be put into lists of things for which all else is instrumental. Intrinsicality is relative to the specific situation: "If the need and deficiencies of a specific situation indicate improvement of health as the end and good, then for that situation health is the ultimate or supreme good. It is no means to something else. It is a final and intrinsic value."[39] In general, growth is the only moral end. Dewey's focus on relating good to the transformation of the problematic situation here becomes so total that it leads him into what is in effect a moral tirade: "Happiness is not, however, a bare possession; it is not a fixed attainment. Such a happiness is either the unworthy selfishness which moralists have so bitterly condemned, or it is, even if labelled bliss, an insipid tedium, a millenium of ease in relief from all struggle and labor. It could satisfy only the most delicate of molly-coddles. Happiness is found only in success; but success means succeeding, getting forward, moving in advance."[40]

The theoretical lessons here offered are amplified in *Human Nature and Conduct*,[41] and in some respects more sharply clarified. We shall see in a later chapter how lingering problems about habit are there resolved, and the place of intelligence confirmed and strengthened. Good is treated in a chapter entitled "The Good of Activity."[42] Very relevant is an immediately preceding chapter on "The Present and Future." On the face of it, Dewey's concern with consequences would seem to cast value into future relations. But in fact his point is that intellectual preoccupation with the future is a way in which we secure efficiency in dealing with the present. Knowledge of relations through consequences enhances the meaning of the present. The good is in the present, not in a postponed future. Even in production, "actually, morally, psychologically, the sense of the utility of the article produced is a factor in the present significance of action due to the present utilization of abilities giving play to taste and skill, accomplishing something now."[43]

Dewey's basic conclusion is of course the familiar point that morals is concerned with situations in which alternative possibilities are faced. Here the formulation of better or worse enters, with decision directed to what is better. "The better is the good; the best is not better than the good but is simply the discovered good."[44] It follows also that morality is not a separate department of life; it may pertain to any conduct. Moreover, it is a continuing process. Dewey maintains therefore that "every situation has its own measure and quality of progress, and the need for progress is recurrent, constant."[45] Such progress involves increasing present meaning; in fact he is tempted to offer a categorical imperative "So act as to increase the meaning of present experience"[46]; but he immediately warns us that we would, to follow it, have to turn from the law to unique and localized situations. He is confident that there is no ending to such concern: "No matter what the present success in straightening out difficulties and harmonizing conflicts, it is certain that problems will recur in the future in a new form or on a different plane."[47]

The lessons repeated in these two books—the problematic focus, the particularity and uniqueness of each situation, the relation of moral concepts to the reflective process of choice in the effort to resolve the situational problem, reflex relation of the envisaged future to the meaning of the present—could only have strengthened Dewey's confidence that the concept of *value* belonged properly with reflective judgment and not with immediate satisfying experience. He takes up the cudgels again in 1922 in the philosophical journals. He is less concerned now with the logical aspects of practical judgment than in meeting the criticisms that he has neglected intrinsic value. His move is initially to show that he has not ignored the phenomenon of immediate satisfying feeling, of what he had hitherto called prizing or esteeming in contrast with appraising or estimating, and to explain why that does not merit the title of *value*, or if it does, then only in a secondary sense. There are a number of tactical moves worth noting.

These are evident in a long article that renews the attack, "Valuation and Experimental Knowledge."[48] He hastens to concede an immediate sense of *value*, that whether immediate or contributory, value may be found without judgment or the implication of cognition: "If immediate, we prize, cherish, directly appreciate, etc., and these words denote affectional or affecto-motor attitudes, not intellectual ones."[49] In some cases, he goes on, judgments merely state or record values— they are about values and utilities. "In other cases, there is no given or determinate value about which we may judge. We have recourse to estimation, to appraisal with respect to an absent uncertain value." This would seem to suggest that to speak of the immediate as value is to think prospectively about an estimation of it. As direct report, to speak of a value is to say something *about* value and not to make a value judgment.

A second move follows shortly. The term "value" has many meanings in its ambiguity and loose usage and so, we may suspect, the immediate is one of a crowd rather than a sole rival to the reflective. Dewey lists six significations starting with "immediate good in its immediacy or isolation—largely an intellectual abstraction for any grown-up person."[50] The second is a utility, the third a good in consequence of judgment (our previously examined post-reflective habit), the fourth same as third but for a utility, fifth the same as the third plus incorporating in its quality the results of prior reflective judgment, sixth an immediate utility with a sense of integration with the immediate good of its end. A footnote at this point refers to Picard's pointing out that sometimes we judge something to be of value but in spite of this do not in fact like it; thus "judgment in its theoretical aspect does not of itself determine a new intrinsic value (value being defined as a case of liking)."[51]

The use of the term "intrinsic value" in this footnote would seem to put to rest any charge that Dewey is ignoring it. But Dewey points out that in appraising or estimating what we formerly value "we no longer accept past values as final, as unquestioned values"[52] but evaluate with respect to their goodness in new and unique situations. Again, note 8[53] tells us that Perry, Robinson and Prall thought he was denying the existence of judgments *about* values in behalf of valuation judgments. That note is intended to be reassuring, though on Dewey's terms, not theirs, for the interpretation of the critical term is "*about* values"; and Dewey has asserted that to call these value-judgments would be like calling judgments about potatoes potato-judgments. But footnote 9 marks a sudden reversal and seems to wipe the slate clean and start all over again. Dewey refers to Brogan's article "The Fundamental Value Universal"[54] in which value was defined in terms of "better than" and the meanings of other ethical terms formally brought into line. Dewey says, "On this view, which I accept, liking would have to be understood as *preference*, selection-rejection, interest as 'this-rather-than-that'." And so not merely has the ground lost to intrinsic value been recaptured at one logical blow, but even liking (the mildest prizing) invaded. Moreover, if what is there discussed is the meaning of the ethical term (good) then what more need be said?

Yet Dewey went on to say it over and over again. In the Nov. 8, 1923 issue of the *Journal of Philosophy*[55] Dewey argues with Prall, in a paper on "Values, Liking, and Thought". In "The Meaning of Value"[56] in the same journal of Feb. 26, 1925, he continues the argument with Prall. A significant shift in the ground of the argument, however, takes place in "Value, Objective Reference and Criticism."[57] Here he is not just concerned with the logical type of judgment, but with the nature of value. He does make use of Ogden and Richards' remarks about approving of approving, but the point is that he finds the objective reference in the non-immediate character of valuing, for liking may be well- or ill-grounded. And he makes the explicit claim that prizing and the rest should be moved over to the judgmental side: "Wherever there is appreciation, esteeming, prizing, cherishing, there is something over and above momentary enjoyment, and this surplusage is a sense of the objective relationships of what is enjoyed—its status as fulfilling prior tendencies and contributing to further movements."[58] Thus it is not a mere statement that it has been liked but an investigation of the claims to be appreciated. Apparently then, even "about value" is not enough. The question is now shifted to the psychologic exploration of what is going on, which of course ties in with the epistemological view that the cognitive permeates even apparently immediate quality.[59]

Dewey's chapter on "Existence and Value" in his *Experience and Nature* (1925),[60] presents a balanced outline of his view. He comments on the recent rise of a theory of value and reckons with all the tendencies of isolation, dualism, etc., that become embroiled in it. Immediacy is again recognized but as trivial. With the general view being offered of philosophy as inherently criticism, there is no need to follow it through in particular for value. Immediate qualities of good and bad pass into the regulation of further appreciation. In general the chapter deals with the wider contours of a naturalism in which reflective criticism is the pivotal center.

The logical aspect reappears in *The Quest for Certainty*[61], chapter 10 of which is "The Construction of the Good." But the chapter is preponderantly a clear statement of the psychological and epistemological approach that Dewey has already fashioned in dealing with the good. Unfortunately, its few remarks about the desired and the desirable, the satisfying and the satisfactory, gave rise once the logical positivist movement was in full swing in America to the suspicion that Dewey had not adequately related the factual and the valuational. But to any careful reader it is clear that Dewey was not attempting a Millian inference about the desired and the desirable (if Mill be taken himself to be doing that, which is extremely dubious except to a Moore or a Bradley). For Dewey, the desired is not an isolated psychic phenomenon. Value is not assigned "to objects *antecedently* enjoyed, apart from reference to the method by which they come into existence."[62] Without thought enjoyments are not values but problematic goods, he says, and they become goods when they issue from reflective or intelligent behavior. This is clearly an experimental process in the problematic context to which desire is originally addressed, not a logical inference from the fact of desire.

This completes our account of the changes in Dewey's notion of the good between *08* and *32*. But it did not end his concern with the theory of value. The works beyond *32* are not within our present ken, but a glance is of interest. *Theory of Valuation*[63] became a classic exposition of his mature view of value. It criticized Perry and the traditional static naturalistic interpretations, including the positivist imperativist and emotivist interpretations, and it presented the psychological basis of his now overall familiar theory. It made also clear—an aspect we have not had occasion to consider—the way in which the means-end dichotomy is softened in the context of an interpretation of value as appraisal. And in its broad character it tied in with, and even in turn influenced, the growing movement of decision theory in the logic of probability. But once Dewey's view was out in such a systematic context—and especially as it intruded a pragmatism in the largely positivistic *International Encyclopedia of Unified Science*, in which it appeared—fresh lines of battle were drawn up between the Deweyan view and the positivist analysis. For the latter, focused on judgments of intrinsic or ultimate value, being ready to regard only instrumental value judgments as scientific, and so was driven to interpret value utterances as disguised imperatives or emotive. A fresh batch of articles flowed from Dewey's pen, somewhat reminiscent of the older batch on values, but more firmly, after *Theory of Valuation* focused on his fundamental theses. One ("Inquiry and Indeterminateness of Situations") in the *Journal of Philosophy*[64] was a response to D. M. Mackay's criticism of the idea of an indeterminate situation. A second a month later[65] considers "The Ambiguity of 'Intrinsic Good'" and warns of the shift from immediacy, that the thing has the quality, to a doctrine of essential natures. A year later[66] Dewey publishes "Valuation Judgments and Immediate Quality" in a response to Philip Blair Rice. And when Rice writes "Types of Value Judgments" wanting a plurality of types, Dewey answers[67] with "Further as to Valuation as Judgment." Two subsequent articles criticize emotive theory. "Some Questions About Value"[68] appearing in the same year as C.L. Stevenson's influential emotivist treatise, *Ethics and Language*, suggests that the emotivist view enshrines the prevalent cultural pattern of settling disputes by violent conflict. The psychology of emotion in the emotivist theory is questioned: emotion as a "quasi-gaseous stuff" is endowed "with powers of resistance greater than are possessed by triple-plated steel."[69] The criticism is amplified in "Ethical Subject-Matter and Language."[70] Ethical sentences may have a different interest from that of science, but a difference of interest is not a component of the subject-matter. Such differences may lead to different organization, as between physics and physiology. "It is quite another thing to convert the difference in function and use into a differential component of the structure and contents of ethical sentences"[71] as Stevenson does. There is a paradoxical element in that this criticism of Stevenson might very well have been addressed by the critics of Dewey's conception of practical judgment three decades before that. But Dewey gets directly to the psychological point: Stevenson is making the fundamental assumption that feeling is an affective state immediately revealing its whole nature to introspection, without using induction. For Dewey, as made clear in *32,* the underlying psychology of moral judgment in its contextual situation is a vital determinant of ethical theory, and ethical theory itself is moral in that it is a continuation of ethical reflection that patterns the cultural ways of dealing with practical problems.

Right

32's most serious break with *08* is of course the independence of right and duty. It is the most serious because the good and the right were, in *08*, the marks that defined ethics, and because a great deal of effort went into deriving the right from the control aspects of the pursuit of the good. In *32* there appears to be a clear distinction between ordering ends in their conflict with the emergence of the ideal or end that is the object of aspiration and the kind of restraint involved in duty. "Regarding the notion that the right is the means to the good, it may be said that it is certainly *desirable* that acts which are deemed right should in fact be contributory to good. But this consideration does not do away with the fact that the concept of *Rightness*, in many cases, is independent of the concept of satisfaction and good."[72] The new element is that of *exaction* or *demand*. This comes from a moral authority, and so presupposes an authoritative claim. This should be neither as coercion nor as unrelated to desires. "The way out is found by recognizing that the exercise of claims is as natural as anything else in a world in which persons are not isolated from one another but live in constant association and interaction."[73] Dewey illustrates with the demands of the parent on the child: "they may issue from the very nature of family life in the relation which exists between parent and offspring."[74] Dewey makes considerable use of this notion of "the very nature of." For example, in generalizing from familial and political situations, he says that "Right, law, duty, arise from the relations which human beings intimately sustain to one another, and that their authoritative force springs from the very nature of the relation that binds people together."[75] We recognize here the independent second root, the phenomena of association and group regulation of claims that arise among people. Sometimes, instead of the very nature of the relation, Dewey speaks of inherent relationships[76] or intrinsic ties,[77] or relations intrinsic to the situation.[78]

What was presented in *08* as the nature of right and duty here becomes regarded as a basic function of the independent concepts. Their effect is "to lead the individual to broaden his conception of the Good; they operate to induce the individual to feel that nothing is good for himself which is not also good for others. They are stimuli to a widening of the area of consequences to be taken into account in forming ends and deciding what is Good."[79]

The use of such notions as intrinsic ties and the very nature of the relationships does not mean that Dewey is offering a rationalistic or intuitionist conception of obligation. We saw previously in examining the general character of the structural shift that while he maintains the independence of the category or conception of the right, the question of what is right in particular cases is another matter. And just as an independent category of right may carry out functions for the good, so it may even be concerned with goods in some special or independent relationship. It is here that we see how Dewey has emancipated himself from the individual focus that channelled all moral theory through the concept of the self. For the independent phenomena that are the base of concepts of right and duty and obligation are group phenomena, not individual phenomena. "In principle, therefore, Right expresses the way in which the good of a number of persons, held together by intrinsic ties, becomes efficacious in the regulation of the members of a community."[80]

The meaning of "intrinsic ties" or "the very nature of the relationship" is therefore neither mysterious nor obscurantist. It is simply the case that group life requires institutions and patterns or a network of relationships, and the claims that arise from members of the group against other members have to be assessed to determine whether they are required by the specific pattern of relationships. The justification of the requirement comes from a consideration of the group good. Presupposed in the independence of the category of right, etc. is therefore the notion of a common good not external to the individual. Dewey says: "it is a *fact* that a vast network of relations surrounds the individual: indeed, 'surrounds' is too external a term, since every individual lives *in* the network as a part of it."[81] That in some sense the individual is a social being and the social good operates somehow within his good was already a clear outcome in *08*. The underlying issue of individual and social in the development of Dewey's thought will be traced in a separate chapter below.

What contributed to this crucial change in the position of right within an ethical theory, other than the shift we have already explored in orientation from channelling everything through a self to a broad view of human life? The centrality of the notion of relationships in the emerging picture provides a focus of inquiry for it seems to be the differentiating feature rather than the more continuous view of the individual as a social being. On this matter useful clues are to be found in a paper by Tufts, "The Moral Life and the Construction of Values and Standards", published in *Creative Intelligence, Essays in the Pragmatic Attitude*.[82]

Tufts proposes to examine four factors in the moral life: life as a biological process; interrelation with other human beings (he lists associating, grouping, mating, communicating cooperating, commanding, obeying, worshiping, adjudicating, etc.); intelligence and reason; judgment and choice that give rise to a self and approved objects. In the second of these, which here particularly concerns us, he says that so much has been written recently on the social nature of man that it is now obvious. "But I believe that in certain points at least we have not, yet penetrated to the heart of the social factor, and its significance for morals."[83] He goes on to expound this: "So far as the moral aspect is concerned I know nothing more significant than the attitude of the Common Law as set forth by Professor Pound. This has sought to base its system of duties on relations." The Pound article he is referring to is "A Feudal Principle in Modern Law", an introductory lecture of a series of eight upon "The Spirit of the Common Law" presented in February of 1914 and published in *International Journal of Ethics*.[84] Tufts was at that time Managing Editor of the journal.

Roscoe Pound contrasts the feudal principle that affixes duties and liabilities independently of the will of those bound, in terms of relations, with the current high valuation of individual liberty and property and determination of duties on the basis of transactions. The latter individualism reached its high water mark in the last quarter of the nineteenth century. Pound finds the feudal principle operative in the Common Law, and the individualist accentuated by the entry of Roman Law. Thus the latter speaks of a letting of services, while the former of the relation of master and servant; the latter of family law, the former of domestic relations. In the nineteenth century, says Pound, the Roman idea of contract became popular in jurisprudence, and (quoting Maitland) contract became "the greediest of legal categories." Pound regards Henry Maine's thesis about the evolution from status to contract as a generalization from Roman legal history only. It is belied by the present course of English and American law in which the feudal principle of relations is gaining in scope. Pound offers the general sociological observation that the concept of transaction or contract suffices for a pioneer agricultural society, but "In the industrial and urban society of today classes and groups and relations must be taken account of no less than individuals."[85]

Tufts is ready to draw a far-reaching conclusion for ethics from this material: "If right and duty have their origin in this social factor there is at least a presumption against their being subordinate ethically to the conception of good as we find them in certain writers. If they have independent origin and are the outgrowth of a special aspect of life it is at least probable that they are not to be subordinated to the good unless the very notion of good is itself reciprocally modified by right in a way that is not usually recognized in teleological systems."[86] Shortly after, Tufts takes this stand categorically: "Right is not merely a means to the good but has an independent place in the moral consciousness."[87] And again, "Right means just 'right,' nothing else. That is we mean that acts so characterized correspond exactly to a self in a peculiar attitude, viz., one of adequate standardizing and adjustment, of equilibrium, in view of all relations."[88]

How far can we assign a similar change of view about right to Dewey at this time? We can at least say that some of the influences from the awakening philosophy of law were then operating upon him. He wrote the entry on "Law" in the *Cyclopedia of Education*[89]; but this was not specifically directed to legal matters, it rather referred briefly to the early conception of law as order construed in jural fashion as governing particulars, then the positivist conception that saw scientific law as a statement of an order and jural and moral law as commands or imperatives, and finally he suggested an instrumentalist interpretation that brought the physical and social together in a notion of "*use as a method of procedure* in dealing with further cases, with future possibilities."[90] In 1914 he writes on "Nature and Reason in Law,"[91] examining the way in which the relation of these traditional conceptions identified the reasonable and the natural with the antecedently given, the customary, rather than the exercise of intelligence to remedy deficiencies. He adds: "From the side of the employer, it meant *Beati possidentes*, To him that hath shall be given; from the side of the employee, *Vae victis*, From him that hath not shall be taken away even that which he seemeth to have."[92] He illustrates from problems of risk in implied contract and problems of liability. The general tone is much like Pound's in that older individualistic legal interpretations are being criticized as requiring revision in the light of the newer social conditions.

We do have, however, more direct evidence that Dewey at this point was taking an active personal part in the revival of philosophy of law. In his autobiographical *A Dreamer's Journey* (1949) Morris Raphael Cohen describes the organization of a Conference on Legal and Social Philosophy which held meetings in April of 1913 and 1914, and December of 1914 and 1915. Dewey was chairman and Cohen secretary.[93] The first meeting dealt with "Law in Relation to Social Ends" and Pound opened it with a talk on "The Philosophy of Law in America." Although Dewey did not write a book on legal philosophy, (as he did on political philosophy, social psychology, and education) his interest in it apparently was fairly constant. We can reasonably assume that he was aware of Pound's focus on relations as distinct from contract in its pertinence to the contemporary world and his own position ran parallel to it. That the juristic formulation played some part in his use of the idea of relations for right and obligation in *32* is plausible. But we cannot make the direct inference that he was led in the period of 1912–1917 to the independence of right as Tufts apparently was.

We have therefore to look between 1917 and the period of 1926–32 (the time when he definitely set down the thesis of the three roots) to see what inklings there may be of the independence of right. On the whole, Dewey's attention in ethical theory was turned primarily to the concept of value and the good, and to reconstructing (as we shall see later) ideas of the individual and the social; and even in dealing with the social, it is the social nature of the individual that concerns him rather than at this point the relational structures to be found within the group. We suggest, however, that the new conception of the right emerged some time between 1918 and 1923 and that it was fairly clear by 1923.

In Dewey's brief syllabus for his lectures of February and March 1919 in Japan[94] he has a section on "Relation of Rights and Duties, or Freedom and Law."[95] He regards this as "conditions of effective furtherance of a community of experiences, of common ends and values." His emphasis is on liberating the capacities of individuals, without which society is impoverished. "Law is a statement of the order upon which fruitful association depends." This summary is barely developed in *Reconstruction in Philosophy* itself,[96] the amplified publication of the lectures. In the same few years, Dewey was preparing *Human Nature and Conduct*, beginning as lectures in 1918 but not published in developed form till 1922.[97] In a chapter in the last part, on "Morality is Social" Dewey does get to consider the category of right. But he is chiefly worried about those who cut off the right and turn it into a transcendental authority. He regards such a notion as "the last resort of the anti-empirical school in morals and that it proved the effect of neglect of social conditions."[98] Dewey's own brief discussion of the category asserts that "Right is only an abstract name for the multitude of concrete demands in action which others impress upon us, and of which we are obliged, if we would live, to take some account. Its authority is the exigency of their demands, the efficacy of their insistencies. There may be good ground for the contention that in theory the idea of the right is subordinate to that of the good, being a statement of the course proper to attain good. But instead it signifies the totality of social pressures exercised upon us to induce us to think and desire in certain ways. Hence the right can in fact become the road to the good only as the elements that compose this unremitting pressure are enlightened, only as social relationships become themselves reasonable."[99] And if one argued that this is just social pressure, not morals, Dewey says that social pressure is just a name for the interactions always going on. His concern is to show that considerations of right originate within life, not outside of it. Clearly he is moving toward the thesis of three roots, but he is still in the thick of the woods. The spotlight has moved from a direct relation of the right to the good to a realization of conflict between them in human situations, and the demand for intelligent reconstruction is there. But the place of the good in relation to the problematic still carries the flavor of the reconciling ideal.

In 1923 Dewey prepared a long syllabus for a course at Columbia in social philosophy, entitled "Social Institutions and the Study of Morals" (Philosophy 131–32). Social philosophy is described as the ethical evaluation of social phenomena and, as previously, he is looking for a path between the positivistic that registers existing valuations and the transcendental appeal to an outside possibly utopian norm. The intermediate path is of course the intelligent study of the social phenomena themselves in the light of their immanent problems. The reflective valuation is itself an integral part of the social phenomena among which goods and bads and selective bias already exist. Social philosophy can help render more enlightened and efficacious the continual social criticism and projection of social policy. It does this in a way "analogous to judgments of health and disease developed in medical science and hygiene."[100] Dewey points to the social policy character of presumed economic laws and to the history of the value components, leading to the conclusion that social theory is comparable to engineering, not physics. He goes next into a study of association as seen in human groups and their characteristics, and the place of fundamental needs as the basis of association, group formation, and interests that reflect those needs. Then, turning to the social problems that require reflective choice, he finds their origin in group conflicts of interest and the subtle ways in which these find expression.

The description of ethics that immediately follows deserves extended quotation:

Group activity and interest has three generic consequences. 1. In the first place it extends, secures and liberates the activities of its members. It confers upon a member immunities, privileges, satisfactions, liberties, claims and rights which he would not otherwise have. 2. It imposes upon him expectations, requirements, demands, burdens, liabilities, injunctions and prohibitions, obligations. 3. It gives rise to admiration, esteem, approval, respect, reverence, because of position, power in behalf of group interests, whether the function is actual or putative, and to ridicule, disesteem, blame, penalty, etc. Objectively the traits and acts favored with social esteem are virtues; those occasioning group disesteem are vices delinquencies, transgressions.
These three things are the specific subject-matter of morals. Conflict among then gives rise to moral problems.[101]

Dewey goes on to locate within group relations the habitual and reflective components of ethical processes:

Actually, prevailing standards in a group express the rules or regulations which habitually control the granting of indulgence, immunity and rights, the insistence upon duties and the conferring of repute and honor. Moral laws and standards are names for the uniform and enduring ways of acting that any group has in this respect. Criticism of them is equivalent to taking the standpoint of another social group, actual or possible, having other habits of praise-blame and other systems of rights-obligations. Discriminating personal "conscience" is prophetic of social change.[102]

He goes into some detail on the criterion of criticism and how ideals emerge in intellectual form from concrete forms of existence, how division of interests yields rivalry of standards and ideals, and he stresses that conflicts of interests among individuals when they are significant for moral theory, are the consequences of group conflicts.

The threefold division of generic consequences of group activity and interest here presented parallels closely the later three roots of morals. There is a difference in the description of the root that is conceptualized as the good, in that it is here presented not in the quasi-biological terms of wants and needs and satisfactions (in this syllabus that basis has previously been described) but in the social terms in which the goods come to the individual, that is, as liberties and supported claims. The treatment of right and virtue is precisely equivalent to the second and third roots. There is also a difference in their all being presented as a consequence of group activity and interest, but that is because the context is one of social philosophy and has already approached the place of ethics through the social theory of groups. This indicates no difference in the account of what ethical theory is about. We have only to add to this 1923 statement the correlation with the history of schools of ethics and the thesis of the three roots, with its emphasis on conflict, and reflective resolution as an immanent process is fully matured. (And it carries us beyond the independence of the right to the changes that have taken place in the theory of virtue.)

Virtue

The recognition of a separate root from which the concepts of virtue and vice emerge is perhaps the most dramatic shift in *32*, especially when we compare it with the abstract derivation of virtue from freedom in the *Syllabus* and the derivation of virtue from social good in *08*. The first section of chapter 13 in *32* ("Approbation, the Standard and Virtue") is headed "Approval and disapproval as original facts."[103] This is a direct reversal of the way approval was treated in *08* as an affective consequence of the recognition of a social good. Dewey is quite aware of the shift: "Reflection tries to reverse the order: it wants to discover what *should* be esteemed so that approbation will follow what is decided to be *worth* approving, instead of designating virtues on the basis of what happens to be especially looked up to and rewarded in a particular society."[104]

It is interesting to note that even before *08* Dewey had rejected a theory of this sort. In reviewing a Festschrift by students of Charles Edward Garman (where Tufts had written an essay on "Moral Evolution" that will later concern us), Dewey commented on the position taken by Sharp:[105] "His thesis is that the fact of approbation is the fundamental phenomenon of moral life." Sharp, however, identified moral approbation as being directed to the agent's purpose or intended aim, and so to the system of his desires as related to his action. It is thus a complex thesis that Dewey finds begging or evading the real issue. But he does accuse Sharp of making without justifying it "the transition from the *fact* of approbation to the *ideal* of a certain kind of approbation, which is precisely the crux of all valuational or approbational theories of conduct."[106] And he recommends more attention to the machinery of Adam Smith's "impartial spectator." Dewey does, of course, describe in *08* the attempt to make approval and disapproval central in the British moral theory of Shaftesbury, Hume, and Adam Smith.[107]

While Dewey in the *Fries letter* points to his study of eighteenth century British ethical theory as playing a part in developing his idea of the three independent roots, it is possible that complex concerns with the notion of *character* also had their place. *08* was quite careful at the outset to envisage character broadly so that it did not prejudge the results of psychological inquiry of the sources of conduct. The complexities involved are considered in Dewey's entry on *character* in the *Cyclopedia of Education*.[108] The elements of character are three: discriminating judgment as to relative values, emotional susceptibility to values presented in experience, and force in execution.[109] Knowledge, and so intellectual skills, play a part in judgment. Historically medieval thought sharply separated will from intelligence and in recent thought the contrast has been rather the emotions and the intellect. Dewey thinks we are recovering a more integrated conception than that of arbitrary will and blind emotion. He finds the distinction between knowledge and emotion somewhat arbitrary.[110]

It is clear that already at this point Dewey's view of character embraced cognitive affective purposive and volitional tendencies, that he might make distinctions but would not allow absolute or sharp separation of faculties and so of intellectual and moral virtues. Hence, if virtues are construed in the traditional way as states of character, they would embrace an organization of the different elements and their conditions. Different structurings would be possible. If in *08* virtues were routed through the good (the social good) as central, in *32* the origin is found in the affective-expressive element of approval and disapproval. But the latter is not to be construed as pure affectivity or feeling—that was the mistake that Dewey in his value discussions attributed to emotivism. Dewey does not tell us precisely the constituent mixture of what enters into approval in the account of virtues in *32*. But there is sufficient indication that it has a cognitive element consisting in the habits of identification developed in the past. The very acts of approval and disapproval thus express already patterned affective-cognitive reactions. The cognition which had priority in *08* and lost it in *32* is not cognition as such, but the intellectual consideration of the good as steering the feelings and emotions.[111]

In the shift that took place regarding the basis of virtue Dewey did not abandon the lessons that emerged from his reorganization in *08*. *32* continues to recognize the moral character of praise and blame and approbation, that is, that the very use of such sentiments and expressions itself requires evaluation; also that though they are spontaneous reactions within a group they function to shape others. He retains the view that there is a conservative impact in particular pictures of virtues and vices because they express conceptions of merit and desert that are measured by the current reactions of others. Thus "virtues and vices in morals as far as dominated by custom are strictly correlative to the ruling institutions and habits of a given social group."[112] And although the basis of his doing so has changed, he still presents his positive account of virtue by examining the traits which an interest must have—whole-heartedness, persistence, impartiality, and so on. This prevents virtues from being treated as possibly separate traits and also prevents their identification with the specific forms that virtues take under changing historical conditions.

One feature in Dewey's treatment in *32* that calls for explanation is that he discusses the notion of a *standard* in relation to the problems of this third base. On the face of it, one might have expected that each root would generate its own standard—higher ends to evaluate more specific ends, principles to help in evaluating duties, more pervasive virtues to evaluate specific virtues. Instead, Dewey here uses the notion of a standard to work out the relation of approbation to ends, that is, judgments expressing the third root to judgments expressing the first root. (We may compare the way he related duty to good in specific cases while keeping the categories distinct.) He defines a standard as follows: "The principle upon which the assignment of praise and blame rationally rests constitutes what is known as a *standard*."[113] Again, "Although end and standard are two distinct conceptions having different meanings, yet it is the very nature of a standard to demand that what is approvable according to it shall *become* an end. In other words, it calls for the creation of a new end..."[114] Dewey goes on to argue that unless the standard arose from a different source from that of ends "it could not exercise a controlling influence on the latter." In effect, the standard represents, in reflective morality, the fact that men have become conscious of the principles underlying their spontaneous praise and blame; this, as in the theory of Hume and Adam Smith, is what furthers social well-being. Here in spite of initial differences in meaning and concepts, approbation theory and Utilitarianism converge.

Actually, there are signs of a development in Dewey's notion of *standards*, in which association with one root is succeeded by association with a second and then a third where it comes to rest. In his course on *Logic of Ethics* in 1909[115] Dewey says of standard: "It is the retrospective use which gives us the standard." The standard, he says, arises because of conflict in ideals and values. After right as a concept has broken away from good, it would appear to take over standard-setting. Thus in the quotation from the 1923 syllabus on social philosophy, the habitual and reflective components of ethical processes are located within group relations, so that standards are coupled with moral laws. And indeed, in the Fries letter after *32*, the superscripts over "the good, right and virtue" are respectively "end, standard, approbation", still aligning standards with right. Perhaps it is the relation of virtue to character that finally allies virtue and the operation of standards. It is surprising too that there is on the whole so little reference to education in the discussion of virtue. The need of every group to undertake the cultivation of character in a succeeding generation forms a stable base for the third root, quite as important as the natural process of mutual appreciative response, praise and blame.

We have examined the three independent factors or variables in morals and seen what effect the recognition of the independence had on the major moral concepts, and in some degree on their relations. We have not examined the three corresponding theoretical systems in the history of ethics that Dewey reckons with. There is little change in his criticisms of them in *08* and *32* except insofar as the outcome in the reinterpretation of their leading concepts has been changed. It is essential next to look at the social problem in the comparison of the two editions and then to the ideas of social and individual that were recurrent themes in both works.

Notes

1. 1911, MW 6: 437–40.
2. Ibid., 437–38.
3. Ibid., 439.
4. Ibid., 440.
5. 1903, MW 3: 3–39; categories, 23–26.
6. Ibid., 24.
7. LW 7: 181.
8. Ibid., 184–85.
9. Ibid., 185.
10. LW 7: 287.
11. Ibid., 302.
12. The notion of the self is, of course, another matter. It has its psychological basis and social origins and has a varying career in human history. For a brief assess-

ment of it see Dewey's entry on Self in *Cyclopedia of Education* (1912–13, MW 7: 339–343). Part of the story is a changed conception of childhood.

13. MW 3: 145–52.
14. For Dewey's analysis of interest, see his *Interest and Effort in Education* (1913, MW 7: 150–97). Such remarks as "Genuine interest is the accompaniment of the identification through action, of the self with some object or idea, because of the necessity of that object or idea for the maintenance of a self-initiated activity" (159) mark the beginning of a shift in the theoretical center of gravity. Eventually, as in *32*, interest will be talked of more in terms of reflective ends. Dewey's entry on Interest in the *Cyclopedia of Education* (MW 7: 252–60) is a succinct statement of his view as of 1912–1913.
15. Wilbur Marshall Urban, *Valuation, Its Nature and Laws, Being an Introduction to the General Theory of Value* (New York: Macmillan, 1909).
16. *General Theory of Value, Its Meaning and Basic Principles Construed in Terms of Interest* (New York: Longmans, Green and Co., 1926). In a later work, *Realms of Value* (Cambridge, Mass.: Harvard University Press, 1954), Perry reckoned with the diverse movements that had intervened and carried his own approach into the provinces of value.
17. 1913, MW 7: 44–46.
18. Ibid., 45.
19. Ibid., 364–65.
20. 1915, MW 8: 14–82.
21. Ibid., 14.
22. Ibid., 15.
23. Ibid., 16.
24. Ibid., 26.
25. Ibid.
26. Ibid., 29.
27. Ibid., 32.
28. Ibid., 35.
29. Ibid., 42.
30. Ibid., 67.
31. 1918, MW 11: 3–9.
32. Reprinted in MW 11: Appendix 2 and 3.
33. Ibid., 7.
34. 1919, MW 11: 341–49.
35. Ibid., 347.
36. 1920, MW 12: 172.
37. Ibid., 173.
38. Ibid., 176.
39. Ibid., 180.
40. Ibid., 182.
41. 1922, MW 14.
42. Section I of Part 4: Conclusion.
43. Ibid., 136.
44. Ibid., 193.
45. Ibid., 195.
46. Ibid., 196.
47. Ibid., 197.
48. 1922, MW 13: 5–28.
49. Ibid., 4.

50. Ibid., 7.
51. Ibid., 7, n. 4.
52. Ibid., 11.
53. Ibid., 11, n. 8.
54. *Journal of Philosophy* XVII, 1920: 96.
55. 1923, MW 15: 20–26.
56. 1925, LW 2: 69–73.
57. Ibid., 78–97.
58. Ibid., 96.
59. A comment of Dewey's on Perry in manuscript notes (102/63/4, manuscript 3, p. 6) is enlightening: "Professor Perry has been regrettably reticent in expounding his notion of desire. There is little or nothing in his statements inconsistent with the idea that desire is a behavioristic attitude; there is considerable that implies such a notion. But there is no account whatever as to the bearing of such a notion on that of the 'object' or the fulfilment of desire. And without such an account the identification of value with the object of desire or fulfilment leave us with the vaguest notion of the meaning of value."

      Another remark of Dewey's elsewhere rounds out the criticism: the object of desire simply means the recognition of conditions under which desires as active, urgent tendencies will be carried through to their completion and fulfilment. In short, for Dewey, to understand the object is to see its function in terms of context.
60. 1925, LW 1.
61. 1929, LW 4.
62. Ibid., 206.
63. 1939, LW 13.
64. *Journal of Philosophy* XXIX, 11, May 21, 1942: 290–96.
65. Ibid., XXIX, 12, June 4, 1942: 328–30.
66. Ibid., XL, 12, June 19, 1943: 309–16.
67. Ibid., XL, 20, Sept. 30, 1943: 543–52.
68. Ibid., XLI, 17, August 17, 1944: 449–55.
69. Ibid., 455.
70. Ibid., XLII, 26, December 20, 1945: 701–12.
71. Ibid., 702.
72. 1932, LW 7: 216.
73. Ibid., 218.
74. Ibid.
75. Ibid., 219.
76. Ibid., 218.
77. Ibid., 228.
78. Ibid.
79. Ibid., 225.
80. Ibid., 228.
81. Ibid., 317–18.
82. 1917, New York: Holt, 354–408.
83. 1932, LW 7: 361.
84. Roscoe Pound, "A Feudal Principle in Modern Law," *International Journal of Ethics* (October 1914): 1–24.
85. Ibid., 24.
86. 1932, LW 7: 363.
87. Ibid., 372–73.

88. Ibid., 382–83.
89. Dewey, entry on "Law" in the *Cyclopedia of Education* (1912–1913, MW 7: 269–71).
90. Ibid., 270.
91. MW 7: 56–93.
92. Ibid., 61.
93. Morris Raphael Cohen, *A Dreamer's Journey*, 1949. A specific article by Cohen on Roscoe Pound appears in Cohen's *Law and the Social Order* (New York: Harcourt Brace and Co., 1933).
94. 1919, MW 11: 341–49.
95. Ibid., 349.
96. 1920, MW 12.
97. 1922, MW 14.
98. Ibid., 222.
99. Ibid., 224.
100. Dewey, "Social Institutions and the Study of Morals", p.3.
101. Ibid., 9.
102. Ibid., 10.
103. An explicit treatment of the relation of right to good in this new vein is found in a few sheets of ethics notes in 1925 (102/64/9, Ethics, notes, 1925 January. AMs and TMs, 4 pp.):

   "The concepts of Rights—its relation to that of good, confusion—it may be quite true that the specific acts deemed right should be contributory to the good, but this does not prove that the concept of rightness equals contribution to good...rightness means the fact of the subjection of human conduct with respect to purposes and choices, decisions, claims, exactions, demands, requirements, outside the individual making the choice—It is permitted, allowed, licit authorized—and their contraries—and there is no method of reducing these concepts to those of it is good or contributory to good."

   1923 and 1925 are late, compared to Tufts in 1917, for the recognition of the independent status of right. There is one passage which may be proof of an earlier date, perhaps even 1917. In a Columbia University course on Psychological Ethics (syllabus: 102/62/9, TMs, 43 pp.) Dewey says (p. 35) that the idea of 'right' is clearly connected with that of justification; 'wrong' with that of 'no business', no 'call', lack of justification. "It may be true that justification is ultimately to be found in consequences, and hence that what is right is equivalent to what conduces to good; but it does not follow from this that the concept of right is equivalent to that of a means to good, but only that *reflective* morality has a certain point of view from which to criticize the judgments of right and wrong current in customary morality. In the latter, the claim, the demand and justification for certain acts are directly social—the ways of acting which the group demands from a member as a condition of full membership..., e.g. exogamy."

   This material comes in an envelope dated 1911. But the text contains a reference to the *Journal of Philosophy* of 1917, as well as to *Democracy and Education*, published in 1916. It cannot then be earlier than 1917.
104. 1932, LW 7: 237.
105. 1907, MW 4: 221–22.
106. Ibid., 222.
107. *08*: 260.
108. 1911, MW 6: 381–88.

109. Ibid., 382.
110. Ibid., 385.
111. The understanding of cognitive affective relations is unavoidably more difficult when the sharp separation of the two aspects is softened. The interpretation of "approval" becomes the crucial question. In the same syllabus for Psychological Ethics, which we noted above must date after 1917, Dewey wrote (p. 35): "We do not punish *because* we have disapproved, but the punishment *is* the disapproval. (To introduce a formal disapproval before the punishment means simply that the act is getting reasonable or reflective, not that it has ceased to be an overt act. In other words it signifies the intervention of doubt or uncertainty as to what action to take.)"
   In any case, Dewey continually regarded approval as "a very active thing"; habits of judgment are not cold and inactive (e.g., 11A5. "Ethics and the Psychology of the Self", a series of six lectures given at Smith College, Jan. 1911. Archives of Smith College, First Lecture, p. 3).
112. 1932, LW 7: 254.
113. Ibid., 237.
114. Ibid., 246.
115. Dewey, course on Logic and Ethics (00A1, pp. 67–68, lecture of Nov. 22, 1909).

6

Custom and the Odyssey of Habit

In the early chapter on "Customary and Reflective Morality" we examined the use made of *custom* and *habit* in *08* and *32*, the apparent conflicts in the former and the resolution in the latter. Some of the constituent themes have been traced in the later chapters: the changes in the relation of individual and social, and the withdrawal of the linear thesis about the evolution of morality. Especially with the changed view of individualism, it would appear that the notion of custom is left in a shambles. Can we not put the pieces together by threading our way through the different periods of Dewey's thought, as we did in the preceding two chapters?

We may note first that none of the contrasts that appeared in the pitting of customary against reflective morality (listed in chapter 3 at the end of our consideration of Part I of *08*) has actually been eliminated. Significant differences do occur between the presence or absence of group cohesion, between automatic acceptance and thoughtful consideration, between static and dynamic in stretches of social history, and the rest. What has been shattered is the bundling of all these contrasts in the single opposition of a customary morality and a reflective morality. It is not hard to see, retrospectively, that the tune was called by the notion of reflection, whose role in morality was the immediately initial interest of the book, in both *08* and *32*. Reflective thought is the performance of the individual, it is active, it probes complexities, it works out new paths, it is dynamic. Does it follow that these properties are mutually implicated, that they have to hang together; even more, why should it follow that there has to be a notion opposed to reflective thought that will combine all the opposites—that will issue from the group, involve passive acceptance, stick with unanalyzed simplicities, cling to the old, remain static? These are the properties assigned to customary morality.

It is also clear by this time that the consolidated treatment of customary morality in *08* came from assuming the convergence of three distinct inquiries: one into the moral growth of a person from childhood on; the second into the evolution of morality from primitive society to contemporary civilized society; the third, unlike the temporal inquiries into psychological and historical development, a synchronic analysis of the proportions of the habitual and the reflective in present conduct at a given time. Let us look at each of these and the apparent results as we saw them in *08* and the theoretical background that led to the assumption of converging results.

Moral growth was modelled on the psychological process in which impulse, becoming rationalized and conceptualized, takes the shape of desires and needs that embody the results of experience. There is thus a layer of habit at this basic level. The conflicts of this layer of impulse and habit gives rise to conscious intervention and reconstruction and the outcome is the habits and self pattern of character. Habit thus has a role throughout, and for this reason we distinguished the pre-reflective habits from the post-reflective habits with reference to any part of the process. But since changes compel a constant concern with revision and reconstruction, the post-reflective habits of one stage become the pre-reflective habits of a later point. To consider habit in general as what in society becomes custom (by being valued or regarded as compelling) is thus to focus from the point of view of reflective thought upon the pre-reflective. At the highest stage of the moral development moral concepts have taken shape and are consciously operative in the reflection.

Moral evolution, we have seen, was taken to go from the simple, uniform, undifferentiated to the complex individualized differentiated in which the moral was separated from the legal, conventional, etc. and became more imbued with reflection. This has been sufficiently described. We saw that by analogy with the "ontogeny recapitulates phylogeny" thesis the so-called "culture-epoch theory" assumed that the pattern of moral development and the pattern of cultural evolution were identical. Dewey accepted this in general in 1896 and held to it as late as 1911, as we saw in his two papers on the culture-epoch theory, though he insisted that the two sides should be separately investigated and that the educational consequences depended more on the psychological theory. That Dewey held quite firmly, and quite early, to the role of custom in primitive morality may be seen from his article on "Moral Philosophy" in *Johnson's Universal Cyclopaedia* in 1884.[1] He writes: "In primitive societies morality is identified with the customs of the community; and these customs, receiving religious sanction, are thus binding religiously as well as morally. This fact tends to retard the growth of any theory of conduct. Custom when consecrated by religion is the essence of conservatism."[2] Greece, he says, won freedom from "slavish subserviency to the fixed habits of the past" by discussion of means and ends relating to community welfare. The discussion of the Sophists abstracted such topics from the habits and traditions of any particular community.

The third enterprise is less explicitly formulated. It consists in analyzing the components of the customary and the reflective in conduct at a given point. For example, we saw Tufts saying that the post-reflective habits embodied "more intelligence," and Dewey speaking of "the customary factor in the present." This mode of analysis is already suggested in the Syllabus of 1894[3] where the distinction is drawn between habits ("the mediating experiences are completely *absorbed* into the initiating impulse; the two sides, the immediate and the mediate, no longer have any separate existence.") An example is having learned to walk, or to talk; general lines or plans of action (which furnish limits within which other acts fall); and particular variable acts (where the expressions of an impulse are "so numerous and complex as to be uncertain"). These three aspects could be discerned in any action: how much is habitual, how much part of a plan, how much variable and requiring reflection. We have seen that Tufts pointed to the greater complexity of modern life as ensuring the higher degree of necessary reflection. The assumption of convergence of this third inquiry with the earlier two would apparently be that the advanced stages developmentally and historically require this greater reflection. But while this may be the case in a general sense, it underestimates the degree in which complex patterns may be digested into habitual symbols in the modern world as well as the extent to which complex patterns (we suggested earlier the illustration of kinship) may be handled in primitive societies.

The net result is that the character of habit is still in *08* too complex and its quite contrary properties too capable of invocation in different contexts to support the picture of custom painted for customary moral-ity. Eventually, we know, Dewey will stabilize his ideas about habit and refine them considerably, in *Human Nature and Conduct* (1922), and this will govern the changed ideas of *32*. But perhaps it is worth noting some of the references to habit and their import for custom both before *08* and after that up to the 1922 resolution.

In 1891,[3] in writing of "Moral Theory and Practice", Dewey is intent on avoiding the notion of sheer practice without theory. He says: "Whatever may be the case with savages and babes, the begin-ning of every ethical advance, under conditions of civilized existence, must be in a further 'examination of life.' Not even customary moral-ity, that of respectability and of convention is freed from dependence upon theory; it simply lives off the funded results of some once-moving examination of life." Apparently then, customary morality can always boast at least an ancestry of reflection. But this does not certify its reasonableness. In a review of Royce's "On Certain Psychological Aspects of Moral Training"[4] Dewey says that "The psychological iden-tification of imitation with immediacy of action, and of habits with reasonableness of action, seems to me, however, very questionable. Habit, as such, (apart from a need of changing it) is, upon the whole opposed to conscious reflection . . . " Dewey thinks that a function once it is mastered or become habitual passes into unconsciousness.[5] In the evolutionary context (1898, "Evolution and Ethics"[6]) Dewey brings out both sides of habit. "Without habits we can do nothing. Yet if habits becomes so fixed that they cannot be adapted to the ends suggested by new situations, they are barriers to conduct and enemies to life. It is conflict with the end or ideal which keeps the habit work-ing, a flexible and efficient instrument of action." Thus habits and aims are cooperating factors in the maintenance of conscious experi-ence. But once again in the context of evolution ("The Evolutionary Method as Applied to Morality"),[7] "more acts of habit just harden an original custom. It is only through *failure* in the adequate working of the instinct or habit—failure from the standpoint of adjustment—that history, change in quality or values, is made."

In the writings after *08* the relation of habit and idea becomes a frequent theme, especially with the quickening interest in logic and the psychology of thought. Again it is the context of interest that deter-mines which face of habit is shown, whether the drag on change or the constancy in experience. For example, in "The Influence of Darwinism in Philosophy"[8] Dewey writes: "Old ideas give way slowly; for they are more than abstract logical forms and categories. They are habits, predispositions, deeply engrained attitudes of aversion and preference." He goes on to suggest that intellectual progress comes rather from change of questions, so that we get over problems rather than solve them. In his article on "Experience and the Empirical" in the *Cyclopedia of Education*[9] he depicts the shift in the notion of experience as it moves from the Greek interpretation as "the cumulative effect, intellectual and practical, of a repeated series of acts and sufferings of a like nature" to the Renaissance interpretation as "the incursion of the new, the fresh, the conquest of the unknown." In the former, experience is so linked to habit and routine that it is thought incapable of providing true universals; hence the appeal to the rational as something transcendent. As we have seen, and shall explore further in our chapter on Dewey's mode of analysis, the tie-in of an established idea to rule and rule to habit becomes the basis of Dewey's constant differentiation of *rule* and *principle*, the former having a rigid absolute character and the latter an analytic character tied to experiment and reconstruction. Perhaps this was a lesson he came to by combining his own view of habit as a drag with Peirce's identification of an idea as a rule of action. In the *Cyclopedia* article just mentioned he says that the contemporary pragmatic view of experience goes back to the Greek in regarding experience as a practical matter, but it interprets science not rationalistically but as concerned with experiment and the possibility of the control of experience, and it invokes the lessons of biology about the process of life.[10] Experience thus has two phases, the conservative with the limitation furnished by habit and the progressive focused on discovery and invention. Which dominates at a given period of history is largely a matter not of the biological or psychological structure of experience, but of the social standards of the period.[11] In his 1916 paper on "The Pragmatism of Peirce"[12] there is a slightly different focus: "pragmatism identifies meaning with formation of a habit, or way of acting having the greatest generality possible, or the widest range of application to particulars."[13] "Meaning or rational purport resides in the setting up of habits or generalized methods . . ."[14] Later on Dewey quotes from Peirce's earlier articles that "the belief of a rule is a habit. That a habit is a rule, active in us, is evident." And "That every belief is of the nature of a habit, in so far as it is of a general character . . ."[15] The focus thus falls on the formation of a habit as well as the functioning of the habit when established. Habit thus includes the post-reflective as well as the pre-reflective.

We have seen how the Chinese experience suggested to Dewey that custom may in some cases be what reflection could reaffirm, the lesson that preserves rather than retards. But since the social situation of the contemporary world is the crisis that calls for reconstruction, it is not surprising that *Reconstruction in Philosophy*[16] deals with habit and custom on their conservative side. Technologies are said to promote the experimental attitude once arts are removed from "the rule of sheer custom."[17] His account of classical Greek philosophy is that it is a metaphysical substitute for custom as the guarantor of moral and social values that were being threatened.[18] Custom makes claims of finality and immutability and breeds a pervasive authoritative tradition.[19] When the bonds of customary institutions are relaxed, the contract theory of the state rapidly gains a place.[20]

We come now to *Human Nature and Conduct*[21] which presents Dewey's mature theory of habit and custom. The cast of characters in the book is by now familiar enough—Impulse, Habit, Intelligence. But each one is refined and sharpened, and their relations are carefully worked out. The book is obviously the end product of a long period of reflection, at least three decades of concern with the character of psychology itself, with the successive strata of psychological theories and outlooks. It carries further the earlier view that psychology is either biological or social. In the cast of characters, Impulse represents biology, Habit is the surrogate for the social, and Intelligence is the category reflecting the individual agent in practical reflection. Which member of the cast is, however, in the position of the star?

Impulse might have claimed temporal priority. After all, biology is on the scene first, and society works on the biological equipment of the infant. Dewey in fact asks at the beginning of Part II, which deals with impulse, why habit, which occupied Part I, was discussed first. Why was the derived discussed before the primitive? His answer is simply (and paradoxically) that "in conduct the acquired is the primitive. Impulses although first in time are never primary in fact; they are secondary and dependent."[22] This is, of course, not a postulate but the outcome of a long development in psychological theory. The early part of the century had seen social psychologies attempting to furnish lists of instincts to explain determinate modes of behavior and ascribe inevitability to specific institutions. Dewey had criticized and rejected such simplicities. "When this volume was first produced," Dewey writes (1929) in his Foreword to the 1930 reprint of the book, "there was a tendency, especially among psychologists, to insist upon native human nature untouched by social influences and to explain social phenomena by traits of original nature called 'instincts'. Since that date (1922), the pendulum has undoubtedly swung in the opposite direction. The importance of culture as a formative medium is more generally recognized."[23] There is today, he adds, a tendency to overlook the basic identity of human nature. But basic impulses play a definite role. Though they are immediately shaped into habit and particular conduct always involves the interaction of complex habits, impulse arising when not satisfied plays the role of pivot: "Impulses are the pivots upon which the re-organization of activities turn, they are agencies of deviation, for giving new directions to old habits and changing their quality."[24] Thus impulses, fed by habits, are the means of reconstructive growth, which knowledge comes to make possible. "The hen precedes the egg. But nevertheless this particular egg may be so treated as to modify the future type of hen."[25] Impulse is plastic, and human docility is not to be equated with simply learning the customs of adults; it is also the source of original action.

Unlike impulse, intelligence does not make a bid for primacy. We shall examine its character in the next chapter, and its relation to reason. But it clearly functions in the Deweyan framework within a scheme in which there is conflict of habits or an unsettling of habit by impulse, and it is the agent of reconstruction.

The star of the book is accordingly habit. Dewey tells us as much in his Preface (February 1921) to the original 1922 edition of the book: The book "seriously sets forth a belief that an understanding of habit and of different types of habit is the key to social psychology." Impulse and intelligence "are secondary to habit so that mind can be understood in the concrete only as a system of beliefs, desires and purposes which are formed in the interaction of biological aptitudes with a social environment." The reference to different types of habit is most significant. It means the end of the wholesale treatment of the notion, and the distinction of the variety of its forms and functions.

The introduction to the 1930 edition reconfirms this outlook. If Hume had not become known as a subjectivist, the book might well be seen as following in Hume's footsteps in its concern with habit and custom, adding to Hume's emphasis on these what Hume failed to see, "that custom is essentially a fact of associated living whose force is dominant in forming the habits of individuals."[26]

Once we recognize that habit is the center of the inquiry, we can readily see one major respect in which it differs from its fellow categories. Impulse tends to set itself off from the others, from intelligence because it is native and from habit because it is biologically primary and because it stands ready to disrupt unsatisfying habits. Intelligence likewise sets itself off, not merely conversely from impulse but also from habit because it is essentially occupied with the reconstruction of habits. Habit, however, is a thoroughly imperialistic concept. Once its multiple forms are distinguished it can invade both impulse and intelligence. This is quite literally what happens in the book. Here are some of its conquests:

"All virtues and vices are habits. . . . "[27]

"All habits are demands for certain kinds of activity; and they constitute the self. In any intelligible sense of the word will, they *are* the will. They form our effective desires and they furnish us with our working capacities. They rule our thoughts, determining which shall appear and be strong and which shall pass from light into obscurity." In approaching this conclusion Dewey has explained the power of habit on us because "we are the habit."[28]

Habits also shape the rise of ends. "Only as the end is converted into means is it definitely conceived, or intellectually defined, to say nothing of being executable."[29] "Now the thing which is closest to us, the means within our power, is a habit. Some habit impeded by circumstances is the source of the projection of the end. It is also the primary means in its realization. The habit is propulsive and moves anyway toward some end, or result, whether it is projected as an end-in-view or not."[30] Habits are apparently at their work constantly; we are told that during waking life each habit operates all the time, like the members of a crew doing their work and only becoming central focus on occasion.

It is not surprising, consequently, that "Character is the interpenetration of habits."[31] That is why character can be read through acts. (But interpenetration is never total.) The moral situation is defined by the mutual modification of habits. When an act has consequences for habit and character it may require judgment from the standpoint of the whole body of conduct, that is, moral judgment.[32]

Dewey is conscious of the fact that he is extending the customary use of the term "habit". "But we need a word to express that kind of human activity which is influenced by prior activity and in that sense acquired; which contains within itself a certain ordering or systematization of minor elements of action; which is projective, dynamic in quality, ready for overt manifestation; and which is operative in some subdued subordinate form even when not obviously dominating activity." Habit is a better term for this than attitude or disposition.[33]

There still remains the story of the penetration of habits and the mode of functioning (the habits?) of habits. In discussing character and conduct, Dewey makes the fundamental point that "patterns exist only within and for the sake of reorganization", that they are instrumental.[34] This is presumably the basic lesson of evolution for moral theory. It is graphically put: "morality becomes legitimately subjective or personal when activities which once included objective factors in their operation temporarily lose support from objects, and yet strive to change existing conditions until they regain a support which has been lost."[35] Thus habits, no matter how good they may be, will need modification in the kind of world which is ours.

The conquest of thought proceeds by stages. The first advance is to recognize that the separation of habit and thought goes astray. It reduces habit to the mere reiteration of the past. It underlies the separation of body and mind, practice and theory, and makes thought abstruse and irrelevant. Eventually the book reaches the frontal assault on intelligence itself (Part III). "Concrete habits do all the perceiving, recognizing, imagining, recalling, judging, conceiving and reasoning that is done."[36] Consciousness "expresses functions of habits, phenomena of their formation, operation, their interruption and reorganization." But habits cannot do all the work alone: "A certain delicate combination of habit and impulse is requisite for observation, memory and judgment. Knowledge which is not projected against the black unknown lives in the muscles, not in consciousness."[37] We may "know how" by our muscles, but that is not really knowledge. But the reach of habit even here is not to be denied. For it is the conflict of habits and the release of impulse that occasions the conscious search. Yet habit does not merely initiate search and leave some other agency to make decisions. "Choice is made as soon as some habit, or some combination of elements of habits and impulse, finds a way fully open. Then energy is released. The mind is made up, composed, unified."[38]

Let us not here go further in this mop-up of the campaign of habit. This requires tracing the nature of reason in Dewey's development, and how it blossoms into intelligence. Let us instead focus more specifically on what conclusions Dewey draws about custom.

Two chapters (Part I, chapters 4 and 5) are devoted to the relation of custom and habit and of custom and morality. Dewey is opposing the view that custom comes from the consolidation of individual habits. On the contrary, individuals form their habits under conditions set by prior customs. Yet Dewey is not asserting the priority of "society" to *the* individual; that is metaphysical nonsense.[39] What we have is prexistent association of human beings prior to every fresh birth. He attacks also the psychologists (like Le Bon) who look for a crowd psychology that is in some sense inherent in the group and not in the individual; he looks rather for the interplay of habit and emotion under the existent conditions and habits.

Given the relation of habit and thought rather than their separation, it is easy to see that a distinction can now be made between habits that are reasonable and those that are not. (We are far from the early criticism of Royce in 1894 for associating reasonableness of action with habits.) It follows that custom too can be released from the charge of being the drag of the past. Even reason can be seen as "a custom of expectation and outlook, an active demand for reasonableness in other customs."[40] The rise of this new custom in human affairs has a revolutionary influence on other customs.

What are we to make of this all-encompassing nature and role of habit? Has it become almost a metaphysical category for the discussion of mind and human life? Perhaps so, but in the kind of naturalistic metaphysics that Dewey develops shortly after, in *Experience and Nature*.[41] Indeed, the metaphysical role of the *stable* and the *precarious* in the latter, as major categories, parallels that of *habit* and *intelligence* in the social psychology, the one providing the stabilities of life and thought, the other dealing with the transformations in uncertain conditions. This does not mean, however, that Dewey has substituted a metaphysics for a social psychology. If metaphysics stabilizes the categories that are found of use in various fields, then Dewey has been working out in *Human Nature and Conduct* precisely what he said he was doing, an introduction to social psychology, not a social psychology. It is a schema, reflecting the growth of knowledge, not a body of specific knowledge. The detailed growth of social psychology would have to decide how far that schema was preferable to alternatives. And Dewey is quite explicit about the features that the schema conveys—

above all, continuities rather than sharp dichotomies. Philosophically, it is Hume's outlook refined by realizing the active character of mind and habits, the permeation of thought in all human activity and consciousness (the lesson of philosophical idealism against the separation of sensation and thought and of reason and experience, but reinterpreted for a naturalistic view of mind and matter).

If such an interpretation of what Dewey is doing is plausible, then it is worth glancing at the use of the schema in a number of contexts. It will, of course, take a level of generality that is appropriate to the subject-matter in each case. Thus, in the 1923 syllabus,[42] Dewey applies it to economic theories about the relation of moral justification and the system of exchange. He says: "The essential fallacy is that the theory assumes that original and natural wants determine the economic phenomena of production and exchange. In fact, before they become economic wants—effective demands—they are reshaped by the existing distributive-exchange system. The market and business determine wants, not the reverse; the argument moves in a vicious circle."[43] He goes on to consider the psychology of wants and concludes: "Only with respect to the objects of a distributed system of activities does each object have a definite value. So far as this system is not apprehended in thought, it exists in the system of *habits* as these are determined by the economic status of the person in an objective economic system; the standard of living appropriate to a certain economic class."[44] It is this standard of living that assigns place to each particular want and satisfaction. Dewey thus appears to be suggesting that the economic analysis is sidetracked into a question-begging psychological approach when it should be examining its context in the sociology of a habit system. The moral evaluations are thus routed in a different direction.

In social philosophy we have already seen the way the schema functions in *Individualism Old and New*. In one respect, the old and the new become the general categories corresponding to the pre-reflective and the post-reflective categories of individualism and individuality. It is a call for reconstruction of a broad philosophical outlook in the light of changed contemporary conditions.

That Dewey applies a similar schema to philosophic thought in general and to the role of philosophy in the history of civilization was already clear in *Reconstruction in Philosophy* (1920). It is reaffirmed in general in *Philosophy and Civilization* (1931): "The life of all thought is to effect a junction at some point of the new and the old, of deep-sunk customs and unconscious dispositions, that are brought to the light of attention by some conflict with newly emerging directions of activity. Philosophies which emerge at distinctive periods define the larger patterns of continuity which are woven in effecting the enduring junctions of a stubborn past and an insistent future."[45]

The schema operates as a general background of Dewey's thought in specific materials. Take as a final example, in the field of legal theory, his review of Allen's *Law in the Making*.[46] Allen has custom the chief law-making force. (This is, of course, an old view in legal theory, and we may digress to note that it is often question-begging. When a custom is affirmed as law it is obviously supported. When a custom is overruled it is argued that the procedure of judicial decision is at least customary. And when customs change it is argued that customary values lie behind the change.) Dewey gets immediately to the point of decision and notes that "Customs do not become laws in any juridical sense until they are authoritatively stated or formulated, and that the occasion of such statement is always a dispute. Customs themselves conflict, and the source of law may be in the need of adjudicating such conflicts rather than in the bare fact of customs themselves." A rule of law is thus not mere reduplication of the custom. The custom is given a new status and is the beginning of a new custom. If all customs were mutually consistent and universally adhered to we would not get law. Dewey might have added that we would not need law.

We have not suggested here that the schema emerged for the first time in 1922. Much of it was implicit throughout and constitutes a central part of Dewey's philosophical contribution. Our interest is in the shift from *08* to *32*, and it is clear that after the full articulation of 1922 and its use in subsequent major works, the view of habit and custom in *32* can no longer be that of the mere drag of the past.

Notes

1. 1884, EW4: 132–51.
2. Ibid., 132.
3. 1891, EW 3: 96.
4. 1894, EW 4: 198.
5. It is worth noting that Dewey's analysis of emotion in 1894 (EW4: 185) refers to habit only as a source of the conflict: "The emotion is, *psychologically, the adjustment or tension of habit and ideal...*"

6. EW 5: 48.
7. 1902, MW 2: 34.
8. MW4; 1910 revision of "Darwin's Influence on Philosophy," 1909:14.
9. 1911, MW 6: 445–46.
10. Ibid., 447.
11. Ibid., 448–49.
12. MW 10.
13. Ibid., 73.
14. Ibid., 74.
15. Ibid., 77.
16. 1920, MW 12.
17. Ibid., 86.
18. Ibid., 89.
19. Ibid., 92.
20. Ibid., 104–05.
21. 1922, MW 14.
22. Ibid., 65.
23. Ibid., 223.
24. Ibid., 67.
25. Ibid., 68.
26. Ibid., 224.
27. Ibid., 16.
28. Ibid., 21.
29. Ibid., 29.
30. Ibid.
31. Ibid.
32. Ibid., 31.
33. Ibid.
34. Ibid., 39–40.
35. Ibid., 40.
36. Ibid., 124.
37. Ibid.
38. Ibid., 134.
39. Ibid., 114.
40. Ibid., 55–56.
41. 1925, LW 1.
42. MW 15: 229–72.
43. Ibid., 264.
44. Ibid., 265.
45. Dewey, *Philosophy and Civilization*, (New York: Minton, Balch and Co. 1931), 7.
46. *Columbia Law Review*, 1928, XXVIII: 832–33.

7

Individual and Social Reconsidered

In *32*, in the chapter beginning Part III—which it is well to remember is the revised counterpart of one in *08* entitled "Social Organization and the Individual"—Dewey wrote:

> We shall accordingly substitute the consideration of definite conflicts, at particular times and places, for a general opposition between social and individual. Neither 'social' nor 'individual', in general, has any fixed meaning. All morality (including immorality) is both individual and social:—individual in its immediate inception and execution, in the desires, choices, dispositions from which the conduct proceeds; social in its occasions, material, and consequences.[1]

And shortly after he follows up with a case study of Historic Individualism.

If this is the mature outcome of the quarter century inquiry, what are we to make retrospectively of the many arguments in which social and individual in one garb or another were contrasted and made the keynote of answers to one or another question? We saw this happening particularly in the historical pattern where the emergence of the moral and its separation from the cake of custom was characterized as the growth of the individual, the reflective, as against the group social, the unthinking customary. But there were also other theoretical issues in which something like the opposition appeared: the meaning of "moral"; qualities of self and the character of virtue; social organization, with the individual vis-a-vis social institutions. Perhaps we can find some *contextual* meaning to the contrast of individual and social—where the context is the intellectual problem—rather than some *general* meaning.

113

Let us begin with the historical picture, whose major outlines were already studied. The developmental theme is the passage from unthinking custom through consciousness of customary to individual reflective judgment. The various aspects are worked out in some detail in *08*. The conditions which show the importance of group standards are education of the young, and their preparation for full membership in the group; restraining refractory members and adjusting conflict of interests; occasions of danger or crisis. Now in a generally stationary society the second and third occasions may be minimal, but the first should be recognized as a perennial task. There are thus permanent elements in the succession of generations to suggest some degree of consciousness about the moral ways (even though the moral as such is not differentiated). Primitive societies often do have initiatory rites or initiatory teaching of the ways of the people, even though it is less transcribed than the New Yorker cartoon has it where the elder substitutes a book of Margaret Mead's describing the culture. It should be also noted that the Deweyan account of consciousness as stimulated by the problematic is easily satisfied by the situation of need for educational transmission in some conscious form.

We are approaching the nerve of the distinction of customary and reflective morality in terms of social and individual by asking what the consciousness of the ways has to be like to become reflective. This is worth exploring in a thought-experiment.

Suppose we have two primitive societies (A and B) in neither of which there has been reflection about morality. But they do have property patterns and we are going to frame one to be in some sense individualistic (B) and the other in some sense group-oriented (A). Let us give them a simplified economic base: both have an adequate animal food supply, but for A it comes in bursts and there is no way of preserving the food (e.g. our refrigeration). Theoretically A is worse off than Locke's savages whose accumulations of acorns as private property was stopped only by the capacity of the acorns eventually to rot. (But a whale would not last that long.) Now A is a hunting society and its precarious luck is maintained by the strict injunction that every kill is to be shared on kinship lines: this itemized part of the animal for the killer, that for the one who first sighted the animal, that for the mother-in-law of the killer, that for his cross-cousin, etc. Everything gets used up before it can spoil, and they all manage to live on till the next kill. Now society B has made one economic advance: it has domesticated the pig. Here the quarry in hunting goes to the person who captured it; no one else may so much as touch it. He may give to the others at will, but that is generosity or hospitality; he has the alternative of "refrigerating" what he does not use by feeding it to the pigs. He can then feed on pig-meat when hunting is low, or become expansively hospitable in a lavish pig-feast when the food supply is good.

We have then two contrasting property-patterns, one of socially mandated distribution, the other of individual ownership plus hospitality. They both work fairly well in the underlying social task of ensuring survival. The sense in which the one pattern is social, the other individual, has nothing to do with the contrast of group-mandated and individual reflective morality, for both are group mandated and whatever we could say about the social pattern in consciousness or lack of consciousness we could also say about the individualistic pattern. So let us dismiss this aspect at present as a different dimension of the general social-individual contrast—perhaps labelling it the *collectively-oriented* and *individualistically-oriented* social institution. Which pattern comes historically first, if either, is an empirical-historical matter. Probably for our examples the one with domestication of pigs is later. But our present concern is with the development of consciousness and so far neither exhibits this.

Now suppose an unthinking member of A meets an unthinking member of B at a feast in some third society in which A comes as a distant kin and B as an institutionalized "blood-brother" to the man giving the feast. Somehow they now learn of each other's ways. There is now consciousness of their own and some other ways. What happens? That is, has it become problematic and in what way?

We know what has been the reaction in some primitive societies, and it is a reflection of the kind of character they have developed. There are rigid self-enclosed societies and more open pragmatic societies. The former may now think of the other as weird, if not explicitly sinful; the latter may think of the other as simply different, but the ways practiced in their own society are *their* ways and thus the proper ones for them. Sometimes there is a readiness to borrow here and there. A might want to learn from B how to domesticate a pig and allow private ownership for pigs but not change any rules about the other animals. (Of course we can see an inner conflict in the offing.) Or A might introduce the pig and have it also shared when killed— that is, obligatory hospitality feasts. At such a point a member of A, faced with the alternative, might be in effect making the moral judgment that his customary ways are better. It thus verges on reflective morality, insofar as it is individual decision about what is better. But it is what is better for the group, not for the individual himself.

Our thought-experiment thus suggests that there are at least three different forms of the general social-individual contrast in the historical pattern that *08* presents. One is the contrast of the *unthinking* and the *thinking* with the latter beginning to involve some decision about what is better. The second is the institutional pattern already noted—the *collectively-oriented* and the *individualistically-oriented*. The third is the motivational contrast that has just emerged between thinking of one's own well-being or thinking of the common well-being; let us call it the *egoistic* and the *communal*. Now how far is *08* implying a line-up of the individualistic in all three aspects as an actual historical transformation in our world? We have to turn then to the text once more.

In chapter 5 of *08*, dealing with the passage from group morality to personal morality, Tufts gives three criteria of "advance" or progress. The first is to "substitute some rational method of setting up standards and forming values, in place of habitual passive acceptance."[2] Our not thinking member of A in the thought-experiment would be moving in this direction; suppose he supports the introduction of the pig but within the old shared framework, not private property, on the ground that the feelings of sharing and the social cohesion of sharing and its patterns are better than the possibly divisive individual ownership. While he maintains the old way it is no longer passive acceptance. The second criterion Tufts gives is "secure voluntary and personal choice and interest, instead of unconscious identification with the group welfare, or instinctive and habitual response to group needs."[3] This does not appear to go far beyond the first criterion, except that using a standard of the common well-being must be conscious choice. Our member of society A must apparently try out in his heart the lure of egoist pig-ownership and reject it consciously. The third criterion is to "encourage at the same time individual development and the demand that all share in this development—the worth and happiness of the person and of *every* person."[4] This brings in something new. It combines what we have seen Dewey later in *08* calls "moral democracy"—a rich individuality for everyone with rich diversity of opportunities. This, of course, combines a universalistic moral community and an advanced material civilization. It is interesting to note that in *32* Dewey calls attention to two fallacies that lead to pitting individual development against attaining the common good: "restricting the number of individuals to be considered" and "taking these individuals statically instead of dynamically"—that is, not attending to what they can become rather than to what in their present position they are.[5] Tufts in *08* does not give a blank cheque to individualism. He does define it as "the assertion by the individual of his own opinions and beliefs, his own independence and interests, as over against group standards, authority, and interests."[6] But he adds that action in this vein may be better or worse than the level of custom and group life.[7] So he concludes that moral progress demands a *reconstructed individual*—"a person who is individual in choice, in feeling, in responsibility, and at the same time social in what he regards as good, in his sympathies, and in his purposes. Otherwise individualism means progress toward the immoral."[8] Perhaps in these terms our member of group A might lay claim to being an individual without having to be reconstructed.

The ambivalence that is evident in Tufts at this point stems from the complexity of issues which are here bunched together. He is describing the growth of civilization, the arts and the sciences and the broadening of opportunities for individuals, the awakening of critical thinking in the individual. But there is also the commercial and political individualism that tends "to shift the emphasis of life from the question, What is proper, or honorable? to the question, What is *good*— good for *me*?"[9] And there is the individualistic inner development in ethical theory—the pleasure of the hedonists which thrusts aside the social and the stoic concentration on the inner self. And of course the account of the modern period embraces the rise of secular aims of wealth and power, political individualism in conceptions of liberty, democracy, and natural rights, and economic individualism with its notions of contractualism and free individual contract.

In both *08* and *32* at the end of the account of the modern period there is a brief treatment of the theoretical interpretations of this period (that is, in *32*, "of modern trends") in ethical systems. *08* mentions Kant and Utilitarianism.[10] That it leaves out the British moral sense theory is to be expected, in the light of the influence Dewey assigns in the Fries letter to the intervening study of this movement. But the omission of Hobbes in *08* does require some explanation. In

32 it is labelled "the *selfish system*"[11] as the simplest formulation of the early individualism, "particularly as it expressed itself in wars for ambition and plunder, or sought protection for private interests under the authority of the State." Hobbes is given as its most famous expounder.

The most likely reason for the omission of the selfish system would be that *08* does not regard it a morality. *08* at times has a proprietary view of what is the moral and what is not. There are a few phrases that suggest that unreflective morality is scarcely morality, being just passive automatic acceptance. Similarly the selfish path is a fork in the road of individualism that reflects its darker side. Tufts describes the vices incident to the reflective stage and the degenerative tendencies.[12] "The vices increase with civilization, partly because of increased opportunity, partly because of increased looseness in social restraint. There is a further element. When any activity of man is cut off from its original and natural relations and made the object of special attention and pursuit, the whole adjustment is thrown out of balance."[13] Selfishness and injustice become more common. Tufts comments that if evolution were all taken to be in one direction, "there would be no seriousness in life."[14] Of course the really serious problems arise when after the industrial revolution the selfish individualism becomes increasingly dominant and the question of capital and labor emerges.[15] By *32* the relations of the selfish system to morality is on the agenda of theory.

The situation then amounts to this: after having made individualism the mark of progress, that is, of the emergence and growth of the moral and of reflection replacing acceptance of the customary, it is time to qualify the result by accommodating the displaced social element in the very definition of the moral. The last section of the last chapter of Part I of *08*—that is, the end of the historical treatment—sums up what has happened to the social order with moral differentiation. The primitive group broke down into several institutions. "The moral, which is so largely unreflective that it could be embodied in every custom and observance, became more personal and subjective. The result of this was either that the moral was now more consciously and voluntarily *put into* the social relations, thereby raising them all to a higher moral level, or that, failing such a leavening of the distinct spheres of the social order, the latter were emptied of moral value and lost moral restraints."[16] This is only the beginning of the return journey of the moral—the appeal to the now adult morality not to forget whence it came. Soon it will go further. The social will become integral to the idea of the moral, and eventually the self that is now the locus of the moral will turn out itself to be social. The journey is a long one with many turns. Let us trace it briefly.

In Part II of *08*, stating the problems of moral theory, Dewey lists among them that of individuality and citizenship. From the rise of intense individualism in the Renaissance on, the problem of the relation of the individual and the social, of the private and the public became not only prominent but "in one form or other has been the central problem of modern ethical theory."[17] The psychological atomism in which the individual became a self-enclosed unit soon became the entity in terms of which all institutions had to be justified. We need not go into this familiar picture nor the effort to restore the social moral through the ideal of the State. By the time that the content of moral judgment has been entered upon—"Would there be any use or sense in moral acts if they did not tend to promote welfare, individual and social?"[18]—and happiness theory worked through, to yield the criterion of "ends of action, desirable in themselves, which reenforce and expand not only the motives from which they directly spring, but also the other tendencies and attitudes which are the sources of happiness"[19], can we be surprised that the next and decisive chapter (chapter 15, Happiness and Social Ends) begins with the blunt assertion that "the only end which fulfills these conditions is the social good."?[20]

As to the good moral character, the conclusion is that "The genuinely moral person is one, then, in whom the habit of regarding all capacities and habits of self from the social standpoint is formed and active."[21]

The same solution works through the complex problems of the place of the self in the moral life (chapter 18), where the issue is focused as self-love and benevolence, or egoism and altruism. Dewey finds it fairly easy to dispose of the argument that having a motive is already being self-directed, that the object of action is self-development or self-expression, and the like. His older experience with the self-realization theory of Green stands in good stead. He will not allow a self that is empty choosing because of its selfhood, nor a self that makes its relation to its object into its normal object, nor a division of all motivation into self-regarding and other-regarding, nor even the assumption that all altruism is good. The fact is that most of these conceptions are riddled with ambiguity and can be stretched or narrowed to prove a point. Dewey's strategy is to keep his eye constantly on the objects that are being pursued or chosen, the kind of self that is being developed. As we saw earlier, he regards as the essential factor in morality "the constant discovery, formation, and reformation of the self in the ends which an individual is called upon to sustain and develop in virtue of his membership in a social whole. The solution of the problem through the individual's voluntary identification of himself with social relations and aims is neither rare or utopian."[22] He calls for the formation of a voluntary self "in which socialized desires and affections are dominant, and in which the last and controlling principle of deliberation is the love of the objects which will make this transformation possible."[23]

We have also seen, in discussing the virtues in the previous chapter, that Dewey defines them as habits of character that sustain the common good.[24] By this time, then, the moral in its major aspects or contexts is being characterized by a relation to the social good.

Finally, in *08* there is Dewey's chapter on Social Organization and the Individual (chapter 20) in which he undermines not only the historical pattern, but even the very conception of individualism that was built up in general opposition to the social. We examined this argument earlier, but it is important to look at it here again. It began with the recognition that while the history of morals revealed an increasing stress on individual intelligence and affection, it also revealed a growing emphasis on the social nature of objects and ends to which personal preferences are to be directed. It is almost as if the social, which was the efficient unconscious cause in the early period, becomes after the growth of individual reflection a conscious final cause of action. (Perhaps there is an Hegelian residue in the picture of the growth of self-consciousness by the society operating through the individual.) But Dewey does not stop with this. He also recognizes that the individual does not move from a social order to an individual order, but from one social order to another social order. The second is one in which because of advances of knowledge and civilization and the multiplication of resources and opportunities, and because of the liberation of individual energies, many more things are possible for the individual. It is this change in the character of the society which makes the changed individual. Even his revolt through reflection against the established order does not deny the morality of that order but rather the need for progress with changing conditions. It is not something higher than a socially embodied morality. The variable and complex social order itself generates the habits of individual moral initiative. And the final blow: the virtues of the individual in a progressive society and in a customary society are both just as socially conditioned.

In this climax, Dewey has moved to the formulation that the individual, whatever form his activity takes, is a social being and that the social is constitutive, not just an external objective of a good individual. Any historical account that remains is primarily of the growth of reflective thought in theory and practice, and of the diversification of elements in the society itself and its growing powers and resources. The historical process has been really nothing more than the story of how the yeast of reflective *voluntariness* got added to the cake of custom to (en)lighten it. But the leavening factor (unlike our analogy) must itself be seen as generated in the process, not as an entering alien, and it must not substitute its own rise for its leavening task.

Now what are the theoretical changes that appear in *32*? Several stand out clearly, even where the analyses of *08* are continued.

(1) The whole emphasis on the social is retained and intensified, but it is no longer treated as a reaching out of the individual, through his becoming moral, to incorporate the social. The social stands on its own feet as a set of intrinsic moral phenomena.

(2) With the collapse of the earlier linear historical pattern, the particular historical context is substituted for the particular stage in the historical development.

(3) The problems for morality are consequently elicited from the present historical context and its conflicts and the problems it sets. The result is almost a moral agenda for our time.

(4) There is an unheralded reversal of the vista of unfolding individualism—unheralded because the linear pattern has disappeared, but not unexplained because it is seen to be a demand of our world's conditions—and instead the movement of morality today is said to be from personal morality to social morality.

(5) There is an appreciation of class opposition and a use of it to explain the conceptual lineups in the opposition of moral outlooks.

(6) There is a specific reanalysis of historic individualism and the problems it sets.

(7) Finally, there is a detailed analysis of the "ways in which the social environment enters into the stuff of character" and so of conduct.[25]

We now proceed to examine these seven changes.

(1)   The importance of the social in ideas of the common good is evident throughout: as integral to happiness, as a basic criterion for character, as underlying the controversy over egoism and altruism. It continues the conclusions of *08*. The fact that right and duty have an independent root adds a new independence to social moral phenomena. In addition, *32* exhibits a greater concreteness in explicating the idea of the common good and in invoking sociohistorical context to illuminate theoretical struggles.

The idea of the common good is now enriched by the idea of sharing and participating. "Sharing a good or value in a way which makes it social in quality is not identical with dividing up a material thing into physical parts. To partake is to *take* part, to *play* a role. It is something active, something which engages the desires and aims of each contributing member."[26] Dewey analyzes the support or reinforcement each participant gets in such a communal process and the new meanings and values that emerge. For the individual it is an expansion of experience and learning, "an enjoyment of enlargement, of experience, of growth of capacity."[27]

The use of socio-historical context to illuminate a theoretical inquiry may be illustrated from the egoism-altruism problem. It does not replace the issue or the mode of resolving it or explain it away. Dewey makes clear, as he did in *08*, that the real moral question is what kind of self is being furthered and formed, and that through the kind of objects focused on for conduct. But he also points out that the emphasis of theory on adjusting egoism and altruism took place at a time when an individualistic outlook took individuals to be naturally isolated and social arrangements to be secondary; that this characterized economic theory and practice, so that sympathy and benevolence in morals were the compensation for profit and self-interest in business. Dewey uses this mode of explaining not only to suggest why the period supported such an analysis, but to introduce what he takes to be the correct moral standpoint in evaluating an industry: "whether it serves the community as a whole, satisfying its needs effectively and fairly, while also providing the means of livelihood and personal development to the individuals who carry it on."[28] He adds that this goal could scarcely be reached by the adjustment of egoism and altruism, that is, by thinking exclusively of furthering one's own interests, being benevolent to others, or seeking a compromise between the two. (Not even complete altruism would be an answer.)

(2) The particular context is reached formally through the *content* of the moral ideas or concepts that is provided by the contemporary organization of life. Dewey here contrasts periods of stability and periods of flux. In the former the problems of morals concern more the adjustments of individuals to the institutions of the society; in the latter "moral issues cease to gather exclusively about personal conformity and deviation. They centre in the value of social arrangements, of laws, of inherited traditions that have crystallized into institutions, in changes that are desirable. Institutions lose their quasi-sacredness and are the objects of moral questioning." And he adds, "We now live in such a period."[29]

The theories of each period are to be understood then in terms of its own particular situation. Reverting to his previous analysis of egoism and altruism, he says that under that period's individualistic modes of thought egoism and altruism exhausted the alternatives. But Utilitarianism with its social criterion could question the existing social arrangements themselves. And Kant, from any perspective, could also question the existing organization of political society. "In fact, ever since the latter half of the eighteenth century the interesting and stirring human problems for intellectual inquiry as well as for practical application have arisen out of criticism of existing social arrangements and traditions, in State, government, law, church, family, industry, business, international relations."[30] Moral theories that paid no attention to these areas have become sterile.

Now although there has been some continuity since the latter half of the eighteenth century, set by growing and unsolved problems, it would appear to follow that the successive ethical theories would reflect different stages in the development of these problems and different lines of proposed solution to them. What is the present context of morality?

(3) In the preface to *32* the authors call attention to the growing interest in ethics over the twenty-four year span. Significantly, "economists, sociologists, political scientists, and historians discuss the moral as well as the technical aspects of their subject-matter."[31] The authors call attention to four phenomena that prompt reflection, pointing to "a

world where wars may wreck any national or individual life, where wealth and insecurity go hand in hand, where class still divides, and religion no longer speaks with unquestioned authority."[32] We have to remember, of course, that World War I has intervened, that as *32* went to press, America and the rest of the industrialized world were in the early years of severe economic depression and that America in particular had built up no social institutions to deal with poverty and unemployment; that the Marxian theory of class conflict had governed the Russian Revolution and in America bitter conflicts had occurred and were still to occur in the efforts of workers to organize and secure recognition for unions; that religion as a whole kept out of politics and promulgated the virtues of older times. The moral agenda was then for theoretical and institutional innovation. The chapter that in *08* was cast as Social Organization and the Individual (chapter 20 introducing Part III) now in *32* is directly cast as Morals and Social Problems (Ch. 16). *08* had recognized that social institutions create urgent problems for contemporary moral life. But in *32* the social problems themselves have taken over top billing.

(4)   After a brief introductory review of the pressure of social problems, Dewey speaks of the "change from personal to social morality."[33] He does not mean that morality becomes impersonal or that individual insight, judgment, and choice do not occur. But *"what* men think and believe is affected by common factors, and that the thought and choice of one individual spreads to others."[34] Men have to act together and their action is embodied in institutions and laws. "At the present time, almost all important ethical problems arise out of the conditions of associated life."[35] Indicating the vast changes going on, Dewey points out that personal selves, unless they drift, are forced to take stands on social tendencies, and decide about social conditions in order to solve personal problems. The change from personal to social morality thus concerns the kind of moral questions which are uppermost. Relatively simple questions turn out to call for collective action.

While these reflections lead Dewey to the general discussion of individual and social, we may first notice that he has amplified the whole doctrine of *08*. Whether there is an emphasis on the emergence of individualism or on the shift from personal to social morality itself depends on the specific historical social conditions. The general line of evolution to individualism is gone, although the central importance of individual reflection remains.

Dewey's view of the shift to social morality from personal morality is here modestly formulated. In the 1930s, as new institutions began to emerge to cope with social problems, some—Felix S. Cohen, for example,—wrote of the socialization of morality. By this Cohen meant that many problems that had been morally assigned to the individual were now being tackled through social mechanisms. Socially organized insurance took over through workmen's compensation systems the burden that each person had had to carry when it was believed that the only thing people could do was let the hurt lie where it fell. Provision for security in old age was taken up in a social security system, whereas formerly the social gospel had been one of the obligation to save for old age, or else depend on private charity. Unemployment insurance was directed to loss of work, whereas before the inability to find work had been felt as personal guilt of the male "breadwinner" in the family. Perhaps Dewey's reticence in generalizing the doctrine would have been rewarded when in the 1960s areas that had been firmly established as social began to be regarded as matters of individual choice. The most startling was relations among the sexes and patriotism toward the nation. But once again, these would have to be seen not as intrinsic historical drifts, but as response to and decision about complex present situations in the evaluation of institutions that required change. For example, with women beginning now to be a large part of the labor force, the older institutional attitudes with respect to family, sex, and divorce, were challenge by newer ideals of sexual equality. And patriotism had to cope not only with the inroads of global communication and a broader international perspective, but even more with internal struggles when the nation embarked on what was widely felt to be an unjust war. The lesson would seem to be that no general drift should be hastily inferred—not even of pendular swings—unless a constant basis is provided in the conditions of the society and its surrounding world.

(5) In his discussion of the underlying issue as individual and social, Dewey warns against making an either-or opposition of individualist and collectivist. He does not of course deny that people do line up in this way, but this misanalyzes the locus of conflict. "What

do exist are conflicts between *some* individuals and *some* arrangements in social life; between groups and classes of individuals; between nations and races; between old traditions imbedded in institutions and new ways of thinking and acting which spring from those few individuals who depart from and who attack what is socially accepted."[36] There are also, of course, different convictions about how to settle the conflicts—for example, some say by private voluntary action, some by combined organized action. "No general theory about the individual and the social can settle conflicts or even point out the way in which they should be resolved."[37]

In his analysis of group conflicts Dewey calls special attention to the relations of dominance and inferiority in classes with respect to power and wealth, and how at certain stages of the conflict it takes the form of conserving the old versus the demand for progress. In such a situation one has to beware of regarding social organization itself as the enemy. In some cases the old or established order becomes seen as the individualists while the new in organizing for change become the collectivists. It is such relativity in the assumption of labels that leads to the denial of fixed meaning for "social" and "individual" in general, in the quotation we gave at the opening of this chapter.

It is significant that in this quotation Dewey says not only that all morality is both individual and social, but puts in a parenthesis "(including immorality)". We may recall the view offered by Tufts in *08* that the advance of individualism brought risks and vices of disintegration and alienation. It was almost as if the growth of individualism was moral progress along the historical line, but any concomitant immorality was natural human reaction to the isolation of the moral. For Dewey here immorality and morality are both to be explained in similar terms. They are both individual in their initiation and both social in their response to social conditions.

There is another similar point on which Dewey has earlier taken issue with the historical views of *08*. We saw that one of the elements in the emergence of the moral from the customary had been that it became a separate field, distinct from the legal, conventional, etc. In the chapter on Moral Judgment and Knowledge (chapter 14) of *32* Dewey assigns supreme significance to the question: "Is the moral region isolated from the rest of human activity?"[38] His answer here is of course in the negative—there are no hard and fast lines within conduct separating the moral from the non-moral.

(6)   Dewey's analysis of historic individualism as a doctrinal passage of history does not on the whole contain more material in *32* than the general historical description at various points contained in *08*. It is the way it is done and the lessons drawn from it that are distinctive. It is no longer part of the long march of individualism which constituted part of the emergence of the moral in human history. It is now a very specific set of beliefs embodied in practices—in economics, in politics, in law and so on, that helped unseat practices and beliefs of an agricultural era and shape the outlook of an emerging commercial and industrial era, that at the same time coincided with and helped along in certain respects the rise of a democratic movement, that became hardened as a way of looking at man and nature and institutions and as a consequence impeded people's facing their new problems. The account remains faithful to the statement made by the authors in the preface: "if the authors were to arrogate the decision of difficult questions they would thereby defeat the purpose of ethical study."[39] And so here Dewey is careful to say "The purpose of this historical survey is not to indicate that some anti-'individualistic' principle is correct, so that we should supplant it by a collectivistic formula and program in order to meet the moral requirements of society."[40] It is rather to call attention to the relativism of social formula on the ethical side, how a doctrine can change from progressive to reactionary as well as change its meaning in altered conditions. There also follows that no rule can be laid down in general regarding the scope of public and private action. Each proposed program should be considered on its merits and in an experimental way. Since, he adds, one cannot change everything at once, but some habits have to remain as leverage for changing others, the problem is always one of particular discrimination. "As long as the issue is conceived in a wholesale manner, conservatism will tend to be blind and reactionary and radicalism will tend to be abrupt and violent."[41] It is because an experimental outlook "would eliminate the chief causes of intolerance, persecution, fanaticism, and the use of differences of opinion to create class wars"[42] that Dewey regards, at that time, the question of method to be of greater moral significance than the particular conclusion reached in any one controversy.

(7)   In *08* Dewey's last chapter (Chapter 21, Civil Society and the Political State) maps civil rights and obligations, and their develop-

ment, with some of their problems and how we face them; and again, political rights and obligations, their difficulties and challenges; and finally, the moral criterion for all social and political forms—to set free individual capacities to work for the common good. It is, in a sense, civil society in an Hegelian vein, constituting the substance of the moral self but turned to individual initiative. *32* in its corresponding chapter (chapter 17, Morals and the Political Order) takes a quite different turn. In its last half some of the same specific problems are dealt with—democratic government, liberty of thought and expression, nationalism and internationalism. But the discussion is more directed to the problematic, the concrete issues and threats, the historical specific bases, the way to avoid war. On the other hand, the first half of the chapter is concerned with the basic theoretical point of bringing social environment integrally into the moral and giving concrete meaning to the idea of the common good. We have already examined the latter above, and so deal here with the first section headed "Does the social environment have moral import?"

In fact, Dewey is going all the way back to his earliest attempt in the *Outlines* and in the *Syllabus* to integrate self and environment in a single process. But he is now in a far better position to do it, since the perspective is no longer simply agent-centered, the social has had ample treatment. And so the integration lies in the hypothesis which he says he had been take for granted throughout: "that the social environment has intrinsic moral significance; that it enters intimately into the formation and the substance of the desires, motives, and choices which make up character."[43] And of course to make up character is to permeate conduct. He opposes those who (the Kantians clearly) have the will go it morally alone whatever the environment—unless the meaning of character be extended to include "the whole body of desires, purposes, convictions, manifested in deliberation and choice"[44] in which case the surrounding conditions which arouse desire and direct choice also have intrinsic moral meaning. Such a meaning of character carries us all the way back to *08* in the beginning of part II— "whatever lies behind an act in the way of deliberation and desire, whether these processes be nearby or remote."[45] What lies behind an act is now clearly pinpointed as the social milieu.

Dewey's intention is not merely to tell us of our social composition. The recognition that we are dealing with part of the field which is ourselves in action shows a human complicity and invites responsibility. We can no longer then, says Dewey, view the economic system as existing in the same way as nature does. We see it now as it enters into hopes and fears, desires and purposes. He is then not saying that we are subservient to social conditions "but that the latter are incorporated into our attitudes, and our attitudes into social conditions, to such an extent that to maintain one is to maintain the other, to change one is to change the other."[46]

With the new concreteness, Dewey examines the typical ways in which social environment enters into the stuff of character. One is to determine our opportunities. Another is that different kinds of institutions, traditions and customs stimulate different powers. Still another is to relate persons in different ways—for example, in familial organization, property organization, etc. Finally just as the strong points of institutions reenforce character, so their weak points provoke the criticism out of which reconstruction comes. Thus social conditions enter integrally and intrinsically.

In giving this direct meaning to the social nature of character, as in the refining of the common good in terms of shared experience, *32* has sharpened its conceptual tools for the more effective handling of specific problems. But of course twenty-four years of historical and social experience lie behind the changes.

It is to the signposts of this development as found in the writings of the intervening period that we now turn. They are many and rich in significance as they mark the reasons for a shift in what is sometimes a critical point and sometimes rather a blossoming of a bare previous hint. In considering this development we shall separate somewhat the treatment of the idea of the individual from that of the social, and to see the fuller amplitude of the development we shall dip back before 1908.

Long before 1908 Dewey was aware of the trap that lay for political and social philosophy in the idea of the isolated or atomic individual. In a paper on "The Ethics of Democracy" as early as 1888 he wrote: "The essence of the 'Social Contract' theory is not the idea of the formulation of a contract; it is the idea that men are mere individuals, without any social relations *until* they form a contract."[47] The context is Maine's view of the movement from status to contract in progressive societies; Dewey points out that although Maine had criticized the social contract theory of society, he retained the individual atomism. To see democracy in this way is to equate it with anarchy and to compel the manufacture of a common will in one way or another. We may note that though Dewey questions Maine's underlying conception he does not question the linear view of the development of civilization; in any case, it is perhaps not at this point relevant to his discussion of democracy.

What is more, Dewey is quite conscious of the historical character of the topic. In a review of George B. Adams' *Civilization during the Middle Ages* in 1894, he notes that "Professor Adams recognizes clearly the great significance of the Middle Ages in discovering the individual and bringing him into the light of day."[48] And in his article on "Ethics" in the *Encyclopedia Americana* (1904) in which he takes an historical approach, he says that moral theory since the fifteenth century "is all more or less connected . . . with the struggle toward greater individual freedom, and with the problem of maintaining a stable associated and institutional life, on the basis of recognition of individuality—the democratic movement."[49]

The shape taken by the emergence of individuality in the seventeenth and eighteenth century had already been studied in insightful detail by Tufts.[50] The study is concerned with "the development of individuality and individualism as reflected in modern thought" in the two centuries, and it aims "to interpret the leading categories in terms of the actual life of the writers."[51] Set in an explicit recognition of the role of commerce and manufacturing in altering the character of life, it traces the onward march of individualism in religion and politics, in psychology and morals. Not only has Protestantism transferred authority from outside into the individual, but the center of gravity in the traditional combination of natural law and law of reason has shifted to the individual's reason. The attempts to prove the reasonableness of Christianity shows clearly where the criteria of acceptance now lie. Similarly, the *jus naturale* which traditionally was the natural law that signified the control of society over the individual is turned, as in Hobbes' translation of *jus* as right, into an individualistic right against society. Eighteenth century moral philosophy, from Shaftesbury to Adam Smith, explores the inner psychology of the individual as a basis for morality. Tufts traces the fine shades of each categorial shift. Summing the development, Tufts concludes[52] that after Adam Smith "The way is open for a system which will be enabled to assume the social good as the criterion and end of action, and rely on the social and immanent forces to make the social weal the motive to action."

This is, of course, the conception of the good as social which, we have seen, emerges in *08*.

Nowhere in the Tufts-Thompson study is the question raised whether the conception of individuality that emerged in their period is the early bloom of the full flower of morality or whether it is the ideology of a particular socio-economic period and would give way under different historical conditions. The authors have presented the materials that could point to the latter as well as the former, but as we know from *08* the linear view of the maturation of morality with the growth of civilization was accepted as the interpretation. Hence we would not expect the moral status of individuality to undergo change until the underlying assumption of linear historical development itself gave way. This will be examined in detail in our next chapter.

Some counter-indications are, however, to be found before 1908. In a review essay on Spencer[53], published in 1904, Dewey places Spencer's individualism less in socio-economic transformations than in the stream of intellectual developments from the seventeenth to the nineteenth centuries. He describes Spencer as the reimportation of a Lockean individualism after it has gone through France, the unwavering faith in progress of the French Encyclopedists. His philosophy "shows the individualistic creed dominant, militant; no longer a principle of criticism, but of reform and construction in social life, and, therefore, of necessity a formula of construction in the intellectual sphere."[54] Its evolutionary side is simply the projection of this individualism on the cosmic screen, and is itself distorted into having a fixed and final goal.

Dewey's analysis here shows a thorough awareness of intellectual constructions made out of traditional materials in the attempt to refashion current institutions; he sets the view of "nature's benign aims" and of "the *laissez-faire* theory and its extreme typical expression, anarchism"[55] in such a pattern. But his interest here is completely intellectual history. We are not told here what his judgments are of individualism and its kinds, beyond the open character of evolution as contrasted with the closed finalistic character of the Enlightenment's belief in progress. We may assume that *08*, as already examined, gives us his then current conception, and we have already seen the jostling of individualism and the social within that work. The important point here is that his analysis goes no further than the general recognition that individualism is itself a social phenomenon and a social outlook, not something that is non-social or opposed to the social. Further development of this insight requires the subsequent analysis of the social itself.

Several themes may be distinguished in the unfolding of our topic from *08* to *32*. Constant throughout, and lying behind all talk of individualism and individuality, is the focus on agency, the thoughtful as against the habitual, the actively reflective as against the passive acceptance. This focus has been established in our previous discussion of the reflex arc paper and its centrality; it will be supplemented by the treatment of habit in our subsequent chapter. A second theme stems from the exploration of the social character of the individual and the self. As the idea of the social is clarified and dealt with more concretely, the general appreciation of the role of the social which had been present from the outset is amplified in the development of social psychology and sociology. Properties of the individual as such—for example, initiative, diversity, and originality—move over into sharing and participation in interpersonal relations and variegated groups. This will be examined shortly from the standpoint of the analysis of the social. A third theme, which comes to prominence while the concept of individualism (historically considered) is still intact, is its scope and how penetrating it is in philosophical as well as social thought; many of Dewey's studies see the development of modern epistemology from Descartes on as an individualization of knowledge. A fourth theme, a cumulative outcome clear from at least 1919 on, is the crumbling of the concept of individualism and in due course the search for other concepts and distinctions to replace the social-individual. The fully fashioned reorientation comes, of course, in *Individualism Old and New* in 1930, so that the ideas set forth in *32* need not then be argued but rather explained. Our immediate concern here is to consider the third and fourth theme.

Philosophical inquiry may appropriately be called the river of thought for it has currents moving in opposing directions. Individualism as a concept was being trimmed by attention to the interpersonal and the concrete social, as we have seen above in the study of legal relations and institutional influences; moreover, its own position as the outcome of moral maturity in history was being undermined by the new anthropology. At the same time, Dewey's concern with the theory of knowledge and the attempt to work out a reliable account of scientific inquiry (*How We Think*, 1910) in opposition to both rationalism and narrow empiricism, involved an historical estimate of the rise of epistemology. His view is succinctly stated in his entry on Epistemology in volume II of *A Cyclopedia of Education*[56] (1911): "Epistemology as a distinct branch of philosophy developed out of the growth of individualism. The tendency of nominalism was to make mind or consciousness a possession of individual selves or souls. Then it naturally became a problem how the individual could get outside of himself to know an exterior world." He adds that the problem was accentuated by the development of physical science. Whereas Greek thought regarded the world as one of qualitative diversities, early modern science reduced the heterogeneity to one kind of matter and motion and all other qualities were relegated to mind. He regards the epistemological problem not as insoluble but as artificial. A fuller treatment, both historical and critical, is found in *Democracy and Education*.[57] The isolation of mind meant that practical individualism, with its struggle for a greater freedom of thought, was diverted into philosophic subjectivism. The proper role of the individual or self in knowledge, says Dewey, is the redirection or reconstruction of accepted beliefs. Instead, the subjectivist view broke the social and moral ties of human beings: "Given feelings, ideas, desires, which have nothing to do with one another, how can actions proceeding from them be controlled in a social or public interest? Given an egoistic consciousness, how can action which has regard for others take place?"[58] In his summary of the chapter Dewey still presents the position of *08*: "True individualism is a product of the relaxation of the grip of the authority of custom and traditions as standards of belief."[59] He regards it as a comparatively modern manifestation.

Within a few years—turning to the fourth theme—Dewey's treatment of individualism takes on a different cast. References to it have a more specifically historical denotation, general references are now out of date and readily recognized as vague. The historical shift is obvious: World War I has brought the Russian Revolution, the possibility of Socialism in on the agenda of thought. Dewey himself in 1919 and 1920 is in the Far East, lecturing first in Japan and then for a two-year period in China. He is surrounded by the sense of impending change, vast social change, and the pivotal issue is what direction it may take. Two of the lectures in China[60] are on "Classical Individualism and Free Enterprise" and "Socialism". He reviews some consequences of the industrial revolution, particularly the substitution of mechanical power for muscle power and machine and mass production for handicraft production. One consequence was a political and philosophical individualism, giving the individual the right to determine his own destiny. (Here he expounds the idea of contract, in Maine's distinction from status.) He distinguishes the British political revolution of 1688 from the French social revolution. The English and French socialists who found their axioms in morality are distinguished from the Marxian socialists who postulated a determinism. He also distinguishes those socialists who would strengthen the state from those who identify it with capitalism and seek a voluntary social organization. He points out parenthetically that Marx was not fomenting class struggle but predicting it. In general, socialism centered on the concept of welfare of the total society, rather than individual profit. He adds "This should be our criterion."[61] The topic of the rights of individuals (fully elaborated with many distinctions of types) is presented under the rubric of "Political Liberalism". He does point out that the rights concept is advanced by political individualism, usually in reaction to suppression by despotic governments. Since most western states now represent the will of the people, the question is not to assert the rights but to provide specific opportunities to exercise them. He expresses the hope that China can amalgamate the two steps—the age of self-seeking individualism and then the power of the state to equalize society—because it already has a tradition of state obligation to protect people as parents do (he refers to Mencius) and equalization of opportunity can be achieved by popularizing education and providing specialized knowledge.[62]

Reconstruction in Philosophy, published in 1920, but developed out of lectures given in Japan just prior to the China visit, goes a step further in the analysis of individualism. The concept not only is crumbling, but it is beginning to provide materials for a reconstruction. In the historical discussion (chapter 2) individualism carries its modifying identification: thus it is "religious individualism" that effects startling changes.[63] Again (in chapter 8, "Reconstruction as Affecting Social Philosophy") it is "the individualistic school of England and France in the eighteenth and nineteenth centuries" and it is identified by its common conception of the self as something given, primary, and already there.[64] Hence the individual "can only be something to be catered to, something whose pleasures are to be magnified and possessions multiplied. . . . Now it is true that social arrangement laws, institutions are made for man, rather than that man is made for them; that they are means and agencies of human welfare and progress. But they are not means for obtaining something for individuals, not even happiness. They are means of creating individuals. Only in the physical sense of physical bodies that to the senses are separate is individuality an original datum. Individuality in a social and moral sense is something to be wrought out. It means initiative, inventiveness, varied resourcefulness, assumption of responsibility in choice of belief and conduct. These are not gifts, but achievements. As achievements, they are not absolute but relative to the use that is to be made of them. And this use varies with the environment."

What is the outcome for the general notions of individual and social? Dewey now condemns general discussion in terms of such notions as a waste of energy. It should give way to "specific inquiries into a multitude of specific structures and interactions."[65] "Just as 'individual' is not one thing, but is a blanket term for the immense variety of specific reactions, habits, dispositions and powers of human nature that are evoked, and confirmed under the influences of associated life, so with the term 'social'. Society is one word, but infinitely many things. It covers all the ways in which by associating together men share their experiences, and build up common interests and aims; street gangs, schools for burglary, clans, social cliques, trade unions, joint stock corporations, villages and international alliances. The new method takes effect in substituting inquiry into these specific, changing and relative facts (relative to problems and purposes, not metaphysically relative) for solemn manipulation of general notions."[66]

The outcome is devastating for the traditional notion of individualism. Granted that with the more inclusive and unified organization of the state has come "the emancipation of individuals from restrictions and servitudes previously imposed by custom and class status" this has not meant isolated individuals but fresh recombinations. "What upon one side looks like a movement toward individualism, turns out to be really a movement toward multiplying all kinds and varieties of associations."[67] The real social units, says Dewey, are "groupings for promoting the diversity of goods that men share." And he adds: "They occupy the place which traditional theory has claimed either for mere isolated individuals or for the supreme and single political organization."

In the years that follow, these lessons are found repeatedly. For example, in an article on "Mediocrity and Individuality" in the *New Republic* of December 5, 1922[68] Dewey says: "Individualism is about the most ambiguous word in the entire list of labels in ordinary use. It means anything from egoistically centered conduct to distinction and uniqueness. It is possible to say that excessive individualism is an outstanding curse of American civilization, and that absence of individualism is our marked deficiency." The one refers to economic and legal conditions, the other to intellectual life. "Individuality is a surer word; it carries with it a connotation of uniqueness or quality, or at least of distinctiveness. It suggests a freedom which is not legal, comparative and external, but which is intrinsic and constructive." Dewey is beginning to look for newer concepts and distinctions. He is not yet ready to fashion a moral meaning for individuality to replace the discarded general idea of individualism. And indeed, as the later title, *Individualism Old and New*, suggests, he is working toward a concept that will change and express changing social conditions. But to achieve it requires ideas to replace the antithesis of individual and social. We accordingly interrupt our consideration of individualism at this point to go back and trace the story of the social. Its parallel development in Dewey's thought is integral to the theory of both individual and society in *32*.

Both Dewey and Tufts had insisted on the social character of the self long before *08*. We have seen how Dewey, in the *Outlines of A Critical Theory of Ethics* (1891) and in the subsequent *Syllabus* (1894) worked on a transactional theory of the self embodying the environment. His position is well stated in his "Ethical Principles Underlying Education."[69] The distinction is not between the social and the individual as separate, but between two perspectives—the social and the psychological. "Psychological ethics does not cover part of the field, and then require social ethics to include the territory left untouched. Both cover the entire sphere of conduct. Nor does the distinction mark a compromise, or a fusion, as if at one point the psychological view broke down, and needed to be supplemented by the sociological."[70] He goes on to affirm that society is a society of individuals and the individual a social individual. Psychology gives us "the *how* of conduct, the way in which it takes place", for modifications come from changes in the agent. The *content* is considered from a social point of view, the whole living situation into which it enters.[71] Dewey goes on (59 f.) to comment on the industrial and commercial changes taking place, so that education can no longer be directed toward a fixed place but must prepare the child to take care of himself. There is no point in talking of the harmonious development of powers without reference to the character of social life and participation.[72]

In similar fashion Tufts insists that the conception of the self is always a *socius*.[73] Dewey, in reviewing the book in which this essay appears says approvingly[74] of Tufts' treatment that "'Social psychology' is used not as an annex to the normal psychology of the individual . . . but as a method of interpreting the actual constitution and functioning of the self. At every point of the discussion we find ourselves face to face with an individual into whose structure social factors are already built; and face to face with a social environment viewed as the medium in which the sociality of the past, consolidated into an individual, displays itself, is developed, and, through opposition and effort, reconstructed.''

08 exhibits this general outlook, which makes possible its moral climax in which the mature moral individual uses as his criterion the social welfare of the whole. Our problem now is the influences that concretized this general notion of the social and gave it the direction that emerged in *32*. We find these influences in the growth and operation of the varied disciplines of anthropology, law and education, in the development of social psychology, political theory, as well as social philosophy itself, throughout.

We have already suggested how the new anthropology, from 1911 on, dislodged the linear view of moral development as culminating in individualism, and made possible the reconsideration of the individual-social relation. This anthropological influence will be examined in greater detail in the next chapter.

We shall also see, in studying the emergence of right and obligation from under the shadow of the good, how legal studies in the period from 1911 to 1917 contributed to the focus on interpersonal relations and their character, bringing down the general social into the relational structure of a plurality of institutions.

We have already seen the parallel pluralistic development of the good under the psychological and educational study of *interest*. Dewey's entry for "Many-sided interest" in the *Cyclopedia of Education* (1912-1913)[75] states the significant points in a few lines. The term "interest" denotes "typically important concerns of life—science, politics, religion, art, etc." Herbart took education to aim at developing many-sided interests, and Dewey equates this with "the active and alert identification of the self with these concerns", with "many-sided" indicating the multiple susceptibilities. He adds that the whole notion is the realistic counterpart of "the current idealistic conception of complete and harmonious development of all the individual's powers or faculties." (We see here the early departures from the general idealistic monistic good that will end in 32 with the broad pluralistic concept of the good as the cultivation of interests). The same contrast of the idealistic conception and the concrete reality is found in *Democracy and Education* (1916).[76] After referring to this general notion of the "harmonious development of all the powers of personality" he adds "The conception of education as a social process and function has no definite meaning until we define the kind of society we have in mind." At the beginning of the chapter ("The Democratic Conception in Education") he makes the point already made in *Reconstruction in Philosophy*—that society is one word but the associations of men are multiple and varied in purpose.

Dewey's concern with social psychology plays a great part in the refinement of his idea of the social, from his lecture on "The Need for Social Psychology (1916)"[77] to his full work in the field in *Human Nature and Conduct* (1922). The former is particularly clear in its contention that the source of theoretical and practical difficulties is a wrong interpretation of the relation of individual and social. He scans Tarde's work on imitation, "an ambitious interpretation of almost all the facts of social organization, progress and degeneration in terms of certain rubrics to which he gave a psychological quality"[78] and notes how it dominated social psychology. The schools of Imitation and Suggestibility "gave the dawning science a wrong twist in carrying over into science the old popular and practical antithesis of the individual and the social, and thus setting up two independent and even contrary sciences—individual and social psychology. As a concrete illustration of the absurd results to which this antithesis led, it is perhaps sufficient to refer to those bizarre writings on the psychology of the crowd in which it was assumed that the psychology of the individual left to himself is reflective and rational, while man's emotional obsessions and irrationalities are to be accounted for by the psychology of association with others."[79] Instead of formulating the problem as the relation of an isolated individual mind to a mass or crowd mind, it should be seen as "the relationship of original or native activities to acquired capacities and habits." He states the general descriptive task of social psychology in these terms: "To form a mind out of certain native instincts by selecting an environment which evokes them and directs their course; to re-form social institutions by breaking up habits and giving peculiar intensity and scope to some impulse is the problem of social control in its two phases." The behavioristic movement helped transfer attention "from vague generalities regarding social consciousness and social mind to the specific processes of interaction which take place among human beings, and to the details of group-behavior."[80] From the point of view of behavioral psychology, Dewey concludes, all psychology is either biological or social.

In philosophical formulation, Dewey had long attacked both the extreme of individualistic atomism and that of organicism. In his entry on "Individuality" in the *Cyclopedia of Education* referred to above[81] he says that the concept of the organic was prominent in nineteenth century idealism because it seemed to reconcile individual and universal, whole and part. But he thinks it is not a solution, only "a peculiarly vivid presentation of the terms of the problem." He then suggests that underlying the polar ideas are the facts of stability, order and conservation, and on the other side individuality, variability, freedom, and progress. We have here a foreshadowing of the role that the stable and the precarious are to have in *Experience and Nature* in 1925, his clearest exposition of the metaphysical bases of the warring concepts.

It is by this time more than clear that the concept of the social is being dissolved into the multiplicity of groupings. Take a particularly clear statement in the China lectures[82]: "We are saying that it is more useful—that is, that it conforms more nearly to what we can see to be the case when our observation is thoughtful and careful—to think of society as being constituted of people in many sorts of groupings, rather than being made up of collections of individual persons considered as entities." The vital consequence of this is that conflict should not be seen as between individual and society but of some group interests gained at the disadvantage of other group interests. Even deviance is not the individual against society but better seen as seeking the modification of certain institutions.

The change in outlook is not a verbal one. It reflects the conceptual structure that has been fashioned in the social psychology. Its basic concepts are the biological one of impulse, the socio-cultural one of habit, and the reconstructive process of intelligence. *Human Nature and Conduct: An Introduction to Social Psychology* spells these out in detail, including their implications for ethical ideas. In subsequent chapters we shall deal with habit and with intelligence. Here it is sufficient to note that this framework has completely replaced that of individualism and its growth, individual versus society, even—we shall see—though with many a relapse, custom versus reflection. We are not suggesting that this framework was not implicit throughout since the analysis of the reflex arc. Indeed, it underlay many of the criticisms of atomic individualism and the conflict of passion and reason, in dealing with traditional ethical theories. But its full systematic flowering is found in *Human Nature and Conduct.*

The next half dozen years show occasional restatements of the principles now established, and occasional attempts at systematic refinement of the materials that had been cast from their previous dominance. Take, for example, Dewey's Syllabus for Philosophy 131-132 at Columbia in 1923. The course is on Social Institutions and the Study of Morals. It asserts that the unity of society is purely conceptual, that actually there are a vast multitude of social groups, and refers the student to *Democracy and Education* for this. It begins to study the different properties of groups, with respect to numbers, duration, degree of localization, degree of fixation, extent of conscious characteristic interests. It enters into need concepts, obligation concepts, and how meanings arise. It outlines different consequences in the formation of personal dispositions and desires out of raw human nature. It moves on into the state, economic and ethical doctrines, and so forth. When the question of individual and society arises, it is broken down by exhibiting seven different means of "Individualism": a eulogistic moral sense, involving the ultimate moral worth of personality; the source of independence, sturdiness, initiative; uniqueness and the variable element; the seventeenth and eighteenth century doctrine of political protest; the theory of laissez-faire; ethical doctrine of self-interest or egoism; a metaphysical doctrine involving the separateness of souls, or identifying individuality with private consciousness. Individualistic and collectivist theories are thus broken up and studied in concrete detail.

The period from 1926 to 1930 seems to have been one in which fresh ideas took shape. We have seen the recasting of the relations of ethical concepts expounded in the *Club paper* and the *three roots*. In

1927 came Dewey's most original contribution to political theory, *The Public and its Problems*.[83] Its basic conceptual reconstruction, which alone concerns us here, is to replace the distinction between *individual* and *social* by that between *private* and *public*, for purposes of political and social theory. When the consequences of action extend beyond the agent or agents and become serious to a wider group, a public is formed: "the line between private and public is to be drawn on the basis of the extent and scope of the consequences of acts which are so important as to need control, whether by inhibition or by promotion. We distinguish private and public buildings, private and public schools, private paths and public highways, private assets and public funds, private persons and public officials. It is our thesis that in this distinction we find the key to the nature and office of the state."[84] And again, "The public consists of all those who are affected by the indirect consequences of transactions to such an extent that it is deemed necessary to have those consequences systematically cared for."[85]

On this view publics can rise, change, and disappear; there can be larger more comprehensive publics and narrower ones. The determining consequences take shape in terms of the conditions and instrumentalities of the time. In such a framework Dewey considers the temporal and geographical localization of nations and states, the operations of a democracy, the shift of subject-materials between public and private, forms of associated activity, economic changes and their political effects, present problems, and so on. Throughout it is the conceptual shift that reformulates questions and opens the way to experimental answers in the light of conditions and consequences as they actually are found and take place. A comparison between Mill's attempt in his *On Liberty* to find a principled fixed line between the realm of the individual and the realm of society and Dewey's distinction of the private and the public is particularly illuminating. Although Mill's is an empirical approach, he uses it to state lessons of experience about what should under no or very few conditions be an object of state or social control. He is more successful with freedom of thought and speech because the problems of his day lay in the need for innovative institutional change to make possible the development of the new industrial society, and the source of repression was the older institutions. He is thoroughly unsuccessful in most of his detailed applications, and the fixed line becomes very wavy. Dewey's distinction does not compel a search for fixed lines though it allows stable lessons where they are in fact to be found; it rather suggests experimental efforts to determine comparative consequences, and the experiments are not in terms of control and absence of control but in terms of fashioning different kinds of institutions or making institutional modifications to handle the whole of social development. It admits of major changes in the center of gravity in social thought: as we have already seen, he thinks that the emphasis need fall less on the enunciation of rights than on the provision of opportunities for their exercise; this, however, is open to historical determination. In any case, conditions of action and of inquiry and knowledge are always changing; and history may bring forth much that is new.

In the following year (April 1928) Dewey published an article on "Social as a Category."[86] In one sense, it is bidding good-bye to the category by elevating it to a summit of generality. Perhaps it is a case of old categories never dying but fading away, and one of the best routes in this process is elevation. In any case, Dewey distinguishes between social phenomena in gross, and the social as a category. On the whole it contains few new points, but it confirms the social character of human phenomena, and puts in its proper place the role of thought, even of subjectivity, and morality itself.

It is interesting to note a paper at roughly the same time by Tufts.[87] He too seeks to replace the individual-social dichotomy in ethics, but looks in a different direction: "The old antithesis between individual and society, individualism and socialism, is thus replaced by a correlation between personality and community. For each of these is a task rather than an existence, and each requires the other for its fulfillment."[88] Of course, the personal is not a chance intent but built up in relations and social groups. Here the dissolution of the social into variegated groupings is largely like what Dewey has done. But there is an interesting turn in considering the place of morality: "But instead of constructing a system of impersonal knowledge in which a world of things or events appears as if independent of the knower, these moral judgments construct a personal world, a community. These claim and recognize rights and duties. They pass over into conduct. Their world too becomes objective as will becomes deed."[89] This objectivity is found in institutions.

Dewey's summing up of the issues we have been considering is, of course, *Individualism Old and New*.[90] It embodies, however, a new urgency, for the Great Depression has come, and the older doctrines can no longer rest assured that they are the instruments of prosperity. He is not perturbed by the apparent subjection of individuality in the new economy: "As far as individuality is associated with aristocracy of the historic type, the extension of the machine age will presumably be hostile to individuality in its traditional sense all over the world. . . . The problem of constructing a new individuality consonant with the objective conditions under which we live is the deepest problem of our times."[91] The task is to create a new individualism "as significant for modern conditions as the old individualism at its best was for its day and place. The first step in further definition of this problem is realization of the collective age which we have already entered."[92] Dewey's analysis embodies all the lessons whose emergence we have considered: the rejection of a static individualism, the rejection of the opposition of the collective and corporate to the individual, the cultural character of relations of individuals (for example: "Conformity is the name for the absence of vital interplay; the arrest and benumbing of communication.")[93], the insistence that altruism cannot constitute a solution, the basic role of productive forces, and so on. In his treatment of economic and social problems there is a view of history and its changes which we shall examine in the next chapter. It permeates also his outline of the new individualism. Significantly, as he approaches the conclusion of the book he calls on us to "forget 'society' and think of law, industry, religion, medicine, politics, art, education, philosophy—and think of them in the plural."[94] He does not give a program of institutional change but a concept of individuality to guide it.

Notes

1. *32*: 27.
2. 1929–1930, MW 5: 74.
3. Ibid.
4. Ibid.
5. 1932, LW 7: 348.
6. 1908, MW 5: 75.
7. Ibid., 75–76.
8. Ibid., 76.
9. Ibid., 113.
10. Ibid., 158.
11. 1932, LW 7: 153.

12. 1908, MW 5: 175–78.
13. Ibid., 175.
14. Ibid., 177.
15. Ibid., 149–50.
16. Ibid., 178.
17. Ibid., 204.
18. Ibid., 215.
19. Ibid., 259.
20. Ibid., 261.
21. Ibid., 271.
22. Ibid., 356.
23. Ibid., 357.
24. Ibid., 359.
25. 1932, LW 7: 142.
26. Ibid., 345.
27. Ibid., 346.
28. Ibid., 299.
29. Ibid., 314–15.
30. Ibid., 315.
31. Ibid., 3.
32. Ibid.
33. Ibid., 314–17.
34. Ibid., 318.
35. Ibid.
36. Ibid., 324.
37. Ibid.
38. Ibid., 263.
39. Ibid., 3.
40. Ibid., 335–36.
41. Ibid., 337.
42. Ibid., 338.
43. Ibid., 340.
44. Ibid., 341.
45. 1908, MW 5: 188.
46. 1932, LW 7: 342.
47. 1882–1888, EW 1: 232.
48. 1892–1894, EW 4: 213.
49. 1903–1906, MW 3: 50.
50. James H. Tufts and Helen B. Thompson, *The Individual and His Relation to Society as Reflected in British Ethics* (Chicago: University of Chicago Press, 1898–1904). (The first part appeared in 1896, reprinted in 1898, and the second in 1904. Reprinted, Augustus M. Kelley, New York 1970. Thompson's contribution is the specific study of Cumberland; the rest is by Tufts.)
51. Ibid., 5.
52. Ibid., 58.
53. 1903–1906, MW 3: 193–209.
54. Ibid., 201.
55. Ibid., 202.
56. MW 6: 440–42.
57. 1916, MW 9, ch. 22, "The Individual and the World".
58. Ibid., 306.

59. Ibid., 314.
60. John Dewey, *Lectures in China 1919–1920*, translated from the Chinese and edited by Robert W. Clopton and Ou Tsuin-Chen. (Honolulu: The University Press of Hawaii, 1973).
61. Ibid., 124.
62. Ibid., 154.
63. 1920, MW 12: 105.
64. Ibid., 190–91.
65. Ibid., 193.
66. Ibid., 194.
67. Ibid., 196.
68. MW 13: 289.
69. 1897, EW 5: 54–83.
70. Ibid., 55.
71. This is the point of view from which Dewey criticizes Mark Baldwin's *Social and Ethical Interpretations in Mental Development: A Study in Social Psychology* in a review (1898, EW 5: 385 ff.).
72. 1897, EW 5: 59–69.
73. "On Moral Evolution" in *Studies in Philosophy and Psychology*, a festschrift for Charles Edward Garman, edited by Tufts and others. (Boston and New York: Houghton Mifflin, 1906), 32.
74. 1907–1909, MW 4: 220–21.
75. 1912–1913, MW 7: 275.
76. 1916, MW 9: 103.
77. 1916, MW 10: 53–63.
78. Ibid., 54.
79. Ibid., 55.
80. Ibid., 57.
81. 1912–1913, MW 7: 237–39.
82. Dewey, *Lectures in China 1919–1920* : 73.
83. 1925–1927, LW 2: 235–372. (Originally published by Holt in 1927.)
84. Ibid., 245.
85. Ibid., 245–46.
86. In the *Monist*, xxxviii: 161–77. Republished as "The Inclusive Philosophical Idea" in *Philosophy and Civilization* (1931): 77–92. Also in 1927–1928, LW 3: 44–54.
87. James H. Tufts, "Recent Ethics in its Broader Relations". *University of California Publications in Philosophy*, vol. 12, no. 2: Issued Sept. 12, 1930. (Berkeley: University of California Press): 181–201.
88. Ibid., 198.
89. Ibid., 201.
90. 1930, LW 5.
91. Ibid., 56.
92. Ibid., 56–57.
93. Ibid., 92.
94. Ibid., 120.

Part III

Some Resulting Lessons

8

The Place of History in Ethics as Seen in *08* and *32*

The possible uses of history in ethics are many, for history itself takes may shapes, and in each shape it may serve different functions. Narrative history tells the story of happenings from the perspective of a definite interest; it is this that prompted Santayana's comparison to a man looking over a crowd to spot his friends. A moralist may use such stories, say of great men and their deeds and struggles, to provide moral inspiration or, on the contrary, to show the feet of clay that come with greatness and the moral price of eminence. History is also the unavoidable context of human life. No person lives outside of some time and place and conditions of life. But the contextual role of history itself is manifold. We may fasten on the necessary and un-avoidable in the human context and use it to describe the human predicament—to live with others, to work, to love, to die. Or with a greater specificity, we may look to the special character of the given context—a time of scarcity or abundance, of war or peace, of stability or rapid change, of purposeful striving or gentle enjoyment; and there is no limit to the degree of specificity that may be invoked in relation to different moral questions. Moreover, out of the context and the character of purposes of the day we may often derive a budget of needs or an agenda of problems to be solved that loom large in the moral decisions of the time. Of course context need not always be one shade of determination. It may vary from practical over-determination (as a natural disaster such as a flood or a volcanic eruption may shape our duties with little recourse) to a set of problems that limit alterna-

149

tives and provide urgencies but leave to profound decision the direction of action; and from that to sheerly accidental factors that play a role for no other reason than that they happened and were then and there relevant; often they simply shut one possibility or open an opportunity.

Explanatory uses of history may invoke bits of narrative, but the context is what gives them explanatory significance. Yet context cannot be the complete explanation, for the human purposes and ideas will have their role to play. Only if some more comprehensive theory of historical order or historical necessity or historical purpose supervenes do we find the context endowed with some special explanatory significance. Beyond narrative and context, then, there lies the realm of speculation in the philosophy of history about the order of development or evolution in mankind. The is the type of theory that speaks of cycles in history, or of linear development, of progress or retrogression, of pendular swings; or in a quite different direction, of an open evolution in which novel and unexpected phenomena come into being. It is this realm of theory in which we find dogmas of predictability or of indetermination: that a period of moral seriousness will be followed by one of hedonistic irresponsibility, or the reverse; that the spring of a morality will bring spontaneous morality but its late summer bring on decay; that progress is inevitable or corruption is inevitable; that there is always complete freedom, and anything may happen. These blithe illustrations do not show the seriousness and metaphysical richness that sometimes underlies the different programs for moral evolution involved. Some have an apriori character, some are rested on a line of observation; and some are simply presupposed without a recognition that a historical theory underlies the ordinary judgments. The important methodological lesson here is that some theory *about* historical order underlies any ethical theory; and in particular an ethical theory that rejects a determinate order of moral development is itself a theory about order that requires as much justification as a linear theory of development.

With these preliminary distinctions about narrative, context and historical order, we can proceed to the historical assumptions of *08* and *32*. In general, we have already seen that *08* has a linear theory of human moral development though there are tendencies to move away from it on Dewey's part; and that *32* has broken completely with it, that it uses history to understand the context of morality at a given time and place, and that its view of order is open and in some sense admits of human initiative and decision. Our tasks in this chapter are accordingly as follows:

1. To explore more carefully the linear view of *08* in the light of the intellectual setting of the period. To recapitulate the difficulties it led to already in the text of *08* itself. To track down, if possible, the influences that operated thereafter against the linear view, whether they were changes in anthropology and the social sciences of the succeeding decades or failures of expectation and prediction on the historical scene. To examine the changes made in *32* in actual historical description, in those parts of the book that dealt with historical materials.
2. To examine what replaced the linear view. It has already been suggested that it was contextual use of history, but the precise type of contextual appeal and the specific role it played remain to be seen.
3. To examine whether Dewey derived any lessons about history and ethics from the actual experience of history of the period—whether World War I, or the revolution in Russia or his observation in his visits to Japan and China, particularly in the rapidly changing situation in China.
4. To elicit the resulting model of historical process and change and the place in it of human decision and action that governs the treatment of history in *32*.

(1)   The linear view we have seen is a theory of development of morality to a maturity. It is first immersed in the cake of custom, in which it is unreflective, unseparated, and collective. It matures as reflective, separated, and individual. As it matures there are, of course, traps and dangers. Chief among these is the degenerate path of a spurious individualism of acquisitive greed and self-seeking. But the linear path is not a deterministic one, doubtless as not every child reaches a healthy adulthood.

Again, this linear pattern seems also to describe the odyssey of the individual in his/her maturation. Here too the parental and social influence come as customary or conventional morality and socialization presents it as the way to be followed. Individual reflection and evaluation come later, and flower into a separate responsibility and decision and evaluation.

Again too, the scope or reach of the linear pattern is not too sharp. It may hold of all mankind, viewed collectively, with Israel, Greece, the medieval world and the modern handing on the torch with altered light. Or it may be the selective development of any people or group that in fact move toward maturity, while other people stagnate.

Finally, there is an overall development in the content of morality in all these cases. The more mature uses the criterion of the social good in its pursuit of the good, and finds its individual well-being in the kinds of interests and activities that point to the general welfare.

So much for the historical perspective of *08*. In *32* there are drastic differences, even reversals. The role of the reflective is unchanged, perhaps even enhanced, if only because the other marks are gone. The prominence of the criterion of separateness for morality has given way to the dangers of the isolation of morality. Reflection on morality reaches into any and every area of human life to find what is relevant to its specific problems; it is not an isolated sphere of the operation of its own principles. Individualism has more clearly become a specific movement of thought, feeling, and practice, under specific historical conditions of western man. Whether the movement of morals is from social to individual—that is, from a kind of moral status to a kind of moral contract—or the reverse, depends on the demands of particular historical conditions and contexts. In fact the demands of the period of *32* are for an increase in socialization. Moreover, egoism as a philosophy takes its place within the movement of that historical individualism as a set of beliefs and policies; Hobbes is no longer banned from the roster of competing ethical theories.

As for the scope of the pattern, it is no longer a world development of mankind. Focus is now on western man and the sources that were relevant to the shape that his development happened to take. There is no longer a prescribed global pattern, nor a set pattern for any people that is historically bestirred.

The individual development (from childhood to adulthood) to some extent inherits the cast-off social development. At least the ready assumption of the individual's stage of growth are not cast aside; but perhaps it is because they stand alone, without the support of the social parallel of *08* that makes them seem enhanced.

Finally, the criterion of social outlook in pursuit of the good, while even more a mark of the moral, ceases to have the appearance of a unified developmental outcome. There are serious reasons for this. The finalistic picture of *the good* has given way to a pluralistic picture of the multiplicity of *interests*. And most of all, the notion of the social has undergone the profound analysis that began with Dewey's chapter on "Social Organization and the Individual" in *08*, whose eventual outcome in *32*, we have seen in the preceding chapter. Individual and social are aspects of any moral thought or action; no issue can seriously be posed as individual versus social; the alleged conflict of individual and society is always the tension between specific individuals and specific institutional demands under specific conditions or between different groups within society. What remains of the criterion of social welfare is no longer a distinctive possible content in moral judgment, but an almost definitory breadth in the idea of morality itself—a broader as against a narrower outreach in a human being.

How far, we may now ask, are these developments a function of an altered theory of the order of history? Or first, do we have any indication that the linear view as such gave way rather than that it was bypassed in a host of continuing analyses of moral phenomena? There is evidence enough of the former in the intellectual temper of the age after *08*.

The linear view with its cake-of-custom approach to the initial stages, fitted readily into the turn that evolutionary cultural studies had taken in the late nineteenth and early twentieth centuries. In the background was the broad Spencerian characterization of evolution as a transformation from an unorganized or indiscriminate or chaotic homogeneity to an organized differentiated heterogeneity. With this was combined the assumption of progress in such an advance. Hence it became easy for cultural studies in different areas to begin with the current classification of institutions as the outcome of differentiation and the bearers of progress, and to trace the evolution of each field separately within a basic linear pattern. Thus studies of kinship postulated an initial state of group promiscuity, succeeding stages of polygamy and polyandry, and an ultimate culmination in the monogamous family. Studies of law followed the familiar path of the movement from customary status to individualized contract. Studies of religion went from an indiscriminate belief in animism to polytheism to the summit of monotheism. And so on. So too in morality, as *08*'s early chapters show, the progress is from custom with its collective responsibility to individual reflection in a separated morality.

The consequence of such an historical progression is that no more than a general indication is needed for the movement to the next stage. It almost operates by an inner dynamic parallel to the growing up of the individual. At most there is general reference to growth of complexity. In the description of a succeeding stage the important thing is to present the new ideas or forms and compare them to the preceding ones.

The specific paths depicted by these earlier evolutionary theories were of course the subject of criticism. Dewey, at times, for example, questions Maine's generalization of the evolution from status to contract. But the general idea of moral evolution was reinforced after the turn of the century by the voluminous work of Westermarck and Hobhouse. It is probably this second surge of evolutionary social science that explains why the atmosphere of evolution in morality was unquestioned in *08*.

Now the next two decades after *08* were a period in which a new, critical, and more scientific anthropology emerged. Its revolt against the linear evolution was so strong that for decades the idea of cultural evolution itself was almost exiled from inquiry. Emphasis fell on a stricter ethnography, on study of a whole culture in its detail, as against the so-called comparative method of putting side by side isolated institutional items from different societies. The intensity of this research was due in part to the feeling that modern civilization was beginning to permeate all parts of the globe and soon none of the cultures of nonliterate peoples would exhibit its past with clarity. With this new anthropology went also an attack on the ethnocentrism that had identified progress with contemporary cultural institutions and values. And with its accumulating materials there fell also by the wayside the cake-of-custom premises of the linear view. Even in *08* Dewey pointed out the role of the conventional and the customary in modern life, though he did not go back to look for the individual differences in primitive life.

The new anthropology was largely associated with the school of Franz Boas, who set the path for several decades of critical thought. Interestingly, in *32*, although chapter 2 is unchanged from *08*, its reading list at the end adds to the *08* list, not only Boas' *The Mind of Primitive Man* (1911), but also Lowie's *Primitive Society* and Goldenweiser's *Early Civilization*, both of which carry the same critical lessons. Boas' book is devoted to taking a realistic view of the individual man and his ideas in primitive society. It riddles notions of a uniform primitive mentality, and argues for a broad similarity of individual capacities in primitive and modern society, differentiated largely by different traditional patterns, different opportunities and, under different conditions, different attentiveness. Any association that Dewey had with his anthropological colleagues at Columbia, where

Boas headed the Anthropology Department and insisted on every doctoral candidate going into the field for first-hand research, would have reenforced the critical lessons.

Scattered indications over the decades enable us to track the shift in Dewey's and Tufts' views about the linear evolutionary pattern and what anthropology contributes to the substructure of moral theory. In *08* as a whole, the exposition of such a thesis falls in Tufts' part, while the few contexts in which it or consequences from it are relevant in Dewey's part there seems to be at least tacit acquiescence. However, before *08* it is clear that both share the thesis in one form or another. For example, in 1906 Tufts has a paper "On Moral Evolution"[1] in which he deals with the parallel of child moral development and evolution of the human race in a way similar to *08*. For example, he says "Neither in the case of man in group life nor in the case of the child is there complete individuality. But the cases are otherwise not identical." For in the child it is incomplete organization, while "The lack of individuality in primitive man is rather a positive solidarity of interest, a habit of working, feeling, and living as part of the group" due to objective organization of his life.[2] Thus the idealizing and individualizing process is aided by the growth of division of labor. Now the following year we find Dewey reviewing the Garman volume and commenting on Tufts' paper.[3] There is no word of dissent about the general thesis, but concern about its formulation in such a way as not to have a fixed separation of "higher" and "lower" morality. Tufts, he says "has conceived the earlier stages in such a vitally concrete way as to realize that there are in them factors which are strictly analogous to those of more developed ethical situations, so that the evolution of the latter out of the former can be treated without denying the essential features of morality on the one hand, or falling into very dubious metaphysics, on the other."[4] Tufts in holding to the social character of the individual as individual has been able "to seize upon the genuinely moral problem, elements, and processes in every situation, at whatever plane of historic progress."[5]

In the same way Dewey, even a decade before, had written a paper on "Interpretation of the Culture-Epoch Theory"[6] in which he is concerned less with the theory than with its educational uses. He finds the correspondence of development in the race and in the child not to be an exact one, but he adds in a footnote "It will be noted that I do not question the fact of correspondence in a general way."[7] Because of the inexactness of the correspondence the side of child development requires independent investigation as the basis for educational guidance.

Dewey's acceptance of the thesis in general in part no doubt reflects the general anthropological atmosphere of the period that we have noted. But it is probably more than passive acquiescence, for the matter was one of growing scientific treatment in the two years before *08*. In a paper in 1930, "Recent Ethics in its Broader Relations"[8] Tufts recalls how "one phase of ethical study which is important not simply for itself but for its bearing upon other lines of theory, came to a sudden flowering in 1906-1908. The field known variously as Evolutionary, or Genetic, or Comparative Ethics, was opened half a century ago by Darwin, Spencer, Maine, and Robertson Smith in Great Britain, Wundt and Nietzsche in Germany, Guyau in France, L.H. Morgan in America. But a new epoch, resulting from more thorough anthropological studies, was opened early in this century by Hobhouse, Westermarck, Sumner, and Levy-Brühl."[9]

If we take Boas' book in 1911 as the turning-point to a fresh anthropological perspective, it is interesting to note that Dewey's second paper on "Culture Epoch Theory" in the *Cyclopedia of Education*[10] still does not question the theory. He looks to its intellectual sources in German historically oriented philosophy, in the educational thought that saw the child traversing first the simpler way of past stages, and in the embryonic analogy of ontogeny recapitulating phylogeny. Some pedagogical writers, he tells us, have marked their stages as "complete and almost unconscious absorption of the individual in the group", "individualistic reaction and protest", and "voluntary and conscious loyal reattachment of the individual to the interests and well-being of the social group." Others have followed an intellectual cue: "predominance of emotional imagination" as in myth and animism, "development of a matter-of-fact interest, expressed in tendency to observe, to collect, to make utilitarian construction", "conscious reflection" with abstraction and generalization. Still others present typical industrial periods: hunting and fishing, nomadic and shepherd life, agriculture, metals and manufacture, general commerce. Dewey welcomes the attempts to treat the curriculum in relation to "the actual unfolding of the psychology of child nature, and at the same time to connect this psychological growth with indispensable sociological considerations." He offers some qualifications from the purely educational point of view, chiefly that education is concerned with the present and the past is relevant as it helps clarify and appreciate the present. The child is not to be led "*through* the epochs of the past" but "*by* them to resolve present complex culture into simpler factors . . . "

Democracy and Education[11] at least criticizes the foundations of the theory itself, while still concentrating on the educational consequences. But here the theory has been somewhat narrowed, and with so many aspects it is hard to see how far the more general idea of linear development of morality is being rejected; what is clearly rejected is the coordination of historical and psychological development. The several claims about the earlier hold of custom, the development of individuality as the mark of progress, are asserted casually during this period. Even as late as 1919-20 in a course of lectures on ethics in China[12] Dewey in dealing with virtues presents "three stages of moral evolution": 1. Custom as morality. 2. Inner good will and kind heart. 3. Each one forms his own character and helps others build theirs. Although called stages of moral evolution, these are presented from the point of view of the individual, though he clearly thinks that some whole people fall in a stage, as well as lots of people everywhere.

On the other hand, "Chinese National Sentiment"[13] states a forthright rejection of a uniform development from savagery to civilization: "We have made ourselves believe that all development from savagery to civilization must follow a like course and pass through similar stages. When we find societies that do not agree with this standard we blandly dismiss them as abnormalities, as survivals of backward states, or as manifestations of lack of political capacity."[14] It is not arrested development, but "extraordinary development in a particular direction, only one so unfamiliar to us that we dispose of them as a mass of hopeless political confusion and corruption." We shall see, in the following chapter on custom and habit, that Dewey learned important lessons from his observations in China, which considerably refined his analysis of custom. If the contrast of custom and reflection for the most part remains, it ceases to appear in evolutionary robes. *Reconstruction in Philosophy* (1920) has an occasional treatment of a conflict with custom, but in a specific context as the Greece of Plato's day. Or it criticizes nineteenth century German philosophy for enumerating a definite number of institutions and assigning each an essential and immutable meaning and arranging them in an order of "evolution".[15] The emergence of greater individuality as a late product is by no means abandoned—see, for example, the view that in Greek times "Private belief and invention were a deviation, a dangerous eccentricity, signs of disloyal disposition. The private was an equivalent of the illicit; and all innovations and departures from custom are illicit . . ."[16] But at the same time Dewey sends the reader to Boas' *The Mind of Primitive Man* for what is sound and what is exaggerated in the French anthropological school.

In his Syllabus for the Columbia course in 1923 Dewey interprets the idea of fixed evolutionary stages as an attempt to assimilate social science to physical in terms of fixed uniformities. He refers to Comte, Spencer, Morgan and others, and to criticisms by Boas and Goldenweiser.[17] But the paper in which he finally comes to grips with the role of anthropology in ethics comes in 1927: "Anthropology and Ethics", a chapter in Ogburn and Goldenweiser's *The Social Sciences and Their Interrelations*.[18]

The major issues are here faced directly, both in formulation and answer. Differences between primitive and today's cultures have been exaggerated; similarities do not have to be treated as survivals: "For the most part, tradition does not operate and 'survivals' do not occur except where the older beliefs and attitudes correspond to some need and condition which still exists." It is doubtful whether a single continuous line of moral development is to be found, in a philosophical sense.[20] Advances in knowledge, in economic invention and control, have complicated conduct, but introduced new ways to going wrong, so that they cannot be said to mark moral progress. Moral evolution has occurred in the sense that intellectual changes and changes in political and economic conditions have modified habits of life and extended previous moral concepts and refined their content, for example by widening human intercourse and multiplying contacts. Great relativity of contact in morals is compatible with stability with respect to basic needs, as well as the necessary condition of human association.

In the body of the article Dewey examines specifically the views of influential interpreters of moral evolution. Kropotkin saw mutual aid as basic and early man, living closer to the animal world, as impressed by the unified group action of animals. "Thus, the instinct of sociability inherited from lower animals was made into a conscious idea and sentiment."[21] Distortions came with class differentiation, ecclesiastical and military power. To study such changes requires attention to specific alterations in definite social groups. Westermarck is criticized for his uncritical and uncontrolled use of the comparative method in which data are invoked without adequate study of the total situation of each people. His approach from the moral sentiments is also one-sided. He is rather embodying a particular tradition of ethical theory, descended from Hume, than facing directly the anthropological material. Dewey adds that Kropotkin too is influenced by contemporary issues in making equality the primary idea. Wundt is found to have stressed the intellectualist content, the theory of the universe and human relations to it. Such ideas of the gods in religion supplied on the one hand exemplars for conduct and on the other rewards and punishments. Custom as a norm of voluntary action is intermediate between morality and law, moral in the subjective disposition to conform, legal in objective means of compulsion. As these diverge, morals and law are differentiated. Wundt offers three stages of ethical evolution: the first with narrow scope for social impulses and virtues of obvious external advantage; the second under religious ideas, with virtues connected to socially directed internal dispositions; in the third, philosophy and religion making objects and disposition all-human. Hobhouse (whose ideas, we may note, come closest to the view of *08*) "regards the idea of *good* as the central and unifying theme of morals, so that the evolution of morals is an evolution of the content assigned to this idea and of the means by which the assigned content is realized."[22] To be moral, a social development has thus to express the idea of the good. Ethical evolution has been influenced by forms of social organization and of scientific and philosophic thought. Hobhouse advances four stages of moral evolution: the first (pre-moral) in which customary rules hold but without the character of moral laws; the second, in which specific moral obligations are recognized, but without general moral principles; the third, generalized ideas and standards, but without knowledge of basis or function; the fourth, reflection on the needs of life served by morals and the function of forms of personal and institutional conduct, thus producing reflective criteria for judgment.

Dewey suggests four conclusions that may be fruitfully contrasted with the position of *08*. First, the theoretical desire "to differentiate sharply between moral conceptions and practices, on the one side, and manners and economic, domestic, religious, legal, and political relations on the other"[23] cannot be realized. (This, we may recall, was a major mark of moral evolution in Part I of *08*). In early peoples these are fused, and in contemporary peoples they remain in spite of theorists as largely a complex blend, except where associated with religion and law. Second, the emotional factor in conduct is too universal and strong to be made the explanation of differences and historical changes. The latter require appeal to institutional and intellectual changes. Third, there is no justification for an apriori assumption of economic determinism; this points to the plurality of influences and the need for specific investigations. Fourth, "neither side in the controversy as to whether the direction of ethical development has been away from or toward greater individuality, is unambiguously borne out by the facts."[24] He rejects both the romantic view of the free natural man and the "extreme, or at least ambiguous, statements" about "the enslavement of early men to custom."[25] They were enslaved from our point of view, but, from their own, customs were necessary conditions of life; so too we are not aware of many of our own customs as hindrances which succeeding generations may view as intolerably oppressive.

We may conclude that 1927, with *The Public and its Problems*[26] providing fresh categories for replacing the individual-social dichotomy and "Anthropology and Ethics" rejecting or at least throwing in doubt most of the consequences of the linear picture of moral evolution, marked the end of the historical substructure of *08.*[27]

(2) Our second inquiry is what replaced the linear view. Clearly, no other pattern of moral evolution is offered in *32*, although there may seem to be some diluted "survivals" of the earlier picture in Part I. The importance of the linear view had been not so much that it was a theory of history to be accepted or rejected, but that it had prevented the specific historical evaluation of individualism by enshrining it, that it had underscored an abstract sociality in the criteria of the moral. The phenomena that were, so to speak, enslaved by the theory were not eliminated. Thus individualism could be examined in different historical contexts for the conditions under which it was developed. The general social yielded to variegated groupings. Static societies could be examined without assuming that they had to be in an earlier developmental stage; for example, one could look at the role of the customary in China without regarding it as moral backwardness. The answer then to what replaced the withdrawn linear view is simply a more genuinely socio-historical analysis of social phenomena in their spe-

cific socio-historical contexts. We shall examine the character of this contextualism as an analytic method in a later chapter. Here we are concerned with the changes that it brought in *32* when freed of the encumbrance of the linear theory.

The changed approach to history can be seen in the specifically historical chapters of *32* as compared to *08*. The chapter on "The Moral Development of the Greeks" is unchanged, but that on Hebrew morality is rewritten; there is the added chapter on the Roman contribution, and the rewritten treatment of modern trends.

The shift in the treatment of the Hebrew Moral development is very clear. The aim in *08* is to present the emergence of the higher conscious and personal morality. The Hebrews and the Greeks are, by a familiar division of labor, given different aspects to develop (as in Matthew Arnold's well-known "Hebraism and Hellenism", in his *Culture and Anarchy*.) The one cultivates the strong desire to do the right, the other the wisdom to find what is right. The one is individual in its inner emphasis, the other in its trust of the mind. There are, of course— in the treatment of the Hebrews—political and economic factors in the background to account for the growth of a national life or of the clash of interests. But these are not the central focus. That falls on the constitutive elements of the changed morality: a conception in the Ten Commandments of a covenant replacing the demands of custom; the development of a concept of law and authority; a concept of a personal lawgiver; grappling with the problem of evil. The moral conceptions attained are fivefold. One is the sense of righteousness and sin. The second and third attainment are a sense of personal responsibility and sincerity and purity of motive. Both of these indicate an internalization of morality. The fourth and fifth are: a growth in the conception of "life" from material prosperity to love, personal relations, and national feeling, and eventually to the life of the spirit; and a social ideal of love and justice and peace.

Now compare with this the story in *32*. The descriptive content is largely the same and the reading list in unchanged, but the questions asked, the historical focus, and the source of interest are very different. The problem is specifically historical: How explain that the Hebrews, beginning as nomads like their neighbors, should have developed morally as they did? Did their religion raise their morals, or did their morals transform their religion? The answer, Dewey says, is neither; moral problems reflect actual human relations and difficulties in family, in conflicts between standards of desert clan and commercial city, in problems of administering justice, in adjustments with neighbors. The point is not merely that the previous suggestions of economic and political background are expanded and put into the foreground, but that the moral forms that emerge are now seen *not as general emergents of moral evolution but as specific responses to challenges in the specific historical problems and conflicts.* There is a specific pinpointing of causal agencies—the prophets supply a dynamic force that furthers growth. And whereas the discussion of religious agencies in *08* had stayed with the conceptions of covenant, personal lawgiver, etc., *32* moves into the way the religious conceptions reflected the character of the family, how moral ideas found a foothold in ritual and ceremonial practices, as well as how the unity of the view of God was related to political unity. There is similarity in the materials, but the focus has shifted. But of course the discussion of moral conceptions attained is essentially unaltered. Yet, as we noted earlier these too are no longer set in the presumed evolutionary unfolding of morality as such but in the historical development of a western moral consciousness. There is more of historical contingency, and so while in one sense the sublimity of a stage in evolution is removed, in another the real causal role in a more local development has its own momentous character. Who knows what the western moral consciousness would now be like if the Hebrews had not happened to develop the way they did under the conditions of their life? In this sense, the revisions of *32* are not a retreat from history but a movement from one way of doing history to another way—one that, we shall see, will in the end add to the momentousness of the present.

In the chapter on Rome we can see more directly the main lines of the historical approach, for the chapter is new and there is no jockeying of an earlier and a later version. In the very title it is posed as "The Roman Contribution to the Modern Moral Consciousness" and more than half of the chapter deals with the conditions and institutions of Roman society before we get into the moral ideas.

The very first sentence shows the influence of the restructuring carried out in the *three roots* paper we have studied in detail earlier. "If the modern world owes to the Hebrews its religion with the moral emphasis upon inner motives and the ideal of a kingdom of God, and if Greece gave us methods of scientific search for the good, it is to Rome that we are largely indebted for a third factor in the moral consciousness—the law, and the conceptions derived from it."[28] This appears to assign the root that generates the concept of virtue to the Hebrews—the inner or character side of morality. It assigns the root of appetition and aspiration and the concept of the good to the Greek development. And the jural root goes to the Roman. This does not of course mean an exclusive assignment, for each focus finds some place out of the spotlight for the others. But even with this qualification it involves some simplifications. The Hebrew development had already been described as not only turning to the inner but as giving a conception of law and a lawgiver; the second is now underplayed and the inner becomes central. There may be some historical justification here if the claim is taken to be that the heavy work of right and duty in contemporary morality is still done with concepts rooted in the Roman developments; the juridical status of the Hebrew idea would be that of a precursor.

Changes in the treatment of the medieval and modern period show the same shift from exemplifying the preassigned evolutionary development to tracing the specific problems and social movements of a given period for their relation to the specific ethical forms.[29] *08* sets out to give the general attitudes and ideals of the Middle Ages and then moves to "the three lines along which individualism has proceeded to the moral consciousness of today." The medieval contrasts group (e.g. clan) loyalties with the Church ideal, the latter mostly in its other-worldly spiritual virtues. Individualism is exhibited in challenge of tradition; in its conceptions of natural rights and liberties; in the individualizing impact of industry, commerce, and art, yielding not only contractualism and the growth of capitalism but also a reaction in terms of ideas of benevolence and sympathy; and finally, in the growth of the scientific spirit, with its articulation of method and development of education. A final paragraph, on theoretical interpretation of this period in ethical systems, selects Kantian and Utilitarian ethics as expressing the different aspects of these mainlines.

While *08* tried to get at the essential morality of the period and place it in the evolutionary framework, *32* tries to depict the specific political and social conditions and movements, each with its moral components and intellectual outlook. The (equally brief) medieval treatment focuses on the church's establishment of authority and unity, its control of usury and attitude to wealth, and its moral formulation in terms of the law of God. The modern period is considered in terms of growth of nationalism, the rise of the middle class and the development of civil rights, the Reformation in religion, the economic developments of commerce and industry and the theories that accompanied them, the Renaissance with its effects on the arts and the rise of science, the Revolutions and the progress of democracy. There is no unified moral theme imposed on the whole picture; the moral conceptions fit into the specific ongoing patternings. Finally, in the projected interpretations of ethical theory, the Hobbesian *selfish system* and the *Moral Sense* writers are added to the *Kantian* and the *Utilitarian*.

It should not be assumed that the emphasis on specific investigation of complex relations in a given situation, as against broad historical stages or abstract laws of history, militates against systematic results in the area of concrete investigation or foregoes the possibility of finding determinants. Indeed Dewey's criticism of Westermarck and the comparative method loosely used is precisely that it is not systematic. On the whole, Dewey is most successful when he is examining the fine shades of moral outlook conveyed in a specific socio-cultural context or a specific ethical theory. A good example is his early article on "Interpretation of Savage Mind."[30] He offers the same criticism of Spencer's method that he later did of Westermarck's. And he sets out to suggest a method for determining a pattern, resting on the biological assumption that mind "whatever else it may be, is at least an organ of service for the control of environment in relation to the ends of the life process."[31] He selects the hunting life for investigation, and examines it in the context of the Australian aborigines. Its detail encompasses environmental setting, focus in activities, emotional interest, dramatic character of the occupation, transfer of psychic pattern that is developed to other relations of life—art and ceremonial, religion, attitudes to death, courtship and marriage. The paper has much the same quality as Veblen's work in delineating the psychic aspects of modern economic operations or the effects of technology on habits of mind.

(3) Our third topic is any lessons that emerged about the relation of history and ethics from the major experiences of the period. They were momentous enough. World War I and its traumatic impact on intellectual attitudes stand out readily. The general assumption of progress and continued rational democratic advance as the mark of civilization was shattered by the war. If the linear view of history had predicted anything, it was the gradual unfolding of this liberal world

view. But instead of rationality there was now violence and the growth of dictatorship. The Spenglerian mood made extensive inroads. While the later preachings of the doom of democracy in the 1930s concomitant with the advances of fascism come after the *32* edition, the first world war and the economic crises and world depression were enough to unsettle any linear beliefs. It does not follow that Dewey in any way abandoned his democratic outlook; indeed in many ways it was intensified. But its status could not be that of triumphant emergence. It is a more open world in which it is up to man to take the reins.

Dewey did not need to be taught as a fresh lesson that the world was an open one in which man's decisions and actions and the ideas that guided them could shape direction. He had always argued for this. But the lesson could be intensified, perhaps refined, in critical historical crises. In an essay on "Progress"[32] during the war (1916) he asserted that we had confused the rapidity of change with progress, "the breaking down of barriers by which advance is made possible with advance itself."[33] The future of progress now depended on man to say whether he wants it or not, for the conditions were at hand. He calls the belief that evolution gives a cosmic sanction to automatic and wholesale progress in human affairs an infantile and selfish dream. "Progress is not automatic; it depends upon human intent and aim and upon acceptance of responsibility for its production. It is not a wholesale matter, but a retail job to be contracted for and executed in sections."[34] Social machinery is needed. He suggests an international commerce commission, an international tariff board, an international board for colonies, and "one for the supervision of relations with those backward races which have not as yet been benevolently, or otherwise, assimilated by the economically advanced peoples."[35] In the light of his subsequent writings on the Far East, we may suspect that this last recommendation is intended to control the harsh intrusion of the great powers.

From 1919 to 1928 there are papers dealing to a great extent with China where Dewey lectured for two years (1919-21) and with Japan where just before that he gave the lectures that issued in *Reconstruction in Philosophy*, and to a much less extent with Turkey, Mexico, and the Soviet Union. In sum, they were the scenes of revolution, the overthrowal of the old and the birth of the new. Spread large on the canvas of history Dewey saw the same structured situation that had long emerged from his exploration of human psychology and the place of thought: the trio that in social psychology (*Human Nature and Conduct*, 1922) appeared as *impulse, habit, intelligence*. On the historical canvas they appear as *needs, custom, reconstruction*. In both cases the reflection that exhibits intelligence at work or prompts reconstruction is the conflict of habits in the matrix of old or new needs, and when it does not issue in smooth change it can become a critical or even a revolutionary situation.

The needs are, of course, the basic human needs of a population, but taking shape in the matrix of current social happenings. For example, Dewey writes on the Chinese situation in 1919[36]: "The Chinese, as long as they were left undisturbed by other peoples, had all the complex elements of their social equation figured out with unparalleled exactness. Their social calculus, integral and differential, exceeded anything elsewhere in existence."[37] He adds that this fact alone accounts for their endurance for 4000 years. The new forces that upset this balance were battleships, artillery, railways, machines, chemicals. The internal equilibrium had been upset by contact with foreign powers.

The habits can become known if we understand Chinese political psychology. We have to know "the historic customs and institutions of China, for the institutions have shaped the mental habits, not the mind the social habits."[38] We go astray if we make all history fit our western patterns. Dewey had come to China at the moment when the student movement against Japanese invasion was accelerating and directed against the attempted compromises of the central government. His strongest interest appears to be in what will happen to Chinese modes of thought in steering the new forces.

Dewey soon found that his own ideas of habit and custom needed refinement. Although he does not tell us this, it is apparent from what he says about Chinese custom and social conservatism. Hitherto his view of the customary (as in *08*) had been predominantly the weight of the traditional, without reflection and passively followed. The contrast had been the customary and the reflective. But what if reflection in a particular case preserved the customary? Dewey in 1920 writes about Chinese social habits[39] and considers the charge that they are held back by their conservatism; but this, he says, merely repeats what needs to be explained. The long passage is worth quoting: "Conservative they doubtless are. But nevertheless their history is not a history of stagnation, of fixity, as we are falsely taught, but of social as well as dynastic change. They have tried many experiments in their day.

Centuries ago they had a statesman who induced the emperor to commit the kingdom to something as near to modern socialism as possible considering the absence of steam and electricity. China has undergone as many barbarian invasions as any country in Europe. Its survival and its absorption of its invaders do not argue conservatism of the inert kind. No country whose conservatism came from sheer routine, from lack of imagination, could have maintained and extended its civilization as China has done. And experience shows that the Chinese are supple, pliant, accommodating and adaptive—neither rigid nor dull."[40] By contrast Dewey reports that a Chinese friend of his finds the Japanese conservative in spite of their modernization, for they have kept to a primitive theocracy and to personal habits of clothing and daily life. Dewey appears to accept the contrast. In a letter[41] he writes of his growing idea that "the conservatism of the Chinese was much more intellectual and deliberate, and less mere routine clinging to custom, than I used to suppose. Consequently, when their ideas do change, the people will change more thoroughly, more all the way through, than the Japanese."

The question apparently persisted in Dewey's mind. Two years later we find him relating their conservatism to their agrarian life.[42] The Chinese achievement of not exhausting their soil in 4000 years is unparalleled, and helps explain their conservatism, patiently conserving the resources of nature. Western peoples, on the other hand, attack, exploit, and waste the soil.[43] It helps also, Dewey thinks, to explain their attitude to government as unnatural interference in the operations of nature; the real government is the immemorial customs of the people.

In many respects, then, Dewey's concern with custom in China was a critical context in which his own ideas of custom and habit gave rise to conflicts that demanded reconstruction. What kind of reconstruction, we shall see in the next chapter.

We move from needs and habits to reconstruction in the Chinese situation. In an essay on "Old China and New"[44] Dewey writes: "Simply as an intellectual spectacle, a scene for study and surmise, for investigation and speculation, there is nothing in the world today—not even Europe in the throes of reconstruction—that equals China. History records no parallel. Can an old, vast, peculiar, exclusive, self-suffering civilization be born again? Made over it must be, or it cannot endure."[45] A new mind, says Dewey, must be created. He is quite definite about the necessities. For example, the family system is being undermined, not by the desire of some for their own choice of mates or for educated wives, but by the railway and factory system. "They will continue to do so, even if every student take the vow of eternal silence."[46] Modern methods of the industrial system cannot be introduced and the old institutions unchanged. What is to be done? We need not go here into Dewey's analysis of alternative ideas and recommendations. The significant point is his belief that there has to be a reform in culture as antecedent to other reforms, and that for this reason leadership should revert to those who are distinctively Chinese in attitude, not to those who want Western or Japanese importations.

Dewey's emphasis on the vital role of ideas and modes of thought and his perspective on revolutionary situations as those that stir a whole people to reach out to new ways and look for ideas characterizes his contact with other changing worlds of this period. In Japan he had looked for the growth of liberal ideas and somewhat overestimated their strength at the time. Only when he saw what Japan was doing in China and the relations of Japan to the West did he conclude that the liberals would always yield at the last moment to the traditional conservatives in Japan, in serious part because of western attitudes of discrimination against the East as a whole. In Soviet Russia and in Mexico and Turkey, in which he was investigating educational methods, the focus on modes of thought was natural, but his accounts clearly reveal his perspective in general. In Leningrad ("Leningrad Gives the Clue") he writes: "I now realize that any student of history ought to be aware that the forces released by revolutions are not functions, in any mathematical sense, of the efforts, much less the opinions and hopes, of those who set the train of events in motion." And explicitly, he points to "the more basic fact of a revolution—one which may be hinted at, but not described by calling it psychic and moral rather than merely political and economic, a revolution in the attitude of people towards the needs and possibilities of life."[48] Here too he dismisses "outworn absolutistic metaphysics and bygone theories of straight-line, one way 'evolution.'"[49] He feels for the first time some inkling of what may have been the moving spirit and force of primitive Christianity. In Mexican rural schools, "Much of the actual work is, it goes without saying, crude, as crude as are the conditions under which it is done. But it is the crudeness of vitality, of growth, not of smug conventions."[50] He is impressed by the phenomenon of the night schools, to which Indians walk miles "each one bringing a candle by whose glimmering light the studying is done."[51] In Turkey ("Angora, the New") Angora symbolizes the faith in the possibilities of the Asiatic peasant.[52]

If at times Dewey's emphasis on the reconstructive power of a people's awakening may seem to have a romantic tinge by contrast with the theories of historical determinism that he pushes aside, this impression is likely to be mistaken. There is, underlying it, a sober theory of history and the role of ideas in history in relation to productive and technological development, to which we now turn.

(4)   Finally, what is the model of historical process and change that Dewey is developing, and what the place of human action and decision? It is possible to indicate the growth of this conception from long before *08* to the threshold of *32*.

The pivotal conception of *reconstruction* is long-standing. An early paper[53] with the title "Reconstruction" deals with the development of theology and the religious life of the churches; it is an address before the Students' Christian Association of the University of Michigan. It clearly has already the structure which we find later in the concept. It speaks of and illustrates "a time of unusual ferment"—a background of problems that may look disconnected but express large tendencies at work for centuries, as well as the tendency to deal with superficial symptoms. It deals with the meaning of a critical change in life, and of the reconstruction of activities, the analysis of causes, and the determination of what to do. The idea is generalized over different phases: "Reconstruction is a periodic need of life. It represents, in history, the conflict between ideas and the institutions which embody those ideas. In animal life, it stands for the conflict between function and the structure which exercises the function; in the life of the individual, it is the conflict between habits and ideals; in general, it is the conflict between ends or aims and the means or machinery through which those ends are realized."[54] The ideas and functions and aims require a system of objective powers for their exercise. The structure of habits or institution has to be animated by a purpose. When a conflict arises in these various sides reconstruction is necessary.

This picture is almost completely the later structure of reconstruction. Perhaps it gives a more prominent place to the ideal than later when it is absorbed in the general milieu of purposes and values. But Dewey is already careful to point out that we oversimplify if we assume that the ideal always leads the way: "this overlooks the fact that ideas finally become embodied in outward life, that aims become realized as habits. To suppose anything else is to suppose that our ideals and our aims are without hands and feet, that they never succeed. Such is not the case. Any aim worth striving for is always at some definite period or other realized; if not wholly, at least sufficiently realized to demand a further development of the idea. The execution of our purposes creates a new purpose. It makes necessary the transmuting of the accomplished institution or habit into a means, an instrument for the outworking of the new idea. This is the period of reconstruction."[55]

Interestingly, the address ends with a consideration of the radical and the conservative. The true conservative is true to the spirit of the past, not to its outward form. "No one can moor himself to the past. The present is the true past. It is the past in its fuller expression, in the revelation of its deeper meaning."[56] Loyalty to it demands accepting its onward movement. Similarly, the radical who looks to the future without the meaning of the past is engaged in futility. "The only force, the only instruments with which he may carry out his projects of progress are the traditions, the institutions of the past in their adjustment and reconstruction."[57]

The centrality of the present is a fundamental element in the structure. It is central because that is where reconstruction is taking place. But it is not the present as such but the meaning of the present that is vital. That provides the selection of lines along which decision is guided. It issues from the established habits in understanding the situation in which reconstruction is to take place. The source of the generating conflict is on the whole left open. Sometimes it is seen as impulse struggling against established habits; but since impulse is usually already given a determinate form in desire, impulse is shaped and has habitual components. More often then, the conflict is between established habits, ways, institutions; or it is between the old and the new, where the new already has roots in the sense of the present. We know that this conceptual scheme, almost complete in this 1894 disquisition about theology and the church will reappear in the feedback model of "The Reflex Arc in Psychology" in 1896. In a general view of the decade, it is clear that not the problems of theology but the problems of psychology are inspiring the model. The source of the model is the analysis of consciousness or thought, the vital present of a human being. But it is fed too by, and applied to, the analysis of history.

The importance of the present is stressed also in Dewey's account of how history can best be taught.[58] History is dead if treated simply as a record of the past. "The ethical value of history teaching will be measured by the extent to which it is treated as a matter of analysis of existing social relations—that is to say as affording insight into what makes up the structure and working of society."[59] Past societies examined show us components of our present complex life. Studies of historical progress rest on the assumption that the influences we find at work are the kind that operate fundamentally throughout.

It is not, however, merely the contemplation of the present that is involved. Over and over again we find Dewey stressing the practical role of ideas, the fact that ideas make a difference in the course of the present. Increasingly Dewey begins to tilt at metaphysical theories that keep human knowledge at bay and see thinking as outside contemplation of the real. A fascinating case of this is his review of Santayana's *The Life of Reason*.[60] Dewey is both admiring and disturbed. "I know of no writing in modern philosophy which evidences more just and kindly appreciation of the forces of human life, taken simply, frankly, and naturally . . . "[61] But Santayana is always running down all other philosophical interpretations. By the end of the review it is clear that what troubles Dewey is the futile role assigned to thought: are the objects of science and mathematics *the* reality "while the purposes and endeavors, and achievements of human experience are only an evanescent and superficial mirror in which *the* Reality happens, for our passing delectation and confusion, to reflect itself?"[62] Dewey might have, though he does not, recognized that Santayana's theory of mind here was a kind of epiphenomenalism, that mind was but a last bubble in the ferment of matter. He appears to find Santayana wavering, and points to the alternative that knowing is itself an operation of reality.

In his paper for the James festschrift ("Does Reality Possess Practical Character?")[63] he faces the issue directly. "Why should the idea that knowledge makes a difference to and in things be antecedently objectionable?"[64] He suspects it is because the assumption is being made that the universe is static. In going on to develop a pragmatic conception he points to the continuity of common sense and science, for "Common sense regards intelligence as having a purpose and knowledge as amounting to something."[65] Indeed natural science can be regarded as doing the same kind of work as a farmer or mechanic, that is, a craftsman, on a vaster scale, arranging things "with reference to their most efficacious services."[66] Common to all awareness is the problematic structure: "Awareness means *attention*, and attention a crisis of some sort in an existent situation; a forking of the roads of some material, a tendency to go this way and that. It represents something the matter, something out of gear, or in some way menaced, insecure, problematical and strained."[67] This is not merely emotional or subjective, but in the facts of the situation. Psychological language describes attention as "a phenomenon of conflicting habits, being the process of resolving this conflict by finding an act which functions all the factors concerned . . . "

In other contexts Dewey correspondingly refuses to see the existence of different philosophies at the same time as futility. In his "Philosophy and Civilization", a paper delivered in 1926 at the Sixth International Congress of Philosophy[68], he assigns philosophy a transforming role in the history of civilization. It is cultural and marks a change in culture. Since every epoch has diverse currents and aspirations, "the divergence of philosophic systems instead of being a reproach (as of course it is from the standpoint of philosophy as a revelation of truth) is evidence of sincerity and vitality."[69] He adds that if the ruling and oppressed elements in a society had the same philosophy one might suspect its intellectual integrity: "The life of all thought is to affect a junction at some point of the new and the old, of deep-sunk customs and unconscious dispositions, that are brought to the light of attention by some conflict with newly emerging directions of activity. Philosophies which emerge at distinctive periods define the larger patterns of continuity which are woven in effecting the enduring junctions of a stubborn past and an insistent future."[70]

Dewey's systematic elaboration of his naturalism with respect to mind belongs to *Experience and Nature* (1925) and to *The Quest for Certainty* (1929, especially chapters 5 and 6 on ideas). We need not pursue this aspect further here. From the standpoint of the historical model, once the active role of ideas is certified, the question of the major determinants in the structure of the situation becomes comparably important. Dewey's answer is not hard to seek. Invariably the problem-producing factors in history, setting the stage for some change as necessary, are the economic in the sense of the productive and technical. We have seen his many references to industry and technology both in general accounts in *08* and *32* and in the specific analyses such as that of China and the rest of the revolutionary world. It is only necessary now to distinguish his view from that of an economic determinism, which he also constantly rejects. His point is simple. Economics does determine, but only where the reflective or ideational is withheld or rendered impotent. The importance of the economic is central as a means of life: "the life which men, women and children actually lead, the opportunities open to them, the values they are capable of enjoying, their education, their share in all the things of art and science, are mainly determined by economic conditions. Hence we can hardly expect a moral system which ignores economic conditions to be other than remote and empty."[71] (*The Quest for Certainty*) But the attempt to treat economics in isolation as embodying physical-like laws, apart from questions of policy, is simply the revenge that it takes when industrial life is not treated as a means. In *The Public and Its Problems* (1927) Dewey pointed out that "Economic agencies produce one result when they are left to work themselves out on the merely physical level, or on that level modified only as the knowledge, skill and technique which the community has accumulated are transmitted to its members unequally and by chance. They have a different outcome in the degree in which knowledge of consequences is equitably distributed, and action is animated by an informed and lively sense of a shared interest."[72] Dewey is clear that the idea alone cannot produce the results. For example, the idea of political democracy alone did not produce democratic governmental practices; it influenced the political movement, but the latter "was the outcome primarily of technological discoveries and inventions working a change in the customs by which men had been bound together."[73] In *Individualism Old and New* (1930) where the by now general categories of the old and the new are being applied to the American scene in its crisis—after the studies of the revolutionary world—Dewey again startles by asserting that "Economic determinism is now a fact, not a theory."[74] What he means is that society is rapidly becoming corporate, so that older conceptions of laissez-faire individualism are irrelevant. But the shape of what can be done is not determined. He goes on: "But there is a difference and a choice between a blind, chaotic and unplanned determinism, issuing from business conducted for pecuniary profit, and the determination of a socially planned and ordered development. It is the difference and the choice between a socialism that is public and one that is capitalistic."

Dewey's model of historical process is thus a present situation whose meaning in terms of the past is to a greater or less degree clear, problematic because of a conflict of established habits and the demands of a new situation, the situation changed from the old largely through productive and technological shifts, ruling out some possibilities and allowing others, and open to human decision and effort in terms of the ideas that people entertain and the knowledge they possess. The ideas themselves are not abstractions but express and are expressed in institutions and habits that are operative factors in the social life of the people. (For example, the technologies that have emerged embody the scientific knowledge that existed and made them possible, but together with the social institutions that allowed the scientific knowledge to be applied.)

The chief remaining issue that Dewey might be asked to face is whether there is not a scheme of determinism that would cover the ideas as well, since obviously ideas arise at some time and to some but not at other times and to others. So far as we have already explored the model it might be argued that if knowing is part of the real world and not an outside view of it, then it is always interactively involved in techniques and institutions and life activities. It does not have to be separated off as the end product of either determination or of an independent reason or of some sense of freedom. Ideas in their occurrence are areas of ferment in reality; they might perhaps be compared to the yeast in the baking, which is not a different kind of reality, but only a part of it having some active powers. But in any case, Dewey does have theories of reason and of freedom, tied into his conception of learning and its character. Both the nature of habit, of reason, and of freedom will be explored in subsequent chapters.

Notes

1. In the Garman festschrift, 3–39.
2. Ibid., 20.
3. 1907, MW 4: 220–21.
4. Ibid., 220.
5. Ibid., 221.
6. 1896, EW 5: 247–253.
7. Ibid., 248.
8. *University of California Publications in Philosophy*, vol. 12, no. 2. Issued Sept. 12, 1930. (Berkeley: University of California Press): 181–82.
9. Ibid., 181.

10. 1911, MW 6: 408–12.
11. 1916, MW 9: 78–82.
12. *Additional Lectures in China, 1919–1921*, ed. Robert W. Clopton and Ou Tsuin-Chen. (University of Hawaii, 1970), Institute of Advanced Projects Title 4; Microfilm 4648: 569–646.
13. MW 11: 215–27.
14. Ibid., 215.
15. 1915–1919, MW 12: 194.
16. Dewey, *Experience and Nature,* 1925, LW 1: 164.
17. Ibid., 7.
18. 1927–1928, LW 3: 11–24.
19. Ibid., 11.
20. Ibid., 21.
21. Ibid., 13.
22. Ibid., 17.
23. Ibid., 19.
24. Ibid., 20.
25. Ibid.
26. in LW 2.
27. *The Public and Its Problems* (1925–1927, LW2: 355–57) invokes the logical analysis of the fixed stage theory that was suggested in the 1932 syllabus. Dewey quotes Mill on the laws of social phenomena being derived from those of individual human nature. Evolutionary ideas did not change this picture where "evolution" was itself understood non-historically: "it was assumed that there is a predestined course of fixed stages through which social development must proceed." (357–58) Social science was thus committed to fixed uniformities. Such a logic, Dewey adds, is fatal to free experimental social inquiry; instead, Dewey compares laws of social life to laws of engineering, dealing with means to be found for desired results.
28. This assignment of a distinctive moral contribution to Rome may be compared to Dewey's article on "Moral Philosophy" in *Johnson's Universal Cyclopaedia* (1894, EW 4: 140–41). Dewey says: "The Latin influence furnished no new ethical analysis. It supplied neither a new idea of the supreme good, nor a further demand for personal righteousness. What it did afford was a vast and coherent system of practical means for realizing the ideal elsewhere developed." (1932, LW 7: 125.)
29. 1908, MW 5: 135.
30. 1902, MW 2: 39–52.
31. Ibid., 41.
32. 1916–1917, MW 10: 234–43.
33. Ibid., 235.
34. Ibid., 238.
35. Ibid., 243.
36. "Chinese National Sentiment," 1918–1919, MW 11: 214–27.
37. Ibid., 220.
38. Ibid., 215.
39. "What holds China back?" 1920, MW 12: 51–54.
40. Ibid., 52.
41. John Dewey and Alice Chipman Dewey, *Letters from China and Japan*, ed. Evelyn Dewey (New York: Dutton, 1920), 308.
42. "As the Chinese Think," (1922), 1921–1922, MW 13: 217–27.
43. Ibid., 223.

44. 1921, MW 13: 93–107.
45. Ibid., 94.
46. Ibid., 104.
47. "Leningrad Gives the Clue," 1928, LW 3: 204.
48. Ibid., 204.
49. Ibid., 205.
50. LW 2: 202.
51. Ibid., 204.
52. 1924, MW 15: 134–35.
53. 1894, EW 4: 96–105.
54. Ibid., 97.
55. Ibid.
56. Ibid., 103.
57. Ibid., 104.
58. "Educational Principles Underlying Education," 1897, EW 5: 54–83.
59. Ibid., 70.
60. 1907, MW 4: 229–41.
61. Ibid., 229.
62. Ibid., 240.
63. 1908, MW 4: 125–42.
64. Ibid., 127.
65. Ibid., 129.
66. Ibid., 130.
67. Ibid., 138.
68. 1927–1928, LW 3: 3–10.
69. Ibid., 8.
70. Ibid., 6.
71. *The Quest for Certainty*, 1929, LW 4: 225.
72. *The Public and Its Problems*, 1927, LW 2: 333.
73. Ibid., 326.
74. 1929–1930, LW 5: 98.

9

From Reason to Intelligence

Since reflective thought is the counterpart of habit, one might have thought that reason would have a prominent place in the *Ethics*. Perhaps this tends to be assumed because Reason (now capitalized) has had so prominent a role in ethics from the seventeenth century on: first in rationalism, then in battles with feeling or sentiment, then in Kantian practical reason, then in Hegelian identification with God and the march of history, then as the essential characteristic of the human. Its role has varied from the intuitive-axiomatic to the swashbuckling. In the twentieth century it has been the target of attack, particularly in psychological and social analysis. Psychoanalysis strengthened the concept of "rationalizing" and social theory fashioned that of "ideology". But at the same time such ideas could be used to distinguish a purer reasoning from pseudo-forms. Indeed psychoanalytic theory in its accounts of the growth of the ego and of the superego made it possible to think of multiple and varied functions that had hitherto been bundled under the single concept of reason.

The approach through multiple functions is the readiest one for tracing the place of reason in *08*. It is a fairly simple story. At the outset there is the notion of thought and reflective thought, taken in an ordinary commonsensical way. In viewing the moral as growth there are the stages of the rationalizing process, the socializing process, and the full development of moral conduct. One may be tempted in the light of Jamesian and Deweyan psychology, to think of so early a rationalizing process as the conceptualizing of the world and making an order of things and processes. Here the rationalizing process is simply the greater use of intelligence to satisfy basic needs and impulses. "It will show itself in skilled occupations, in industry and trade, in the utilizing of all resources to further man's power and happiness."[1] Later, work, arts and crafts, and even war are seen as rationalizing agencies. (War vanishes from this list in 32 presumably because World War I has shown that war no longer delivers the appropriate virtues.) The rationalizing process is thus simply thinking that is necessitated in the rough and tumble of needs and impulses because they are automatically satisfied without developing forms of activity and association. Of course the traditional idea of a Platonic reason that opposes passion is recognized[3]; but, as we have seen, this conception of an independent rationality is not even considered. The real basis of all concepts of rationality is the need for a position of control for which competing ends in human life are projected.[4] "The distinctively moral situation is then one in which elements of value and control are bound up with the processes of deliberation and desire; and are bound up in a peculiar way: *viz.*, they decide what kind of a character shall control further desires and deliberations. When ends are genuinely incompatible, no common denominator can be found except by deciding what sort of character is most highly prized and shall be given supremacy."[5] The theory of reason is thus channelled through the theory of the good and self-realization or character formation.

The career of reason is traced through the development of practical problems and the emergence of consequent ideas. Thus the complexity of the Roman Empire with its requirement of codification and administration makes the problem of control dominate that of value and the good, and a jural ethics is strengthened.[6] The intellectual outcome, from both this and the medieval developments of Christian theology, is the moral theory of natural law. "From the laws of reason, regarded as the laws of man's generic and hence sociable nature, all the principles of jurisprudence and of individual morals may be deduced."[7] Reason here battles against man's sensuous nature. Thus, as we have seen, emerges the ethical theory that, instead of seeing law as an instrument for the good, sees the good as depending on the law and expressing what the law prescribes.[8] In the chapter (16) on "The Place of Reason in the Moral Life: Moral Knowledge" discussion leads inevitably to the conflict of reason and desire and to Kantian theory. "Reason which promulgates ends must be of a different sort from the intelligence which simply searches for means." Dewey, of course, carries through a familiar critique of the Kantian doctrine that so sharply separates the moral end from the technological means, and that equates reason with the provision of formal rules or laws; he finds the surreptitious rational end of the scheme to be simply the social good. Hence Kant's theory of reason has to be transformed. In the remainder of the chapter Dewey considers reason as applied to a particular situation, and carries out a critique of intuitionist ideas of direct perception, of moral sense, and of reliance on rules.

In the theory of the virtues, instead of reason we find wisdom: "the heart of a voluntary act is its intelligent or deliberate character. The individual's *intelligent* concern for the good is implied in his sincerity, his faithfulness, and his integrity.[10] There is even a certain assimilation of Greek wisdom and modern conscientiousness: "'Wisdom 'ended to emphasize achieved insight; knowledge which was proved, guaranteed, and unchangeable. 'Conscientiousness' tends rather to fix attention upon that voluntary attitude which is interested in *discovery*."[11] With the growth of the habit of reflection, to be thoughtful and serious-minded become major character values.[12] Conscientiousness takes increasingly the form of interest in improvement and progress.[13]

Throughout, it is clear, reason in *08* is low-keyed in its operation. It is not a peremptorily prescriptive super-ego, not an isolated and commanding power. It is simply the expression of the needs that stem from conflict and complexity for patterns of control in a changing world, to be worked out with appropriate tentativeness for subsequent experience.

In *32* there are no basic changes in the conception of reason, only perhaps a greater explicitness in its alignment with intelligence and reflective morality. The sensitive point, we expect, is the way reason is to be aligned with the new conception of right as stemming from an independent factor, a separate root in the interrelations of people; this major development was explored in an earlier chapter. Dewey does speak of the new element that the right introduces, that of exaction or demand. And he says: "There has to be an idea of the authoritative claim of what is reasonable in order to convert the Good into the Right."[14] But recognition of this as a conversion process simply invites an understanding of how reflection, given the social nature of the human being and the permeating role of interpersonal relations, can make the move from what attracts to what obliges. As in *08*, Dewey criticizes the jural and Kantian transformation of reason into a force hostile to natural ends and feelings. We have already seen how far

Dewey, in his complex relation of the right and the good, carries out his promise to show that "it is possible to maintain the distinctness of the concept of right without separating it from the ends and the values which spring from those desires and affections that belong inherently to human nature."[15]

In a similar way, the recognition of the third independent factor of affective appreciation does not establish a separate kind of reason. The content of virtue is still at any time allied to the customary and in greater or less degree lagging behind the standard that a reflective morality would set. "Reflective morality instead of leaving praise and blame where they were except for putting under them a rational basis tends to shift the emphasis to scrutiny of conduct in an objective way, that is with reference to its causes and results. What is desirable is that a person shall see for himself what he is doing and why he is doing it; shall be sensitive to results in fact and in anticipation, and shall be able to analyze the forces which make him act as he does."[16] Thus approval and disapproval are brought under a standard and not left as ultimate. The use of praise and blame itself becomes directed and judged for its goodness or badness.

The chapter (in *32*) on "Moral Judgment and Knowledge" is consequently much richer and more thoughtful than that in *08* on "The Place of Reason in the Moral Life: Moral Knowledge". The latter is still overshadowed by the conflict of reason and desire. In *32*, however, focus is on the general place of reflection in the affective responses of human beings. Intelligence reshapes and reconstructs, it enlightens and enriches; it does not supplant. Thought and knowledge are not "mere servants and attendants of emotion" (the obvious echo of Hume's reason as the slave of the passions); they exercise "a positive and transforming influence."[17] Immediacy in all its forms in the expression of the three roots can be modified by the critical and constructive work of thought. This holds for prizing or the sense of value, for conscience and the sense of obligation, and for appreciation and the impulse to praise and blame

In understanding Dewey's ethics the recognition of a continuity, even a constancy, between *08* and *32* is as significant as the discovery of a difference. The interpretation of reason as the office of intelligence is such a fundamental constancy, only rendered more explicit in the later work. It remains here only to look back before *08* as well as note the intervening contexts between 1908 and 1932 in which Dewey and Tufts moved from a variegated set of rational functions to a highly integrated theory of intelligence, and how they differentiated it from traditional conceptions.

The backward turn invites a glance into the *Syllabus* (1894). It shows, with almost stark simplicity, the continuity of reflection with the initial mediation of impulse. The impulse is checked or arrested, and action delayed; the impulse is thus brought into relation with other impulses, habits and experiences.[18] As reflective ideas determine the conditions of expression of the impulse they have the character of controlling power. Dewey even speaks of an intention as "*reflection, or the control of the impulse by reason*" in so far as it shows the impulse to be mediated.[19] In the contention of the natural satisfaction (the thought of the course that would be taken by the unmediated impulse) and the rational, or mediated satisfaction, deliberation takes place, and eventually decision. The whole root of rationality is thus the envisaging of consequences taking shape as mediated impulse.

From the standpoint of both psychology and education, Dewey devoted ample attention to the manifold powers of thought. In the *Syllabus* he had cast a longing glance at the Greek conception of intellectual virtues, and cited "continuity of thought, power of concentration, clear-sightedness, sincerity", as all particular forms assumed by conscientiousness.[20] And *How We Think*[21] was the beginning of systematic works in the nature, psychology, and structure of thinking, to be amplified in the 1933 edition and to lead into *Logic: The Theory of Inquiry* in 1938. What we may expect, therefore, is a continually more systematic picture of reason, blossoming as intelligence. The entry on "Control" in the *Cyclopedia of Education*[22] looks on mental powers as methods of control, with the senses operating as more direct means (touch the most immediate), and thinking, with language as an instrument, being indirect forms. At the same time Dewey was increasingly turning to the history of epistemology for the analysis of experience, the kinds of categories that produced order in it and the varieties of interpretation involved. (Cf. the entry on "Experience and the Empirical" in the *Cyclopedia of Education*[23] and *Democracy and Education*.[24]

The period of 1917 to 1919 appears to be the one in which such developments came to a head, and both Tufts and Dewey make specific distinctions between reason and intelligence and become explicit on the grounds for the wider concept. In his "The Moral Life and the

Construction of Values and Standards" in *Creative Intelligence* (1917), Tufts has as one of several topics "intelligence and reason, through which experience is interrelated, viewed as a whole, enlarged in imagination."[25] In the actual discussion of this[26] he lists different aspects and components of thought that, he decides explicitly, had better be termed "intelligence" than "reason". In morals, both imply considering a proposed or performed act as a whole, in its relations, and with a view especially to consequences; and this involves not only empirical observation on past experience, already formulated concepts, and deduction, but "that rarer quality which in the presence of a situation discerns a meaning not obvious, suggests an idea, 'injustice,' to interpret the situation."[27] There is thus a synthetic or creative element involved as well as analysis, that goes beyond the narrower sense of reasoning and includes imagination and feeling. Even more, there has to be consideration also of other possible acts and their consequences. "To bring several ends into the field of consideration is the characteristic of the intelligent, or as we often say, the open-minded man. Such consideration as this widens the capacity of the agent and marks him off from the creature of habit, of prejudice, or of instinct."[28] Tufts goes on to include under intelligence taking into account how an act will affect others, and also how others will look at it. Such intelligent activity is rooted in social intercourse, and we show this by thinking of a person as stupid who will not take account of the other's point of view. It is also, he admits, part of our understanding of being "reasonable".

Two grounds are given for the preference of "intelligence" over "reason". One is that it does not commit us to a specific doctrine concerning the source of our judgments. Tufts seems to be saying that it is less captured by an already predetermined theoretical approach. Another ground is that "intelligence" points more readily to the constructive and creative efforts toward "enlarged education, new sources of interest, and more open fields for development"[29], whereas "reason" in Stoic and Kantian doctrine has been used for control of the passions by law. He does acknowledge the historical services of reason in the growth of invention and scientific method. All in all, then, Tufts' terminological preference is itself an historical act in the light of the intellectual and practical problems of ethics at that period.

Dewey's systematization of the topic is evident in his preparation for the lectures in Japan that became *Reconstruction in Philosophy*.

The outline, "Dewey's Lectures in Japan", appears in Notes and News, in the *Journal of Philosophy*, XV, no. 10: 253-58, May 9, 1918. Lecture 5 is entitled "The Changed Conception of Experience and Reason."[30] It retraces old ground about how experience which in ancient times meant an accumulation and gradual organization, yielding a practical insight like that of the builder and physician, became under British sensationalist psychology a tool for skeptical criticism rather than construction. Reason was for the ancients a faculty of insight into universals, laws, and principles; for Kant it was a faculty of organizing the chaotic details of experience. But modern psychology, under biological influence, brought out the active and motor factors in experience. Experimental method then emphasized projection and invention rather than accumulation from the past. At this point[31] we have the critical statement: "Reason thus becomes Intelligence—the power of using past experience to shape and transform future experience. It is constructive and creative." Hence the shift from Reason to Intelligence is not simply a verbal shift, nor the discovery of a fresh faculty; it is a philosophic turn to pragmatism, resting on a new psychology.

Reconstruction in Philosophy[32] spells this out in detail. As against ancient teleology, intelligence is regarded "not as the original shaper and final cause of things, but as the purposeful energetic re-shaper of those phases of nature and life that obstruct social well-being";[33] "initiative, inventiveness and intelligently directed labor" are involved for re-creating the world. Since we use our past experience to construct new and better ones, "Science, 'reason', is not therefore something laid from above upon experience. Suggested and tested in experience, it is also employed through inventions in a thousand ways to expand and enrich experience."[34] The conception of reason as a separate faculty from experience is thus unnecessary. "Concrete suggestions arising from past experiences, developed and matured in the light of the needs and deficiencies of the present, employed as aims and methods of specific reconstruction, and tested by success or failure in accomplishing this task of readjustment, suffice. To such empirical suggestions used in constructive fashion for new ends the name intelligence is given."[35] The concept of intelligence thus fashioned begins to affect other ideas. For example, it makes its way into "freedom" which, of course, already had historic ties to reason: "All intelligent thinking means an increment of freedom in action—an emancipation from chance and fatality."[36]

The fuller depiction of intelligence comes, as we have already seen in discussing habit, in *Human Nature and Conduct*.[37] The discussion of habit gave the death-blow to the ordinary assumption that intelligence and habit are opponents. Instead there are both intelligent habits and unintelligent habits, and intelligence itself is a multitude of habits of inquiry, with all the human faculties involved, shaped into an habitual method. Dewey even speaks of reason as signifying "the happy cooperation of a multitude of dispositions, such as sympathy, curiosity, exploration, experimentation, frankness, pursuit—to follow things through—circumspection, to look about at the context, etc. etc."[38] With the flowering of "intelligence" Dewey can thus be generous to the old concept of "reason" whenever he rescues it from older strait-jackets.

Finally, *The Quest for Certainty*[39] is a whole book devoted to intelligence and the life of intelligence, set in contrast with the search for immutable and authoritative truth, the chief philosophic aberration. A brief paper on "Fundamentals", published in *The New Republic*, February 6, 1924[40] strikes a good anticipatory keynote. It is obviously addressed, as a preceding paper on "The American Intellectual Frontier" in *The New Republic* of May 10, 1922[41] had been, to the Scopes case and William Jennings Bryan's attack on teaching evolution. Dewey notes the craving for the unshakeable, but he objects to regarding the anti-evolutionary camp as "fundamentalists". The contrast is rather between modernists and traditionalists, the latter being literalists in their biblical interpretation. "Those traditionalists and literalists who have arrogated to themselves the title of fundamentalists recognize of course no mean between their dogmas and blank, dark, hopeless uncertainty and unsettlement. Until they have been reborn into the life of intelligence, they will not be aware that there are a steadily increasing number of persons who find security in *methods* of inquiry, of observation, of experiment, of forming and following working hypotheses. Such persons are not unsettled by the upsetting of any special belief, because they retain security of procedure. They can say, borrowing language from another context, though this method slay my most cherished belief, yet will I trust it."[42]

The Quest for Certainty integrates the various themes we have examined in different contexts from the previous works. It studies the operation of ideas, the method of inquiry, the continuity of mind with nature and its fermenting as well as its reconstructive work, the philosophic history of the search for the immutable and how the growth of physical science had a reconstructive effect on philosophic thought, and so on. By 1932, it was no longer necessary to argue the case. With only an occasional replay of the long struggle, the lessons of the movement from reason to intelligence can be taken for granted, and the integrated character of intelligence makes its appearance where relevant in *32* without fanfare.

Notes

1. 1908, MW 5: 15.
2. Ibid., 43–45.
3. Ibid., 123–24.
4. Ibid., 193.
5. Ibid., 195.
6. Ibid., 202.
7. Ibid., 205.
8. Ibid., 214.
9. Ibid., 281.
10. Ibid., 375.
11. Ibid., 376.
12. Ibid., 377.
13. Ibid., 379.
14. 1932, LW 7: 216.
15. Ibid., 217.
16. Ibid., 254.
17. Ibid., 263.
18. 1893–1894, EW 4: 244–45.
19. Ibid., 251.
20. *Syllabus:* 355.
21. *How We Think*, 1910, MW 6: 177–356.
22. 1911, MW 6: 393–95.
23. Ibid., 445–51.
24. 1916, MW 9: chapters 11 and 22.
25. Tufts in *Creative Intelligence*, 1917: 358.
26. Ibid., 363–67.
27. Ibid., 364.
28. Ibid., 364–65.
29. Ibid., 366.
30. Dewey, 1918, MW 11: 345–46.
31. Ibid., 346.
32. 1920, MW 12.
33. Ibid., 108.
34. Ibid., 134.
35. Ibid.
36. Ibid., 163.
37. Dewey, *Human Nature and Conduct,* 1922, Part III.

38. Ibid., 136.
39. 1929, LW 4.
40. *The New Republic*, February 6, 1924, MW 15: 3–7.
41. *The New Republic*, May 10, 1922, MW 13: 301–05.
42. 1923–1924, MW 15: 7.

10

The Leaven of Voluntariness

Our subject in this chapter is the familiar and respectable philosophical issue of freedom and responsibility. We have already seen in chapter 3 that the place given the idea of freedom in the *Syllabus* of 1894 is modified in *08* and drastically altered in *32*, and that these changes affect the theory of virtue. But now we have to examine the entire scope of the changes, and to do this carries us even back of the *Syllabus* to the *Outlines* of 1891. The reason for this extended view is that the partial changes of *08* and the final outcome of *32* are part of a general shift, and the parts can best be understood in terms of the total direction. The movement as a whole may be characterized as a pragmatic shift in the theory of freedom and responsibility.

Let us be clear at the outset what is meant by a pragmatic shift. In an obvious sense it is the familiar procedure of understanding an idea in terms of its experiential consequences rather than through an antecedently assigned content. And since consequences are what follow, we do not go too far astray by seeing it as a future-oriented attitude; even logical consequences point to the future experience of results indicated even though they may describe a present and contemporaneous state. But to speak of a future orientation may itself be misleading if it ignores the vital reality of the present. Indeed Dewey constantly interprets envisaged consequences as broadening the meaning of the present by showing significant relations in the present between things and persons, in the self and the environment. And, as we have seen, a similar view holds for the historical reconstruction of the past: its function, as seen in Dewey's educational advice, is to enlighten the present by revealing its significant relations and processes.

187

Now in the traditional relation of freedom and responsibility, freedom is the prior notion characterizing the agent in his action; responsibility is a consequence of freedom. The pragmatic shift is toward finding the meaning of freedom in the phenomena of responsibility, its own conditions and consequences. In a sense, freedom becomes the end to be achieved through judgments of responsibility, but of course its nature is altered in such reinterpretation. The *Outlines* gives freedom the place of a central idea of ethics, but tied into obligation. The *Syllabus* separates it from obligation and makes it the source of virtue, but of course both obligation and virtue are tied into the good through the theory of the self. *08* develops the theory of virtue in relation to social criteria, and freedom begins to be a consequence of social organization, treated alongside of liability and responsibility. (One looks in vain through the whole chapter on "The Place of the Self in the Moral Life," even the section on self-realization, for some treatment of the problem of freedom.) Finally, in *32*, freedom, together with responsibility, is seen as an instrumental idea in the growth and modification of character. Our task in the present chapter is to trace this historical shift in Dewey's works and its effect on the structure of ethical ideas.

In the *Outlines of a Critical Theory of Ethics*[1] the central ethical notion is that of the good. Only when it has been explored at length (in terms of an expanded utilitarian theory and a critique of the Kantian theory) are we introduced to "two other fundamental ethical conceptions—obligation and freedom."[2] There are two sides to the exercise of function. Obligation relates a man to the social whole. But freedom lies in the realization of the individual. "Obligation thus corresponds to the *social* satisfaction, freedom to the *self*-satisfaction." In the chapter on "The Idea of Freedom" (chapter 3) the problem is set forth as moral capacity, "the ability to conceive of an end and to be governed in action by this conceived end."[3] Negatively, direction by conscious ends emancipates one from subjection to particular impulses. Positively, putting various ends before the self gives freedom of choice. These provide the basis of moral responsibility. Since the end adopted is always what the agent considers good or self-satisfying, it involves the agent's ideal of himself or herself. If in choice one recognizes that he or she could have acted otherwise and that would have been the better choice, freedom is implicitly recognized as the basis of responsibility and approbation or disapprobation. Dewey is not here defending indeterminism as freedom. He takes the choice to issue from the character, so that the recognition of responsibility may be at the same time self-condemnation. To say I could have acted otherwise in such case is to seek the modification of character. While all moral action is the expression of self, the self is not fixed. "It includes as a necessary part of itself the possibility of framing conceptions of what it would be, and there is, therefore, at any time the possibility of acting upon some ideal hitherto unrealized."[4] Dewey concludes that only the good person is therefore free in the positive sense of the term, one who is truly realizing individuality.[5] Freedom is concretized in the rights and powers of action one gets in the community.[6] Finally, the virtues are seen as realized morality, and they may be understood as forms of freedom. "A virtue is any one aspect which the free performance of function may take."[7] These are forms of adjusting capacity to surroundings, realized activity as full and unhindered performance of function being the good.

All this is a sufficiently familiar doctrine of a self-realizationist ethic, and we have seen (in our chapter 3) how Dewey came to critical grips with Green's self-realization view in articles in 1892 and 1893. Our point in summarizing the treatment of freedom in the *Outlines* is simply to be able to see how the departures moved from it. It is also worth noting, before moving to the *Syllabus*, that in a paper in 1894 Dewey tried to come to grips with the indeterminist notion of freedom that he had thrust aside. In "The Ego as Cause" (May 1894)[8], he is denying the role of the ego as a separate efficient agent in causation. Taking for granted the psychological description of conflict of desires, interest in competing ends, and deliberation, no outside faculty is required. If we take the consciousness that we could have acted otherwise to prove freedom, it is only because we equate freedom with the presence of alternative ends in consciousness and the consequent deliberation. Much of the objection to determinism, he suggests, comes from looking for a cause of volition, in the sense of efficient agency; but Dewey denies that this is a scientific notion. What it should designate is "analyzing the vague undefined datum of a volition into a group of specific and concrete conditions, that is, factors."[9]

The *Syllabus*[10] like the *Outlines* is self-realizationist and gives the ethical notion of the good the central position, though with a broadened vocabulary (it speaks of the moral categories of Satisfaction, Good, Value). It also retains the two-phase view of conduct—*right* as affording satisfaction and fulfilling organic connections and the agent which it expresses being *free*. But a small step is taken in distinguishing as three main sets of ethical ideas "those centering, respectively, about (a) the *Value*, (b) the *Control*, (c) the *Freedom* of conduct."[11] This is apparently the first step toward a three-family view of moral concepts, though it was a long time before the second and third achieved full independence, if in fact they did fully. We need here only recall that freedom in the *Syllabus* plays a kind of synthetic role with respect to good and obligation. The agent in his discernment of value sets his ends, and in his obligations finds his communal relations. If he is a morally mature character, his interaction with environment and others is morally internalized. Hence moral conduct is to be seen as full self-expression. "Impulse is self, the developing ideal is self; the reaction of the ideal as measuring and controlling impulse is self. The entire voluntary process is one of self-expression, of coming to consciousness of self. This intimate and thorough-going *selfness* of the deed constitutes freedom."[12] And again, "This same identity of self and deed is, of course, the basis of responsibility. We are responsible for our deeds because they are ourselves . . . I am myself, I am conscious of myself in my deeds (self-conscious), I am responsible, name not three facts, but one fact."[13]

It is worth recalling too that in the *Syllabus* the analysis of virtue is wholly tied to freedom, as indeed it was in the *Outlines*. "Virtue may be considered either as a case of substantial freedom, of solid, thoroughly unified action, or as a case of substantial responsibility, of flexible, properly adjusted interaction—the adequate intellectual recognition of, and adequate emotional interest in, the demands of the situation."[14] "Freedom, again, names virtue from the standpoint of good, of value; responsibility from the standpoint of duty."[15]

08 does not announce a dramatic change in the idea of freedom. Rather it ignores it, almost as if having equated freedom with the phenomena of alternative ends entertained, deliberation and decision, it could deal with these phenomena themselves and not worry about the conceptual unification. Doubtless there are surrogates for the problem of wholeness of action. The self is as prominent as it was before in the formulation of ethical problems, character stands out as central, and perhaps individualism with its increasing scope of decision begins to bear the burden of maturing freedom. But this is not explicitly related to the older problem of freedom. Even virtue, that has hitherto rested on freedom, is turned in another direction. As we have seen, virtues are now defined in terms of traits of character that sustain the common good. The net result is therefore that the question seems to be changing its character, so that the old answers are no longer relevant.

The actual discussion of freedom and responsibility, when it comes, is in a significantly different place. It is not in discussing the place of the self in the moral life[16], but in "Social Organization and the Individual".[17] Here freedom and responsibility are discussed together, somewhat hastily, but with a few distinctions. Both are recognized to be greater in a comprehensive and diversified social organization. Liability as a phenomenon reminds the individual that others are concerned with his actions and will react to them; this is the negative side of responsibility. The positive side is the individual's awareness of the justice of the community's interest in his performance, so that he holds himself responsible for his acts. Similarly, negative freedom is the freedom from subjection to others' will, while effective freedom involves control of required resources and appropriate training. The same holds for intellectual powers and powers of self-control. Further discussion of rights and freedoms are cast more in the context of what social philosophy generally thinks of as liberties. The general theoretical conclusion would thus seem to be that the structure of the freedom idea is to be found in the social context and the context of human deliberation rather than in any underlying single central concept.

That this roughly represents the state of Dewey's thought in this period may be seen from his entry on "Freedom of the Will" in the *Encyclopedia of Education*.[18] The problem, Dewey says, "has become so encumbered with the refuse and débris of all kinds of other matters as to be best 'solved' by letting alone."[19] And he lists the items of the débris, that come from theology, metaphysics, law, psychology, etc. Fortunately, he says, none of these affect educational questions. He then lists the items of an educational consensus. In effect he is presenting the elements whose diverse interpretations constitute alleged answers to the free will problem. Only the first item is argumentative: freedom of will in the sense of motiveless choice is unimportant for education since the latter works on the formation of character, valuable and stable ends and effective motives; hence such freedom with its arbitrariness would have to be counteracted in education. The items that are more directly a matter of observation are: the native plasticity of the self as a tendency to growth, variation, readjustment of habit; preferential or selective activity, which is a mark of all organic activity; reflection and the weighing of alternatives. The educator is then enjoined to keep alive plasticity and its properties, preventing fossilized fixation; strengthen constructive preferences and interests; make preferences *reasonable* by developing habits of forecasting consequences of acting on given preferential tendencies, of comparing results, and so enlightening preferences about their deeper nature. It is worth noting that in his earlier entry on "determinism" Dewey had listed some facts relieving the educator of embarrassment in connection with controversies over determinism *vs.* indeterminism, especially the plasticity, or modifiability of disposition and character. He also called attention to the way reflection and deliberation emancipate the agent from "servility to blind impulse and chance circumstances", as well as the role of well-formed habits.

The culmination of the exploration of freedom in the educational arena is, of course, in *Democracy and Education*.[20] Here a whole array of concepts serves as the vehicle for dealing with aims and tasks of education: adaptation, adjustment, growth, direction, as well as development, habit, tradition. For example, adaptation and adjustment came to the fore in the evolutionary accounts of the struggle for existence and descriptions of the survival of the fittest, and have often served as the "essence" of education. They are often treated as if they were neutral scientific concepts and this gives rise to the charge that Dewey's use of them fails to distinguish factual from value uses. (The argument is sometime dismissed with a triumphant illustration that cancers too grow and so growth cannot be an aim of education.) But in fact Dewey is careful to point out the different modes in each of the processes that the concepts indicate. Already in the *Cyclopedia of Education* in 1911 he had done this for "Adaptation" and "Adjustment".[21] Adaptation is such as to be of two kinds, passive and active, differing in degree, not in kind. Spencer had stressed the first and education as adaptation was seen as molding the passive organism to a static environment, thus making the accommodation of individuals to existing polity and customs central. Dewey regards this as a perversion, for education is rather a matter of control that is subordinating the environment to the life functions of the individual. Similarly, adjustment is interpreted wrongly as education leading to class education, fitting individuals to predetermined social positions. These points are made again in *Democracy and Education*[22] in the chapter (4) on Education as Growth. Adjustment to environment should not be taken as wax conforming to the seal impressed upon it, but as active control for the achievement of ends.[23] Otherwise this means fitting ourselves to fixed external conditions. Similarly, adaptation can mean tolerance of the conditions and passive acquiescence, but for a more civilized people it can also mean irrigation and scientific agriculture, not just living off chance products of the land.[24] Again, his own identification of developing or growth with life and its establishment as the basic character of the educational enterprise is translated quite specifically into such assertions as that "the educational enterprise has no end beyond itself" and that it is one of "continual reorganizing, reconstructing, transforming."[25] And the latter, we have seen sufficiently, is his basic characterization of the life process.

Dewey's complex sensitivity to the finer shades in the use of such concepts is perhaps best shown in his remarks about the meaning of "direction," "control," and "guidance" in the chapter (3) on Education as Direction. The passage is worth quoting:[26]

> "Of these three words, direction, control, and guidance, the last best conveys the idea of assisting through cooperation the natural capacities of the individuals guided; control conveys rather the notion of an energy brought to bear from without and meeting some resistance from the one controlled; direction is a more neutral term and suggests the fact that the active tendencies of those directed are led in a certain continuous course, instead of dispersing aimlessly. Direction expresses the basic function, which tends at one extreme to become a guiding assistance and at another, a regulation or ruling."

The discussion that follows shows the clear recognition that when we are analyzing the meaning of such terms we are dealing also with the underlying psychology of human beings, the desirable character of interpersonal relations and the modes of relation they call for.

For the study of education such analyses become translated into proposed answers to questions about teaching as against indoctrination, the appropriate forms of discipline, the relation of work and play, the kind of curriculum that will best release and develop the active powers of individuals. Our interest, however, is in following the general theory of freedom and responsibility for which Dewey already had mapped the elements in the *Cyclopedia* article. We might have thought that after the fullness of its exploration in the educational context Dewey would have moved into the general philosophical arena. But in fact he does not treat the matter outside of *any* context; this would be contrary to his metaphysical approach in which categories are intellectual instruments for use in a diversity of fields. Even in *Reconstruction in Philosophy*[27], whose scope might have admitted a full-fledged theory of freedom and responsibility, we find only three brief points. Two, referring to freedom, are long familiar: that intelligent thinking adds an increment of freedom in action in that it emancipates from chance and fatality[28], and that freedom for the individual means growth, ready change when modification is required.[29] The point on responsibility is of greater significance: to recognize the uniqueness of every moral situation does not destroy responsibility but rather locates it, since it transfers the burden of morality to intelligence.[30] It involves a recognition of the pragmatic shift that will be the central point of the developed theory.

That shift becomes explicit as Dewey moves on to the arena of social psychology, in *Human Nature and Conduct* (1922).[31] It is significant that Dewey concludes Part III, which is on intelligence, with a chapter (9) on "Present and Future." It is the lesson we noted as characteristic of the pragmatic shift. The emphasis on consequences is not intended to make the present instrumental to the future. We do not really know how much of the future can be anticipated, and often our best laid plans have to undergo change, if only through chance factors. What envisaging future consequences does is to deepen the meaning of relations in the present. This is particularly pertinent to understanding Dewey's brief but pregnant discussion of reponsibility.[32] When he says that the reference in blame is *prospective, not retrospective*, it may mislead for it underscores the future reference: "Approbation and disapprobation are ways of influencing the formation of habits and aims; that is, of influencing future acts. The individual is *held* accountable for what he *has* done in order that he may be responsive in what he is *going* to do."[33] This may sound like outside manipulation, at best a craftsman's fashioning of his product. But it has been formulated from only one side of the social interrelations of the human being. Dewey goes on directly: "Gradually persons learn by dramatic imitation to hold themselves accountable, and liability becomes a voluntary deliberative acknowledgment that deeds are our own, that their consequences come from us." So the proper direction of praise or blame is not the effect of an external threat of pleasant or painful consequences, but the learning of the self about its place in a social world. (The chapter is entitled "Morality is social".) And, still from the point of view of the social environment, we have seen long ago that the occasions and modes of praise and blame are themselves subject to evaluation.

Freedom is treated in chapter 3 of that part, entitled "What is Freedom?" Like previous attacks on the issue it has some concern with sidetracking the traditional metaphysical problem and attending rather to human psychological demands in worrying about the issue. Dewey suggests three elements: "(i) It includes efficiency in action, ability to carry out plans, the absence of cramping and thwarting obstacles. (ii) It also includes capacity to vary plans, to change the course of action, to experience novelties. And again (iii) it signifies the power of desire and choice to be factors in events."[34] From this perspective he reckons with social demands for liberty or freedom, and is suspicious of those who glorify only freedom from political and legal repression without attention to conditions of work. The proper relation of freedom and organization is not a matter of abstract principle, but an experimental matter of working out institutions. His objection against those who (presumably the reference is to the Spinozistic-Hegelian tradition about reason) have interpreted freedom as constituted by intelligence, is that they focused on insight into necessity rather than foresight of possibilities.

In sum, the treatment of freedom and responsibility in *Human Nature and Conduct* is toward seeing the operation of these concepts in the social and psychological concerns of people. It has added another perspective to the growing list of contexts from which the problem is being approached, providing an increment of explicitness rather than enunciating a novel doctrine. In the decade of 1922 to 1932 Dewey went on to still further contexts in which he built a wider base of freedom and responsibility. Discussions of social liberty and participation and democracy and individualism, in *The Public and its Problems* (1927) and *Individualism Old and New* (1930), exhibit in the extended field of political and social inquiry the phenomena of plasticity and adaptability, preference and deliberation, and the like, that were long ago laid down as constitutive of freedom. *The Quest for Certainty* (1929), subtitled "A Study of the Relation of Knowledge and Action", is in a sense the growth of the idea of reflective intelligence in the history of philosophy. Even the continuing series of articles during this decade (and controversies entered into long after, whose central focus is in the *Theory of Valuation*, 1939) that we have considered in our chapter on the good above, hammers at the critical-constructive character of judgments of value, as against interpretations that equate value with some already existent phenomenon.

In 1928 Dewey published a paper entitled "Philosophies of Freedom".[35] It is more comprehensively systematic than previous studies, for it attempts to pinpoint the core of the problem of freedom and to relate the different forms in which solutions have been sought. The core, as previously dealt with, is the phenomenon of choice, its significance in human affairs; choice is felt to be freedom itself. It becomes, however, linked to other interests. Praise and blame, reward and punishment, become more important as they are embodied in institutional agencies, and a theory of choice as freedom is elaborated to justify them. Instead of arbitrary freedom Dewey again offers the prospective rather than the retrospective account of responsibility. To hold men responsible may make a difference to their future behavior; we cannot do that to a stone. And in actual practice, we do not do this to infants, idiots, and insane. We begin to do this to a child as he or she grows older, for it will affect further growth. Dewey, however, now moves a step ahead of the merely prospective reference. He recognizes that this could be merely manipulative in ensuring a change of behavior, as in the case of an animal. "The whole story has not then been told. There must be some practical participation from within to make the change that is effected significant in relation to choice and freedom."[36] He goes on to examine choice. It is at least preferential action or selectivity in behavior, but that too is not enough. A human being is complex and preferences reflect a whole life history of the individual in past experiences. There is the possibility of further diversification in behavior—"in short, the distinctive *educability* of men."[37] This alone does not give us everything that makes the change of preference into genuine choice, but it does lead to the conclusion that the formation of a new preference out of a conflict of preference, and not simply one preference outweighing another, is at the heart of choice. And involved in it is the ability to think about the consequences of acting upon the alternative preferences.

In order to develop a comprehensively unified view, Dewey now turns to philosophies of freedom that focus on action rather than choice, on the liberties and freedoms of the political and social and economic arena. This is the arena in which large-scale revolutions have occurred, and progress in freedom advanced. Here Dewey traces the Lockean political sense of freedom as the removal of restrictions on an individual endowed with rights, the economic laissez-faire conception of freedom starting with human wants and the laws of their satisfaction rather than rights, and finally the psychological theories of an original endowment of instincts whose free expression is taken to be the core of freedom (provided that like freedom of others is not interfered with). Dewey recognizes the historical contribution of such views, as he previously did on many occasions; he also offers his familiar criticisms of these kinds of Liberalism. The Lockean view emancipated classes that were in a position to move ahead, not the mass of the people. The laissez-faire approach left the mass of the people at the mercy of the property owners. The free expression view failed to recognize that wants were fashioned by the social institutions and were not merely instinctive. Nevertheless, all of these theories join in presenting the view that freedom lies in the power to act in accordance with choice rather than in choice itself.

The tradition of Spinoza and Hegel is counterposed to the kind of social freedom just considered. Dewey sees it as substituting a philosophy of institutions for one of individual psychological structure. The individual has limited power and limited intellect. Only insofar as he shares the broader power of the whole does he arrive at some measure of freedom. This rests on his intellectual ability and development. "History is the record of the development of freedom through the development of institutions."[38] And thus "Freedom is a growth, an attainment, not an original possession, and it is attained by idealization of institutions and law and the active participation of individuals in their loyal maintenance, not by their abolition or reduction in the interests of personal judgments and wants."[39]

In moving toward a synthesis Dewey points to a connection between choice as freedom and power of action as freedom. "A choice which intelligently manifests individuality enlarges the range of action, and this enlargement in turn confers upon our desires greater insight and foresight, and makes choice more intelligent."[40] Even where the intelligent choice proves a failure, one learns from it as an experiment. Moreover, there are various areas of freedom—family, industry, science, etc.—in which these experiments are taking place. The conclusion Dewey reaches eventually is that "freedom consists in a trend of conduct that causes choices to be more diversified and flexible, more plastic and more cognizant of their own meaning, while it enlarges their range of unimpeded operation."[41] Unlike the liberal theories that define freedom in terms of what is antecedently given, Dewey's view seeks freedom in terms of what we may become. Such a view of freedom is unaffected by a theory of causation. Even if every step of the way were caused, it would still remain that one person's words helped render another persons acts more thoughtful. But capacity to become different is a present capacity, and Dewey recognizes an irreducible individuality that is revealed in what people do. He is moving toward the recognition of effective choice in the macroscopic life of people. He thinks that recent interpretations of science are helpful in looking at scientific laws as dealing with relations of things and not their individuality. And so he thinks the question "Just what *is* intelligent choice and just what does it effect in human life?" can be answered by recognizing that "What men actually cherish under the name of freedom is that power of varied and flexible growth, of change of disposition and character, that springs from intelligent choice, so there is a sound basis for the common-sense practical belief in freedom, although erroneous theories in justification of this belief have often taken an erroneous and even absurd form."[42]

From all this it follows that since thinking is a difficult occupation, it requires careful training and favorable conditions. These include the freedoms of thought and expression and care for the impact of institutions on the encouragement of curiosity and inquiry. "Freedom has too long been thought of as an indeterminate power operating in a closed and ended world. In its reality, freedom is a resolute will operating in a world in some respects indeterminate, because open and moving toward a new future."[43]

The fact that Dewey has by 1928 worked out a general theory of freedom, cast in a historical comparison of theories of the past, makes it likely that no new theory will be found in *32*. What we have is rather a realignment of problem context, keeping an eye on kindred issues and a unified solution. The context is ethics and the shape of morality, not politics or economics primarily. And ethics has continued, as in *08*, to be concerned with the formation of character. While in *08*, the changes in character were set historically in terms of the growth of individualism, in *32* this determinate shape is no longer possible. The theory of freedom and responsibility now finds itself in the last of the chapters of Part II, "The Moral Self" (chapter 15).

To treat of the self at the end of Part II is to tie together the bundle of ethical theory. A self has interests and ideals, recognizes obligations and claims rights, and has standards that include virtues. Dewey here gathers the important issues about the self that have been subject to controversy. He harks back to issues of the unity of self and conduct, the constitutive role of interests in the self, the spurious historical centrality of egoism versus altruism, the centrality of social interest, and finally responsibility and freedom. A few points about the discussions that precede the last show the influence of the kind of analysis that has been growing through the long-run consideration of responsibility and freedom.

In lining up the mistaken dichotomies about the self, such as the separation of means and ends in identifying the self either in terms of consequences or in terms of will and virtue, Dewey reminds us that the self is identified with its acts. This is seen in choice, which is the most characteristic activity of a self.[44] The account of choice embodies the conclusions of the 1928 article: appetite and impulse embody preference or selection, judgment of comparative values and deliberation issue in the new preference which is choice. Such choice both reveals the existing self and forms the future self. "Below the surface, it is a process of discovering what sort of being a person most wants to become."[45] We need not consider again here Dewey's view of motivation beyond reminding ourselves that he takes a motive to be not an external drive to action, but the movement of the self as a whole, which can be looked at in terms of desire and also in terms of the object toward which the movement is directed.

The discussion of egoism and altruism here is an excellent example of how Dewey applies his view of the self. The issue turns out to be not the choice between two motives for action. Neither altruism nor egoism is the natural tendency of human beings. Rather concrete types of selves are developed in relation to the objects at which selves are directed, in effect in response to the kinds of social institutions that shape character. The basic issue is then not whether we think of self or of others in action, but what kind of selves we are developing. Intelligence enters into proper relations with others, as it does into proper development of our own capacities. The furor about altruism in general was a reaction against the acquisitive individualism that hardened in the economic developments of the eighteenth century, with its ruthless effects on large bodies of people. The theory of that time too was individualistic, beginning with an assumption of naturally isolated individuals. Focus on what kind of self is being developed also enables

Dewey to describe the inclusive character of social interest without, as we have seen, making the issue the social versus the individual. Self-realization is not the end, but the growth of the kind of self that embraces "alert, sincere, enduring interests in the objects in which all can share."[46]

The ideas of responsibility and freedom are seen as the culmination of the ethical problems of selfhood. Dewey's treatment here is itself the culmination of his previous analyses. Interestingly, this time he begins directly with responsibility. Approval and disapproval have a prospective rather than a retrospective bearing. The formulation and the illustrative argument are the same as previously, but now directly in terms of learning: a person is held accountable in order that he may learn, in a practical way of remaking the prior self.[47] The theoretical and practical foundations of responsibility are stated explicitly: "the fact that each act tends to *form*, through habit, a self which will perform a certain kind of acts."[48]

That there is responsibility for the use of praise and blame or reward and punishment as modes of helping others learn is also stated explicitly. For example, where punishment produces callousness and subterfuge it is not carrying out the proper function of holding people responsible. "Those who hold others accountable for their conduct are themselves accountable for doing it in such a manner that this responsiveness develops."[49] To be held accountable is a directive force in the growth of the self.

Freedom is now reinterpreted in the same manner as responsibility. It too depends on "the possibility of growth, learning, and modification of character, just as is responsibility."[50] No metaphysical argument for its basis is considered, even for rejection. The appeal is to observed fact about human beings. They learn and they become interested in learning, in developing new attitudes. They can break old habits and fashion new ones. "No argument about causation can affect the fact, verified constantly in experience, that we can and do learn, and that the learning is not limited to acquisition of additional information but extends to remaking old tendencies."[51] A person thus develops different desires and choices, and practical freedom comes when we are aware of this phenomenon and act on it. "In the degree in which we become aware of possibilities of development and actively concerned to keep the avenues of growth open, in the degree in which we fight against induration and fixity, and thereby realize the possibilities of recreation of ourselves, we are actually free."[52] In growth rather than in some ulterior goal lies a new freedom. In the movement of advance there is the experience of freedom.

In this manner *32* dots the i's and crosses the t's of the manuscript about freedom that has been written bit by bit in the almost quarter of a century of travel through the arena of one discipline after another. The voluntariness of action is the present ferment of growth and becoming in the reality that is the present.

Notes

1. 1889–1892, EW 3: 239–388.
2. Ibid., 327.
3. Ibid., 340.
4. Ibid., 343.
5. Ibid., 344.
6. Ibid., 349.
7. Ibid., 383.
8. 1894, EW 4: 91–95.
9. Ibid., 91.
10. EW 4.
11. Ibid., 239.
12. Ibid., 342.
13. Ibid.
14. Ibid., 351.
15. Ibid.
16. 1908, MW 5: chap. 18.
17. Ibid., Part III, chap. 20.
18. 1911, MW 6: 464–66.
19. Ibid., 464.
20. 1916, MW 9.
21. 1911–1912, MW 6: 364–66.
22. 1916, MW 9.
23. Ibid., 49.
24. Ibid., 52.
25. Ibid., 54.
26. Ibid., 28.
27. 1920, MW 12.
28. Ibid., 163.
29. Ibid., 198.
30. Ibid., 173.
31. Dewey, *Human Nature and Conduct*, 1922.
32. Ibid., 216–17.
33. Ibid., 217.
34. Ibid., 209.
35. 1927–1928, LW 3: 92–114.
36. Ibid., 94–95.

37. Ibid., 96.
38. Ibid., 103.
39. Ibid.
40. Ibid., 104.
41. Ibid., 108.
42. Ibid., 111.
43. Ibid., 114.
44. 1932, LW 7: 286.
45. Ibid., 287.
46. Ibid., 302.
47. Ibid., 303.
48. Ibid., 304.
49. Ibid., 304–05.
50. Ibid., 305.
51. Ibid., 306.
52. Ibid.

11

Some Concluding Ideas

The topics to be considered in this concluding chapter are:

(1) The difference (and possible conflict) between *analytic* and *genetic* method;
(2) Dewey after the *Ethics*;
(3) Attitudes to Dewey's work during the twentieth century.

1. Analytic and Genetic Methods

Both these methods have had a somewhat turbulent history in twentieth century philosophy. No one would deny an important place to analysis as a philosophic method. Differences arose about its scope and relation to other methods, and about its application to different fields such as science, history, art, morals, etc. Its place in mathematics was ensured early in the century in the works of Russell and Whitehead, in their *Principia Mathematica*. But its place in other fields—in metaphysics, religion, politics, aesthetics—then became the subject of intense controversy.

In the 1930s and 1940s a philosophical movement labeled "logical positivism" swept in a hurricane fashion through British and American philosophy. Philosophers like Carnap, Neurath, and Reichenbach on the European continent, and A.J. Ayer and J.L. Austin in England, expounded analysis of a specific sort. Logical and mathematical propositions were *analytic*, that is, their truth or falsity could be determined from their meaning alone. For example, the truth of 2+2=4 could be determined for the definition of 2 as 1+1, so that 2+2 became 1+1+1+1, and 4 yielded the same result when spelled out. Hence mathematical propositions were tautologies. Statements of fact were *synthetic*, and could be established as true or false in a scientific manner which relied on sense experience. The most esoteric scientific theory rested ultimately on sensory verification. Their crucial step was to identify the meaning of all factual statements with their mode of such verification. The question then arose about the status of other kinds of presumed knowledge—historical, moral, religious, aesthetic. The answer was blunt and peremptory: if they are capable of sensory verification they are factual; if not, they are pseudo-propositions. For example, to say "Candy is good" was just a way of uttering "yum-yum." "John is a good man" could be regarded as factual if it meant "I like him", but often it was simply a grunt of approval. The positivists found most alleged value propositions to be just expressions of emotion in factual disguise. Ayer translated "Lying is wrong" into "Lying!", where the exclamation mark symbolized an expression of horror.

With the rise of Hitler to power in the 1930s, most of the logical positivists came to America. Some of them taught at the New School for Social Research in New York and others went to the West Coast. Ayer came for a year to New York and taught at the City College of New York in 1960, taking the place of the present writer who was on sabbatical leave for a year. The students at the college refused to accept his view that political arguments (about the public good) had no objective validity. They argued that some of them were better than others as a matter of fact, not of party prejudice.

Other positivists, or (as they came to be called) logical empiricists, got teaching positions in various parts of the country. However, they felt that there was a definite unity in their philosophical approach, the combination of logic and experience to yield knowledge, and tried to organize an encyclopedia to give expression to their philosophical outlook. It was called the *International Encyclopedia of Unified Science* and was directed against the separatism in American science. They hoped to get a specialist in each scientific field to do a study in his or her field that scientists in other fields could understand. Dewey was invited to take part. At first he refused, because he thought they took the narrow view of Ayer about ethics being merely expressive. But once he was assured that they were open-minded and were inviting philosophers with different views to enter the project, he consented and wrote the volume entitled *Theory of Valuation*. The present writer was invited to do the last volume on the theory of aesthetics, but refused on the ground that aesthetics was not his specialty. He was then invited to do a volume on ethics. The result was his *Science and the Structure of Ethics* which appeared in 1961. In 1998 it was republished as an independent volume by Transaction Publishers with a new introduction by Irving Louis Horowitz.

In his *Theory of Valuation* Dewey concluded that values are empirically observable forms of behavior. They rest on desires, which arise only when there is something a person finds lacking in his or her situation; the person assumes that providing it will relieve the want and bring satisfaction. A desire thus embodies an empirical hypothesis which is testable and may be correct or incorrect. There is accordingly no separation of the appetitive or the desiderative and the factual, as positivism had claimed. A philosophic study of these problems is not merely analytic; it has to develop genetic methods for studying the relation of desires to needs and wants, and practical methods for dealing with them.

The knowledge this requires is deep and vast. In March of 1908, shortly before the Dewey and Tufts *Ethics* appeared, Dewey gave a lecture at Columbia University entitled "Intelligence and Morals."[1] His conclusion is "that there is no separate body of moral rules; no separate system of motive powers; no separate subject-matter of moral knowledge, and hence no such thing as an isolated ethical science."[2] He calls for the use of philosophy, anthropology, and psychology to discover man's powers and propensities. The business of ethics is "to converge all the instrumentalities of the social sciences, of law, education, economics and political science upon the construction of intelligent methods of improving the common lot."

Dewey was quite aware of the fact that the pragmatic approach was a new method of acquiring knowledge for advancing human welfare. One of the most fundamental issues in the history of philosophy has been the character of human knowledge. Ancient Greek philosophy gave varying accounts of universals and particulars: some analyzed the former into the latter, while others saw particulars as matter taking on specific form. Later subjectivist philosophies in the western world looked to mind and its ideas to give an account of knowledge. Pragmatism broke with this whole tradition. It saw knowledge neither as a set of universals grasped by the mind nor as a set of particulars grasped by the senses. Moreover, it denied the existence of a special moral sense to do the grasping of moral answers as the eye grasps shapes and hand distinguishes hard from soft. Those bodily and sensory phenomena or activities doubtless play a part in the processes of knowing. But knowledge takes place in a context of action: it is geared to action and is accepted as knowledge to the degree that it helps steer action that is successful in providing practical answers to the problem-situations that generated the questions. "Genetic method" is an appropriate name for such pragmatic method with its probing of context.

The metaphysical aspect underlying these questions had been traditionally viewed as the problem of the relation of mind to matter. This formulation saw them as substances, the one engaged in thinking, the other in motion. The main epistemological problem was how they were related—for example, as two Cartesian substances with their connection a mystery, or as one Spinozistic substance with two aspects and so with definite coexistence. The problem is considerably altered if mind is thought of not as a substance but as an activity. As F.J.E. Woodbridge, a colleague of Dewey's in the Columbia Philosophy Department put it, "mind is not a noun, but a verb: man (the substance) thinks (the activity)." Dewey always thinks of the mental as an activity. It is people's thoughts that he explores, and since thinking is a natural phenomenon, its scientific understanding calls for seeing how it goes on in people's lives, what consequences it has, and how reliable it proves. This again is the genetic method at work, embracing the analytic method and extending the scope of knowledge.

2. Dewey After the *Ethics*

The publication of the 1932 *Ethics* brings to an end the account projected by the title of this book. The story of Dewey's activities and thought from 1932 to 1951 has therefore the character of an appendix to our story. It was certainly the most turbulent setting for his activity, probably the most unsettling period of his life, to which however he responded vigorously.

We have seen earlier how 1930–1932 was a waiting period for American society, with industrial activity slowed to a stop and banks eventually closed. A few areas anticipated the changes to come—for example, liquor became available although formally still banned. Even when Franklin Roosevelt became president, he could not initially carry out his active program for reviving industry. The Supreme Court was still dominated by Hoover appointees and declared his measures unconstitutional. Only when he threatened to have the legislature initiate a constitutional amendment increasing the size of the court with enough of his appointees to overrule the Hoover members did the latter give up and resign.

Surprisingly, Dewey did not support Roosevelt, although he voted for him once. For the most part he supported Norman Thomas, the Socialist candidate. He recognized what Roosevelt did to revive industry and open the way for the upsurge of labor unionism, particularly in the automobile and mining industries. But he apparently believed that more should be done and thought that capitalism would win out by raising prices and cutting labor costs. Nothing short of socialism would solve industrial labor problems.

The problem that most tormented him in the 1930s and early 1940s was the threat of fascism and the growth of communism. In the 1930s he thought that the United States could stay away from the fascism of Italy and the Nazism of Germany, and let Europe deal with the problems. But once Japan declared war on the United States he recognized that America would have to fight on both fronts.

His social activities during this period were varied. He did not throw himself into work in a single direction, as others did in organizing a union of scientists, but wrote and engaged in innumerable debates around specific topics. He joined different groups with varied social aims, he supported the attempt to found a third political party, and he took up the invitation to go to Mexico for the inquiry into Trotsky's guilt or innocence in the charge that Trotsky supported an attempted assassination of Stalin. The inquiry gave a non-guilty verdict.

In the late 1940s Dewey rather despaired of the future of philosophy in America. He had battled during the 1930s and 1940s against the philosophical movements—logical positivism was the most prominent of these—that took philosophy to be essentially the analysis of language and cut it off from all questions of historical treatment of values, their rise and fall. Sadly, he did not foresee that this movement would simply die out by neglect. But he maintained to the end his belief in social freedom for individual thought, whatever direction it took.

3. Attitudes to Dewey's Work During the Twentieth Century

While Dewey was alive and active, his works played an important part in the on-going developments and controversies in philosophy. After his death he was quickly forgotten. This was due largely to the half-dozen years of prominence in the early 1950s of the linguistic schools of philosophy against which Dewey had fought. This neglect was strengthened by a novel tendency in books of philosophy to expound their own position without reference to opposing views. By the 1970s this had become a dominant position. One can look in vain in two books that topped the field in that decade in the extent of use in teaching or in review journals—John Rawls' *A Theory of Justice* (1971) and Robert Nozick's *Anarchy, State and Utopia* (1974)—for any mention of Dewey. This continued for a decade. But in 1981 the series of Dewey's Early, Middle and Later Works published by Southern Illinois University Press changed the picture completely—Dewey has become almost a contemporary figure, for the problems he dealt with have continued to be American social problems. The present writer was once asked (in the University of Pennsylvania library) by a young student who looked in amazement at the full two shelves of Dewey's collected works, "At what college does Mr. Dewey teach?"

Notes

1. MW 4: 39–41.
2. Ibid., 45.

Index

review of
  Adams, *Civilization during the Middle Ages*, 130
  Allen, *Law in the Making*, 110
  Royce, "On Certain Psychological Aspects of Moral Training", 102
  Santayana, *The Life of Reason*, 171
Sociology of Ethics (lecture notes), 47
The Study of Ethics: A Syllabus (1894), 2, 33, 34, 35, 39, 40, 41, 42, 43, 44, 47, 51, 53, 54, 55, 56, 58, 59, 66, 90, 101, 128, 136, 140, 158, 181, 185, 187, 188, 189, 190
Theory of Valuation (1939), 69, 81, 195, 204, 205
Dewey, John, and James H. Tufts
Ethics (1908), xvi, xix, 4, 5, 8, 9, 10, 11, 12, 15, 16, 27, 28, 29, 31, 32, 33, 34, 38, 44, 45, 46, 47, 48, 51, 53, 55, 56, 58, 59, 60, 65, 66, 67, 68, 69, 81, 82, 83, 84, 90, 91, 93, 96, 99, 100, 101, 102, 110, 113, 114, 116, 117, 118, 119, 120, 121, 122, 124, 126, 127, 128, 131, 132, 133, 136, 137, 149, 150, 151, 152, 153, 154, 155, 156, 159, 160, 161, 162, 163, 166, 169, 173, 177, 179, 180, 187, 188, 190, 198
Ethics (1932), xv, xvi, xix, 4, 5, 9, 11, 12, 15, 27, 29, 31, 32, 33, 34, 41, 48, 51, 55, 57, 58, 60, 61, 63, 65, 68, 69, 75, 81, 82, 87, 88, 90, 91, 92, 93, 94, 99, 102, 106, 110, 111, 113, 117, 118, 121, 122, 123, 124, 126, 127, 128, 129, 132, 136, 137, 138, 143, 144, 145, 149, 150, 151, 152, 154, 160, 161, 162, 163, 165, 169, 173, 175, 178, 179, 180, 183, 185, 187, 188, 194, 198, 201
Durkheim, Emile, 4
duty, 10, 24, 25, 38, 52, 53, 54, 55, 59, 68, 70, 82, 83, 84, 85, 92, 122, 163, 190

Early Civilization (Goldenweiser), 154
Edel, Abraham, *Science and the Structure of Ethics*, 205
Edel, May and Abraham, *Antoropology and Ethics,* xiii
Edel, May M., *The Chiga of Uganda,* xiv

Educational Theory, 3
egoism and altruism, 46, 119, 122, 123, 199
egoism-altruism problem, 122
Encyclopedia Americana, 49, 60, 130
ends, concept of in ethics, 6, 8, 9, 11, 17, 24, 25, 28, 35, 42, 45, 53, 54, 55, 56, 57, 59, 66, 68, 69, 71, 76, 82, 83, 87, 92, 94, 101, 102, 106, 119, 120, 164, 169, 170, 178, 179, 180, 182, 183, 188, 189, 190, 191, 193, 199
ethics, etymology of, 18
Ethics and Language (Stevenson), 82
evolution, xvi, 5, 15, 16, 19, 45, 47, 60, 66, 70, 85, 99, 100, 102, 107, 118, 125, 131, 150, 153, 154, 155, 157, 158, 159, 160, 162, 165, 168, 175, 184
evolution, moral, 100
Evolutionary Ethics, 156

Flower, Elizabeth, xviii, 11, 47
Flower, Elizabeth and Murray G. Murphey, *A History of Philosophy in America* (1977), xviii, 11, 47
freedom and responsibility, 59, 187, 188, 191, 193, 194, 195, 198
Frege, Gottlob, 74
French anthropological school, 158
French Encyclopedists, 131
Fries letter. *See* Dewey, John: Fries letter
Fries, Horace S., 3

Garman, Charles Edward, 90, 145, 155, 174
General Theory of Value (Perry), 94
Genetic Ethics, 156
Gifford Lectures, xxi
Goldenweiser, Alexander, 154, 158
  Early Civilization, 154
good, the, 4, 5, 6, 7, 9, 10, 11, 33, 39, 42, 45, 51, 54, 56, 59, 66, 68, 69, 70, 77, 78, 80, 81, 82, 83, 84, 85, 87, 88, 89, 91, 93, 96, 131, 137, 138, 152, 159, 163, 178, 179, 180, 188, 189
Great Depression, xxi, 143
Greek ethics, 4, 7, 8, 18, 27, 30, 103, 104, 133, 158, 161, 163, 179, 181, 205
Green, T. H., xviii, 35, 43, 45, 52, 70, 94, 119, 189